Concepts and Words To Be Understood

alternatives	data	predict
consequences	hypothesis	scientific method
control	optical illusion	variable
controlled experiment		verify

I. Introduction To Science

The science student needs to know that a great deal of information has been collected up to now. Every day new knowledge is being discovered and added. This knowledge has been sorted into subjects. Some of the subjects of science are:

Name of Subject	Area of Study
Meteorology	Weather and Climate
Biology	Living Things
Chemistry	Materials
Mathematics	Numbers
Astronomy	Universe
Physics	Energy
Geology	Earth

The chapters of this book contain some of this knowledge. You will use this "content" to help solve problems.

The attitude of scientists (and you) is very important in their work.

Positive science attitudes are reflected in a person's values. What a person **thinks** is important. Also important is the way a person **looks** at things.

With correct science attitudes, a person would:

- **Identify different ways to deal with people and problems**
- **Make the best choices that would be good for all concerned**
- **Act in such a way as to improve life for him/herself and others**

The successful study of any science requires good attitudes. Good attitudes make problem solving easier.

Also important in the study of any science, is a knowledge of certain skills. Skills are the "tools" of the scientist. Science students also can use these skills to collect information and find answers to problems.

Generally the skills used in classrooms and laboratories are used to:

- **Obtain data through scientific procedures**
- **Organize data into a useful form**
- **Analyze the data**
- **Generalize from the data**
- **Make decisions**

Problem Solving

The main goal of the scientist is to **solve problems**. To do so, he/she needs some basic knowledge (content), correct attitudes, and certain skills. With these three supports, the science student should be able to solve problems successfully. Look at this stool. The legs must be of equal length if it is to be used properly. If one leg is too short, the stool will not stand evenly.

Problem solving in science is much the same. It is difficult if one needs to know much content but has few skills. Poor attitude makes the work harder. A good balance of content, skills, and attitude is needed.

All students should know the **scientific method** to get answers. The steps of this procedure are:

1 - **Recognize the problem**
2 - **Predict an answer to the problem**
3 - **Plan and do a controlled experiment**
4 - **Observe happenings and record data**
5 - **Organize and interpret data**
6 - **Make decisions**
7 - **Verify results**

Planning and doing a controlled experiment (Step 3) make this method different from all others. The **scientific method** not only applies to work in science but also to everyday life. Try using this method to solve other problems and to make good decisions.

1. Problem solving begins with knowing what the problem is.

A problem is something that needs an answer. Problems are stated in the form of a question: Does a cracker contain starch? Is this sample rock a piece of limestone? *Which will speed up faster, a bowling ball or a golf ball when acted upon by an equal force?*

2. Predicting a possible answer to the problem is the next step.

Sometimes this is called a **hypothesis** (educated guess). A prediction is based on known knowledge and common sense: The cracker has starch in it. The rock is limestone. *The golf ball will speed up faster than the bowling ball.*

3. Planning and doing a controlled experiment make the scientific method of solving problems different from all other methods.

In this plan, a comparison is needed. A **control** provides this comparison.

Two experiments are set up with the same conditions. In one experiment only **one** condition is allowed to change. The other experimental procedure does not change. It is the **control**. When both experiments are done, comparisons are made. Otherwise, we would never learn the true cause. The condition that changes is called the **variable**.

One cracker is left alone. A few drops of iodine are added to another cracker. It turns blue-black. A few drops of acid placed on the limestone cause it to fizz. Where there was no acid, there was no fizz.

*The golfer uses the same tee, the same golf club, and the same swing. The **variable** is the ball: (1)bowling ball and (2) golf ball. The two balls are hit, and the results are observed. Using the same force, the golf ball speeded up faster than the bowling ball.*

4. Honesty is required when observing experiments.

Information must be recorded exactly how it happens. For example, look at the following illustrations:

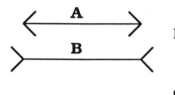

• Look at these lines; which line is longer, line **A** or line **B**?

• Look at the hat; which is longer, the brim (width) or the top part of the hat (height)?

Take your ruler and measure the lines. You will discover that they are both the same length. This is called an *optical illusion; Optical*, because you are observing it with your eyes; *illusion*, because it is something that does not actually exist.

Observe the road or street ahead of you on a hot summer day. You may see what looks like a puddle of water. When you get where you thought the puddle was, it is not there. This is another optical illusion.

Note: *Avoid recording what you think should happen. Observe and record what actually does happen.*

5. After data is recorded, it needs to be organized.

Sometimes data can be recorded easily on a data table. Some information is easier to handle when placed in groups. Numbers might need to be put in order. The scientist (student) needs to decide which way is best.

Whichever way is chosen to organize the data, it must aid in **interpreting** what happened. If after each of 25 trials the cracker turned blue-black when iodine was placed on it, the cracker must have starch in it. This is especially true if nothing happened to the cracker that was left alone (control).

Similar interpretations could apply to the limestone test and to the experiment which used the bowling ball and golf ball.

6. Decision making is a very important step in the scientific method.

Answering some key questions can help make good decisions:

> • **What specific decision needs to be made?**
> • **What are some alternative choices?**
> • **What are the consequences of each alternative?**
> • **Who will be affected by each choice and in what way?**
> • **What values are involved with each choice?**
> • **Which choice is the best choice?**

The data may indicate the prediction is correct. With this, the work would end. Seldom is this the case. Most often the data indicate further work must be done. An experimental condition needs to be changed. Perhaps a change is needed in the way the results were recorded. There are times when the data from one experiment lead to another question. The decision making ability of the problem solver is very important.

7. The final step of the scientific method is to verify the results of the controlled experiment.

Repeating the procedure is one way to do this. Having someone else perform the procedure is another way. If different crackers are used in many different schools with the same results, crackers must contain starch.

Should different pieces of rock fizz with acid on them, they could be limestones. Similarly, if the bowling ball was always the last to get to the line, it must have been slower than the golf ball.

To verify means to prove. Scientists want to prove their findings to be true. Science students must do this also.

Questions

1   Science can be thought of as
   1   an organized body of knowledge
   2   a way of solving problems
   3   an attitude
   4   all answers are correct

2   The study of living things is called
   1   astronomy   2 biology   3 geology   4 meteorology

3   Chemistry is the study of
   1   the Earth   2 energy   3 materials   4 numbers

4   Meteorology is the study of
   1   the universe   3 energy
   2   living things   4 weather

5   Positive science attitudes can be seen in a person's
   1   cells   2 heredity   3 name   4 values

6   Good science attitudes involve
   1   knowing different ways to deal with problems
   2   making choices that are good for all concerned
   3   acting to improve one's self and others
   4   all answers are correct

7   The first thing that needs to be done before a problem can be solved is to
   1   collect lots of materials   3 make a graph
   2   know that a problem exists   4 prove the results

8   When a scientist predicts, he/she is
   1   stating the problem   3 guessing an answer
   2   organizing a data table   4 doing an experiment

9   Another name for a prediction is
   1   controlled experiment   3   hypothesis
   2   data table   4   analysis

10 The main goal of scientists is to
   1   do experiments   3   make good predictions
   2   observe carefully   4   solve problems

11 A control is needed in a controlled experiment because it
   1   leads to good graphing   3   provides for comparisons
   2   speeds up the experiment   4   is easier to record

12 Doing a controlled experiment is really
   1   testing a hypothesis
   2   just stating a problem
   3   going over possible answers
   4   drawing a conclusion

13 Optical illusions can
   1   be relied upon   3   give accurate data
   2   fool us   4   control an experiment

14 To "verify" something means to
   1   look at it a long time   3   record the data
   2   prove it correct   4   state the problem

15 When decisions are made in the scientific method, what is considered?
   1   alternative choices
   2   consequences of each alternative
   3   values involved with each choice
   4   all answers are correct

Questions 16 through 20 are based on the following paragraph:

An experiment is set up to test the effect of cigarette smoke on the growth of plants. It is known that this smoke contains the poison nicotine among other things. 100 cc of smoke are bubbled through the water in a test tube. The test tube is labeled "S". Another test tube labeled "F" is filled with fresh water. Two healthy bean plants have their roots measured and one is placed in each test tube. They are placed on a sunny window sill. The roots are measured each day for 5 days.

16 What do you predict will happen?
   1   The plant in fresh water will *not* grow as well as the plant in smoke water.
   2   The plant in smokewater will *not* grow as well as the plant in fresh water.
   3   The plant in fresh water will die.
   4   The plant in smoke water will grow very fast.

17 The plant in fresh water was included in the experiment to
   1   balance the test tube rack
   2   keep students busy
   3   provide a comparison
   4   provide unneeded data

During the 5 days of the experiment, the following data were recorded:

Root Lengths in millimeters (mm)

Day	Fresh Water	Smoke Water
1	40	40
2	42	41
3	44	42
4	46	43
5	48	43

18 The data seem to suggest that the growth of the plant in the
1 fresh water was slowed down
2 fresh water grew better
3 smoke water slowed down
4 answers 2 and 3 are correct

19 Judging from the data collected, what would be sensible to do next?
1 have a friend do the experiment again
2 try the experiment using different plants
3 extend the experiment for 5 more days
4 all answers are correct

20 A conclusion made based on the data would be that cigarette smoke
1 does not affect plant growth
2 seems to affect plant growth
3 stunts growth in humans
4 is sweet smelling

Questions 21 through 24 are based on the following paragraph:

Knowing the hardness of a mineral can help identify it. Geologists use Moh's Scale of Hardness to do this. "1" on the scale is the softest mineral, and "10" is the hardest. Use the following scale to answer the questions:

1. talc	4. fluorite	7. quartz	10. diamond
2. gypsum	5. apatite	8. topaz	
3. calcite	6. orthoclase	9. corundum	

21 Quartz is a mineral found in granite. It has a hardness of
1 three   3 seven
2 four   4 nine

22 Since "1" on the scale is softest, which mineral on the scale is the hardest?
1 apatite   3 gypsum
2 diamond   4 topaz

Some common materials have been assigned hardness numbers. The fingernail is 2.5. A copper penny is 3.5. A steel knife is 5.5.

23 Your fingernail would be able to scratch
1 calcite and fluorite   3 talc and topaz
2 diamond and corundum   4 talc and gypsum

24 A steel pocket knife could scratch
1 corundum   3 calcite
2 diamond   4 quartz

Questions 25 through 30 are based on the following experiment:

An experiment is set up to show that oxygen is needed for things to burn. Three candles are lit. Two different sized glass jars are put over two of the candles at the same time. Careful observations are made.

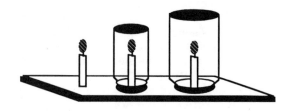

25 What do you predict will happen?
  1 The uncovered candle will go out.
  2 The candle under the smaller jar will stay lit longer than the one under the larger jar.
  3 The candle under the larger jar will burn longer than the one under the smaller jar.
  4 All of the answers are correct.

26 Why was one candle left uncovered?
  1 Only two jars were needed.
  2 The heat from it was needed
  3 This candle was the "control."
  4 It provided light for the test.

27 What is (are) the variable(s) in this experiment?
  1 the uncovered candle
  2 the smaller jar *only*
  3 the larger jar *only*
  4 *both* the larger and smaller jars

28 During the experiment the candle under the smaller jar went out first. The candle under the larger jar went out last. This probably happened because the
  1 larger jar had more oxygen in it
  2 smaller jar had more oxygen in it
  3 both jars had equal amounts of oxygen in them
  4 glass in the small jar was too thick

29 The "control" candle stayed lit because
  1 no jar stopped oxygen from getting to it
  2 there was plenty of oxygen in the room
  3 both answers 1 and 2 are correct
  4 neither answer 1 nor 2 is correct

30 A possible conclusion might be that
  1 things burn better under glass jars
  2 oxygen is needed for candles to burn
  3 candles burn longer under little jars
  4 the jar size had nothing to do with the experiment

II. Science Process Skills

Concepts and Words To Be Understood

inference	observation	quantitative
meniscus	qualitative	standard

A. Laboratory Safety Is A Must

Certain safe laboratory procedures need to be followed by everyone:

- Wear goggles when experimenting.
- Wear aprons and gloves when required.
- Take care when heating things over a flame.
- Never eat in a lab and keep hair tied back.
- Do not "horseplay" in the lab.
- Carry and handle chemicals and equipment carefully.
- Never taste a substance unless directed by the teacher.
- When smelling a sample, hold the substance away from your head and fan the odor towards your nose.

How many pieces of equipment can you recognize?
Compare the picture above with the list below:

1	test tube	4	mortar & pestle	7	tweezers
2	beaker tongs	5	eye dropper	8	tripod
3	beaker	6	rubber stopper	9	funnel

B. Making Careful Observations

Making careful observations is among the most important skills of the scientist. This skill requires the use of all human senses. Scientists not only see things happen. They also observe by hearing, feeling, smelling, and even tasting under carefully controlled conditions.

Observations

Observations describe the properties of things or the features of events. The girl was wearing a blue dress. Blue is a property of the dress. The temperature rose one degree every five minutes. The one degree every five minutes is a feature of the event.

There are basically two kinds of observations:

1) Some observations give the general worth of something (**qualitative observations**). That is, the maple leaf has a <u>dark green</u> color.

2) Other observations give an exact value of quantity (**quantitative observations**). That is, the maple leaf has <u>five (5)</u> points.

When comparing the two, observations obtained by measuring usually are more accurate. They are also more dependable.

Any kind of measurement requires honesty and caution. The reading on a scale must be correct and recorded accurately. To get exact values, measuring instruments are needed. A bathroom scale will give you your weight. A ruler will tell you how tall you are. In a science lab, certain instruments are used to get specific values:

1   **A balance** is used to find the **mass (weight)** of something. What is the reading on the balance? Remember to add the values of both beams. *(Note: This is a kilogram scale. The top beam is in "10's" and the bottom beam is in "units.")*
      Answer: 94.5 grams

2   **Meter sticks** and **rulers** are used to measure **distance**. What is the length of the object on this ruler?

length to be measured

Length in centimeters = 2.20
Length in millimeters = 22.0

Metric Scale Measurement

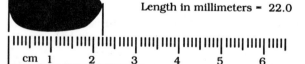

3   A **graduated cylinder** will give the **volume** of a liquid. Reading a graduated cylinder correctly can be difficult.

Notice the curve of the surface of the liquid. This is called a **meniscus**. Always measure at the bottom of the curve (meniscus).

Correct Reading = 41 ml
Wrong Reading = 43 ml

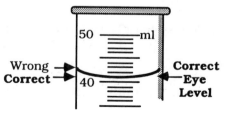

4 **Thermometers** measure **temperature**.

Thermometers with the
Celsius scale are usually
used in labs. Sometimes
the Fahrenheit scale is
used. Science students
should be familiar with
both. Compare the two
scales in the diagram.

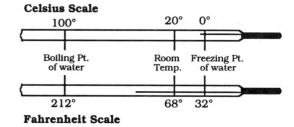

Celsius Scale

100°   20° 0°

Boiling Pt.   Room   Freezing Pt.
of water   Temp.   of water

212°   68°   32°

Fahrenheit Scale

The most reliable observation is one that gives an exact reading. Be sure to
be accurate when reading the scales on these instruments.

Scientists also have to know what an **inference** is. An inference
is an explanation of an observation. It is easy to remember the
meaning of inference if you remember that an
inference is _not_ directly observed.

Look at this diagram of a house. Would
you say that there is a TV inside? You
could "infer" that there is a TV set because
of the antenna. But, do you actually see the
TV set?

You might look out the window in the morning and see the sidewalk is wet.
You could infer that it rained during the night. You did not see the rain fall.
Perhaps your next door neighbor sprinkled his lawn early that morning.

C. Numbers And Measurements

Scientists use **numbers** and **measurement systems** in almost everything
they do. The scales on most lab devices are in metrics. The metric system is
very easy to learn.

All measurement systems need _"standards"_ - basic units to use for comparisons. The metric system standards are:

- The **meter** is a distance (linear) measure. The meter (39.37 inches) is
  equal to one-ten millionth of the distance from the North Pole to the
  Equator.

- The **liter** is a measure for volume (capacity). The liter (1.06 quarts) is
  the same as one cubic decimeter.

- The **gram** is a mass (weight) measure. The gram is the mass (weight) of
  one cubic centimeter of pure water. (28.35g = 1 ounce)

The entire metric system is based on ten (10). Several prefixes that represent multiples or divisions of ten (10) need to be learned. You should know these four prefixes and their values.

Prefix	Symbol	Value (of meter)
kilo-	k	1000
deci-	d	1/10 or 0.1
centi-	c	1/100 or 0.01
milli-	m	1/1000 or 0.001

Standards

The **meter** (m), the **liter** (l), and the **gram** (g) always have a value of one (1). Study the diagram:

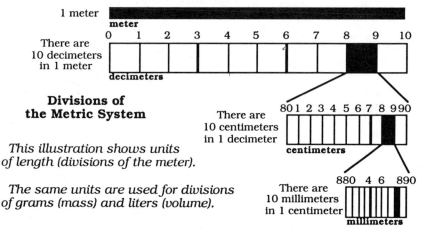

Divisions of the Metric System

This illustration shows units of length (divisions of the meter).

The same units are used for divisions of grams (mass) and liters (volume).

The second ruler shows decimeters. There are ten decimeters in a meter. Each decimeter is divided into 10 equal parts. Each part is a centimeter. Count the number of spaces between 88 and 89 centimeters. There are ten spaces between them. Each space represents a millimeter.

Numbers are used for more than just measuring. They can be used in calculations. You need to know when to add, subtract, multiply, or divide.

Finding the "area" of something is another important process. Area is found by measuring the length and width of something. Then, the two amounts are multiplied. The formula that should be used here is:

$$A \text{ (area)} = l \text{ (length)} \times w \text{ (width)}$$

Example: A small garden plot measures 10 meters by 4 meters. To find the area use the formula and substitute the appropriate numbers.

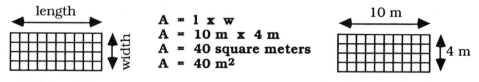

A = l x w
A = 10 m x 4 m
A = 40 square meters
A = 40 m²

Note that the answer is in *square meters* (m²). Area is a flat surface measurement.

Students also need to be able to calculate "volume." The space taken up by an object is its volume or "capacity." This is found by measuring the length, width, and height of something and multiplying. Remember the formula: Volume = l (length) x w (width) x h (height). This will help you.

Example: A pencil box measures 20 centimeters long, 5 centimeters wide, and 2 centimeters high. To find the volume of the box use the formula:

$$V = l \; x \; w \; x \; h$$

Substitute the measurements for the letters and multiply.

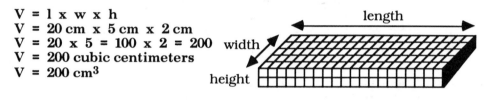

V = l x w x h
V = 20 cm x 5 cm x 2 cm
V = 20 x 5 = 100 x 2 = 200
V = 200 cubic centimeters
V = 200 cm³

Note that volume is three dimensional. The answer here is shown as *cubic centimeters* (cm³).

Measure the cover of this book. What is its area in millimeters? What is the area in centimeters?

Now, measure the thickness. It can be used for "height." Use the length and width of the cover and the thickness of the book to calculate its volume.

If you know the American money system, you also know the metric system. It is based on ten. How many cents (pennies) are there in a dollar? Note that a **cent** is 1/100 (.01) or one-one hundredth of a dollar. **Centi-** is the metric prefix meaning 1/100.

Questions

1   A scientist can make observations by
   1   seeing   3   feeling
   2   smelling   4   all answers are correct

2   A balance is used to find
   1   distance   3   temperature
   2   mass   4   volume

3   To find the length of this paper, what should be used?
   1   balance   3   ruler
   2   graduated cylinder   4   thermometer

4   Which of these devices is a balance?

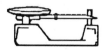

   (1)   (2)   (3)   (4)

5   Body temperature is 98.6°F. What is used to find this?
    1 balance   3 ruler
    2 graduated cylinder   4 thermometer

6   A "meniscus" is the
    1 curve on the surface of liquid
    2 line on a ruler
    3 scale on a balance
    4 liquid in a thermometer

7   What is the reading on this graduated cylinder?
    1 5 ml   3 7 ml
    2 6 ml   4 8 ml

8   Which temperature scale has "0" for the freezing point of water and "100" for the boiling point of water?
    1 Celsius   2 Fahrenheit

9   A measurement system uses standards to
    1 confuse us   3 keep students busy
    2 guess at amounts   4 make comparisons

10   The metric standard for line measure is the
    1 gram   2 liter   3 meter   4 inch

11   The value of the standard unit in the metric system is
    1 one   2 five   3 ten   4 one hundred

12   Kilo- means 1000. How many meters are in a kilometer?
    1 10   2 100   3 1000   4 1,000,000

13   All measurements are what kind of observation?
    1 guesses   2 estimates   3 qualitative   4 quantitative

14   An inference would be
    1 an interpretation of an observation
    2 something you did not actually see happen
    3 both answers are correct
    4 neither answer is correct

15   The temperature of a liquid at the start of an experiment is 35°C. At the end of the experiment it is 45°C. The *difference* in the temperature from start to end would be
    1 10°C   2 35°C   3 45°C   4 80°C

16   An experiment needs 7 grams of sulfur and 10 grams of iron. What is the total mass of the sulfur and iron?
    1 3 g   2 17 g   3 70 g   4 700 g

17   To find the difference between two numbers, you would
    1 add   2 divide   3 multiply   4 subtract

18   In making good decisions about solving problems, a student should
    1 come to class late
    2 do whatever comes to mind first
    3 fool around a lot
    4 keep an open mind

19 If an experiment doesn't work the first time, a student should
    1 forget about it
    2 look for ways to change it and try again
    3 make some excuse for the failure
    4 blame a classmate for the failure

20 The most accurate kind of observation is one which is
    1 estimated   3 inferred
    2 guessed at   4 measured

21 A knee patch measures 4 centimeters by 3 centimeters. What is its area?
    1 4 cm^2 2 7 cm^2 3 12 cm^2 4 43 cm^2

22 A candy bar has a length of 15 cm, a width of 8 cm, and a thickness (height) of 2 cm. What is its volume?
    1 25 cm^3 2 40 cm^3 3 120 cm^3 4 240 cm^3

23 A = l x w is the formula to be used to calculate
    1 area   2 depth   3 height   4 volume

24 V = l x w x h is the formula used to find
    1 area   2 length   3 volume   4 width

25 Which of the following laboratory tools would you use to grind salt crystals into a fine powder?
    1 tongs   3 mortar and pestle
    2 tweezers   4 test tube holder

Concepts and Words To Be Understood

analyze   apply   data table   graph   interpret

D. Organizing Data

Organizing data is another important skill of the scientist.

Data tables are used to put some order into the observations. A data table is a system of columns and rows. It allows for the speedy recording of numbers and other observations and the organization of information.

Graphs are handy tools for science students to compare two variables. A graph is nothing more than a "picture" of data. A comparison can often be **seen** more easily with a graph than with just a paragraph of words or a data table.

Suppose an experiment is planned to show the effect of detergents on the growth of plants. The kind of soil and amount of sunlight will be the same for both plants. Each day of the experiment the "control" plant will get 25 ml of fresh water. The "variable" plant will get 25 ml of water in which 10 ml of a strong detergent were added. The height of the plants will be measured each day at 2 P.M. for 5 days and recorded.

Data Recorded Without The Use Of A Data Table:

On the first day of the experiment, the height of the plant watered with plain water was 10 cm. The plant watered with detergent water was 10 cm high. On the second day, the plant with fresh water was 12 cm high and the detergent plant was 11 cm high. On the third day of the experiment, the fresh water plant was 15 cm high. The detergent plant was 13 cm high. On the fourth day, the fresh water plant grew to 20 cm and the detergent plant was 14 cm. On the last day of the experiment, the fresh water plant grew to a height of 25 cm. The detergent watered plant was 15 cm high.

Data Recorded With A Data Table And Graph:

Note how easy it is to review data with a data table. It is also easier to make the graph from the data on a table.

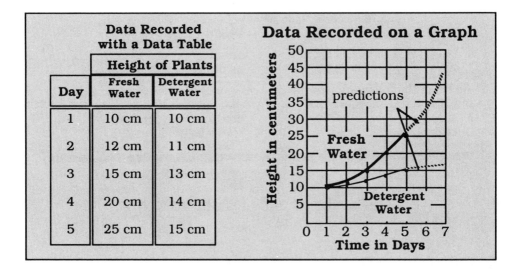

Data Recorded with a Data Table

Day	Fresh Water	Detergent Water
1	10 cm	10 cm
2	12 cm	11 cm
3	15 cm	13 cm
4	20 cm	14 cm
5	25 cm	15 cm

Graphs can also be used to make **predictions**. Suppose you wanted to know the height of the plants at 4½ days. You would make an estimate using the 4th and 5th day points on the graph (interpolation). This would be about 23 cm for the fresh water plant and about 14 cm for the plant watered with detergent water.

Could you predict the height of the plants at 6 days? The fresh watered plant might be 33 cm, while the detergent plant might be 16 cm. To do this, you would note any "trends" showing in the lines on the graph. Then, you would extend the line in the direction of the trend (extrapolation).

The detergent water seems to slow down the growth of the plant (an analysis). In a real experiment, it would be wise to use at least three (3) plants for each condition. Then, take an average reading for the final graph. In this way, if one plant should die from unknown causes, there still would be two others to carry on the experiment.

E. Analyzing And Interpreting

The ability to **analyze** and **interpret** data is a skill all science students need to develop. Here patterns and relationships are looked for. In the plant experiment, the plant watered with fresh water seemed to grow faster than the detergent watered plant.

Any experimental data must be studied. When this is done carefully, the data can be interpreted. Here, the questions are asked, "Does the data support the prediction made at the beginning of the scientific method? If not, why not? Must there be a change in the procedure? Should there be a change in the way the data were recorded? Must the prediction be changed?"

Sometimes experiments need to be performed more than once. This allows the scientist to check for possible errors and/or inaccurate data.

F. Applying What Was Learned

Finally, the skill of **applying** what you learned is considered. After learning that detergents hurt plant growth, it would be unwise to throw detergent water in a garden.

Suppose you did an experiment that proved that tomato plants grow better in full sunlight. How could this knowledge help you if you plan to include tomato plants in your garden?

Conclusion: *As you read this book, try to remember the science process skills listed here.* Each of the units provides some basic knowledge (content). By using these along with your good science attitude, you will become an effective problem solver.

Questions

1   A system of columns and rows used to record data is called a
  1   data table
  2   glossary
  3   laboratory
  4   line graph

2   A data table allows for
  1   a quick reference
  2   the organization of data
  3   easy recording of data
  4   all answers are correct

3   A graph is really a
  1   control
  2   experimental procedure
  3   picture of data
  4   series of columns and rows

4   A student learns that tomato plants grow better in full sunlight. When he/she plants the garden, the tomato plants should be planted
  1   in a place with little light
  2   where they could get lots of light
  3   somewhere that would be shaded half the day
  4   between the rows of corn

Questions 5 through 10 are based on this information:

A student in Chicago recorded the daily high temperature for a seven day period. The results are at the right:

Day	Daily High Temperature in Degrees Celsius
1	15
2	16
3	16
4	17
5	20
6	21
7	23

5   On the graph, *Time (in days)* is represented on which scale?
   1   horizontal scale
   2   vertical scale

6   The vertical (up and down line) contains what readings?
   1   days of the week
   2   daily high temperature

7   Which letter on the graph represents a temperature reading of 20°C?
   1   *A*
   2   *B*
   3   *C*
   4   *D*

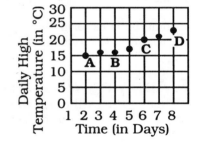

8   Which spot indicates that reading for day 8?
   1   *A*   2   *B*   3   *C*   4   *D*

9   It is most likely that the student recorded these temperatures during
   1   late summer   3   late spring
   2   early winter   4   early fall

10   What do you predict the high temperature might be on Day 8?
   1   18°C   2   24°C   3   35°C   4   39°C

III. Science Vocabulary

The words found in science often are new and seem odd. Knowing the meaning of some word parts can help a great deal in understanding them. Here is a list of some important word parts, their meanings, and some sample words. Learn them before you begin to use this book. Refer to these **Word Parts** as the words appear in the Units that follow.

WORD PART	MEANING	SAMPLE WORD
a- or an-	not	asexual, anaerobic
-al or -ar	pertaining to	skeletal, solar
astro-	star	astronomy
-ate	result of an action	evaporate
atmo- or aero-	air	atmosphere, aerobic
auto-	self	automatic

bene-	well	**bene**fit
bi-	two	**bi**cycle
bio-	life (living things)	**bio**logy
centi-	1/100	**centi**meter
-cide	killer	inse**cide**
convers-	turn about	**convers**ion
counter-	opposite	**counter**clockwise
deci-	1/10	**deci**meter
ex- or **e-**	outside	**ex**trusive, **e**vaporate
geo-	earth	**geo**logy
hydro-	water	**hydro**electric
in-	inside	**in**trusive
inter-	between, among	**inter**cellular
-ist	one who does	conservation**ist**
-ity	condition of	elastic**ity**
-ive	function of	digest**ive**
kilo-	1000	**kilo**gram
kine-	motion	**kine**tic
-logy	study of	meteoro**logy**
-ment	action or state of	environ**ment**
meteor-	atmosphere	**meteor**ology
-meter	measurer	thermo**meter**
micro-	small	**micro**organism
milli-	1/1000	**milli**liter
multi-	many	**multi**cellular
non-, im-	not	**non**living, **im**movable
un-, in-	not	**un**equal, **in**organic
photo-	light	**photo**graph
physi-	nature	**physi**cal
re-	to do again	**re**crystallization
scien-	knowledge	**scien**ce
-scope	look at, see	micro**scope**
sub-	under	**sub**stratum
super-	above	**super**position
syn-	put together	**syn**fuel
thermo-	heat	**thermo**s bottle
-tion or **-sion**	action, process	pollu**tion**, compres**sion**
tox-	poison	**tox**ic
trans-	across	**trans**formation
uni-	one	**uni**cellular

Questions

1   In the word Biology, -ology means "the study of." The word part **bio-** means
   (1) earth   2 life   3 materials   4 weather

2   A microscope is used by biologists. Micro- means small. What does **-scope** mean?
   1 a killer   2 amount   3 materials   4 to look at

3   Words like mental, physical, and social all end in -al. When **-al** is added to a base word, it means
   1 knowledge   2 light   3 pertaining to 4 sound

4   An instrument that would measure **heat** would be a
   1 motor   2 ruler   3 telescope   4 thermometer

5   When **-meter** is added to a base word, the new word would describe something that
   1 digs   2 lights up   3 measures   4 sounds off

6   The base word herb- means plant. What would an **herbicide** do to plants?
   1 clean them   3 kill them
   2 encourage growth   4 provide fertilizer

7   **Hydroelectric** power refers to electricity that is made by using
   1 biomass   3 nuclear power
   2 coal   4 water

8   **Toxins** are
   1 cures for colds   3 poisons
   2 foods   4 wastes

9   **Syn-** means putting together. In the word **photosynthesis**, what energy source is used to put things together?
   1 electricity   2 heat   3 light   4 sound

10 Air is all around us. A word part that can mean **air** is
   1 aero-   2 bio-   3 hydro-   4 thermo-

11 Which of the following means 1000?
   1 **bi-**   2 **centi-**   3 **deci-**   4 **kilo-**

12 The value of **centi-** is
   1 1   2 $\frac{1}{10}$ 3 $\frac{1}{100}$ 4 $\frac{1}{1000}$

13 A **bimetal** bar would be made up of how many metals?
   1 1   2 2   3 3   4 4

14 There are many **unicellular** organisms in nature. Each one is made up of how many cells?
   1 one   2 two   3 several   4 many

15 A **decimeter** would be how much of a meter?
   1 $\frac{1}{10}$ 3 $\frac{1}{1,000}$
   2 $\frac{1}{100}$ 4 $\frac{1}{1,000,000}$

Area 1
Life Sciences

- **Organisms**
  - **Humans**
    - **Microorganisms**

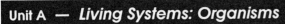

Unit A — Living Systems:
Organisms

Living things have been on the Earth for millions of years. A great variety of organisms is here today because each learned how to survive. They were able to live through floods, famine, and fire.

The cactus and the camel have "adapted" to the desert environment. Each has a good system for conserving water.

Arctic hares can live in very cold places. They have learned how to change when the environment changes.

If a plant or animal is unable to change, it must move to another place. If it cannot change or move, it will die.

What organisms must do to stay alive is the subject of Unit A.

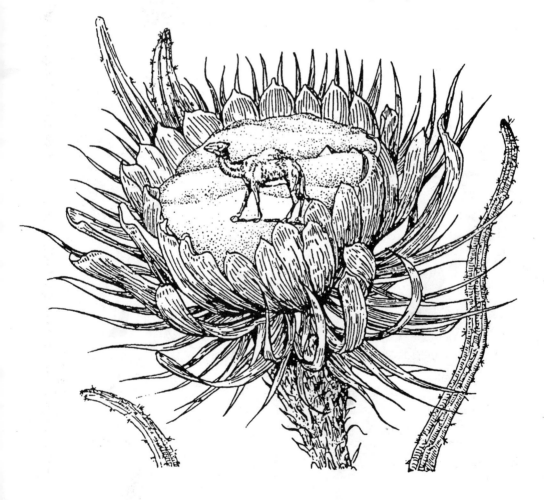

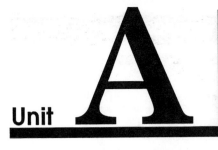

Modern Classification of Living Things*

Kingdom:
Monera — Blue-green Algae
— Bacteria

Kingdom:
Protista — Protozoa
— Algae

Kingdom:
Fungi — Mushrooms
— Molds
— Yeasts

Kingdom:
Plants

Bryophyta
Liverworts
Mosses

Tracheophyta
Ferns
Cone-bearing plants (evergreens)
Flowering plants (oaks, peas, roses)

Kingdom:
Animals

Invertebrata
— Porifera (with holes - sponges)
— Coelenterata (sac-like - jellyfish, coral)
— Worms (tubelike bodies - earthworm)
— Mollusks (soft-bodies - clams)
— Echinoderms (spiny-skinned - starfish)
— Arthropods (jointed-legs - grasshopper)

Vertebrata
— Fish (bass, trout)
— Amphibians (frogs)
— Reptiles (snakes, turtles)
— Birds (ostrich, robin, hawk)
— Mammals (mice, cats, humans)

*Viruses: Biologists have not been able to agree whether a virus is a living organism or not; therefore, viruses will be classified by themselves.

Questions

1. How many kingdoms do most scientists use in classification today?
   1 2   2 3   3 5   4 6

2. Which of the following organisms is *not* classified as an invertebrate?
   1 jellyfish   2 shrimp   3 snake   4 earthworm

3. The classification of most organisms is usually determined by their
   1 size   2 intelligence 3 structure   4 color

4. Mushrooms belong to the kingdom
   1 plants   2 animals   3 protista   4 fungi

5. Which organism is classified as an invertebrate?
   1 dog   2 frog   3 sponge   4 snake

Concepts and Words To Be Understood

adaptation	conservation	habitat	nutrient
chlorophyll	ecosystem	hibernate	organism
classification	environment	microbe	photosynthesis
community	extinct	Monera	Protista
Fungi		succession	

Since the beginning of his time, man has observed his surroundings. He noticed that some things moved, others did not. Some things were good to eat, others were not. All things reproduced, but not always in the same way.

He noted these differences and used them to **classify** or group all the things in his **environment**.

I. Activities Of Living Things

Man has defined certain characteristics that an object must possess in order to be considered alive. In this way, man can identify a living thing from a nonliving one. These characteristics are called **life activities**.

A. Life Activities

Life activities are the necessary processes that a living organism goes through during its lifetime. Some of these processes occur <u>continuously</u> (for example, respiration). Others occur <u>daily</u> (such as ingestion and excretion). Some occur only <u>occasionally</u> (for example, reproduction). In any event, living things are in constant contact with their environment. They also continually exchange materials with their environment.

The following ten processes (life activities) can be remembered by the letters **GRISSLED D & R.** These letters are the first letter of each activity. The letters GRISSLED D & R stand for:

G - **Growth**
R - **Respiration**
I - **Ingestion**
S - **Secretion**
S - **Sensitivity**
L - **Locomotion**
E - **Excretion**
D - **Digestion**
D & R - **Death and Reproduction**

Growth is the ability to increase in size. Sometimes, only an organism's size changes. In other cases an organism's appearance changes as well.

Respiration is the process that makes cell energy from food. Almost all living things need oxygen in order to change food into energy.

Ingestion is the taking in of food, water, and other needed materials.

Secretion is the letting out of a liquid into or outside of the body. (such as, the secretion of saliva, hormones, perspiration, and body oil)

Sensitivity (responding to stimuli) is when an organism reacts to a change in its environment. For example, if a bright light suddenly came into your eye, you would blink. This kind of sensitivity is called a **reflex**.

Locomotion (movement) is the act of moving. Animals go from one place to another to seek food and shelter.

Excretion is getting rid of the waste materials made in the cells of the organism. (such as liquid - urine/sweat, gas - carbon dioxide) Note: the term *elimination* is used when referring to removing feces (solid wastes) from the large intestine.

Digestion is the process of breaking down food into small particles that can be dissolved in water. Then, the particles can be absorbed by the cells.

Death & Reproduction. All living organisms must die at some time. Reproduction is the process by which organisms produce offspring in order for their *species* to continue. All living things come from other living things of the same kind of *species*.

Sometimes, the offspring is exactly like the parent.

At other times, there are slight differences called **variations**.

There are two ways that an organism can reproduce: **asexually** (from one parent) and **sexually** (from two parents).

Questions

1   Which of the following is not a life activity?
   1   digestion   3   thinking
   2   respiration   4   growth

2   Breeding animals and plants to meet modern food demands requires that the farmer study
   1 digestion   2   excretion   3   locomotion   4   reproduction

3   The process of taking in food is called
   1 digestion   2   excretion   3   ingestion   4   indigestion

4   Organisms respond to stimuli
   1   occasionally   3   never
   2   continuously   4   once in a while

5   The gas needed to convert food into energy is
   1   oxygen   3   nitrogen
   2   carbon dioxide   4   hydrogen

B. Asexual Reproduction

Asexual reproduction requires only one parent and produces one or more offspring which are exactly like that parent. Some examples are:

Budding

The parent cell produces a small daughter cell called a bud. This gradually enlarges to a mature cell. The bud may remain attached to the parent cell or break off. When mature, it also will produce a bud.

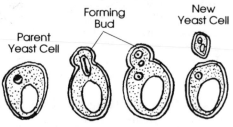

Budding in Yeast

Budding occurs in yeast. If you observe yeast under a microscope, you can watch a bud form and separate from the parent cell.

Vegetative Propagation

Some plants are capable of **regeneration** (to form again) by planting their leaves, stems, or roots.

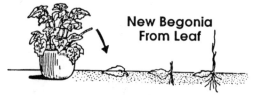

New Begonia From Leaf

Leaf. If a leaf is cut off a begonia plant and placed in moist soil or water, roots and a stem will start to grow. A begonia, *exactly* the same as the first, is produced.

Stems. *Bulbs*, such as the onion, daffodil, and lily will grow well either in moist soil or water.

Bulb

Strawberry Runner

Strawberry and mint plants have trailing stems that grow horizontally. New roots and plants grow at their ends. This results in a row of plants connected by the *runner*.

White potatoes and dahlias are *tubers*. Tubers have "eyes" which are really buds. New plants grow from these buds.

Rambling roses and raspberries also have trailing stems. When these stems touch the ground, a new plant *exactly* the same as the parent plant forms. When a gardener does this, it is called *layering*.

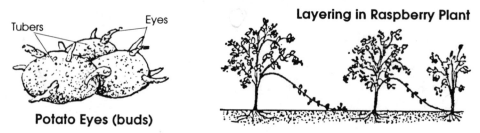

Potato Eyes (buds)

Layering in Raspberry Plant

Roots. The roots of sweet potatoes, carrots, beets, and turnips contain much stored food. These roots will produce a new plant. Again, the new plant is exactly the same as the parent plant.

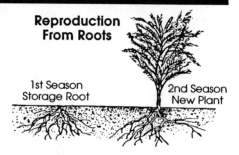

Reproduction From Roots

1st Season
Storage Root

2nd Season
New Plant

C. Artificial Vegetative Propagation

New plants can be grown by **stem cutting** and **grafting**. Stem cutting is just what it says. You cut the stem from a plant such as a geranium, and put it in water or wet soil. It will produce a new plant.

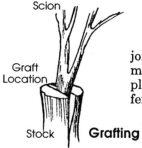

Scion

Graft
Location

Stock   **Grafting**

Grafting. Grafting is when the stem of one plant is joined to the stem of a closely related plant. This is common for reproducing many fruit trees and roses. Some plant nurseries have grafted a tree with five or more different apple varieties growing on the same stock.

Spores. Reproduction by spores is found in the Fungi and Monera kingdoms. Molds and some yeasts have balloon-like structures at the top. These are spore cases. When these cases burst, the spores fly out and spread. New molds or yeasts grow from these spores.

Spores

Spore cases

Bread Mold

Reproduction By Spores

Animals. Asexual reproduction occurs in a few animals by **regeneration**. If a piece of the animal, such as the starfish is broken off, it will grow back the missing part.

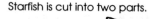

Starfish is cut into two parts.

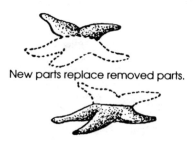

New parts replace removed parts.

Regeneration Of Starfish Parts

Questions

1   Which of the following is *not* an example of asexual reproduction?
    1   grafting   2   layering   3   pollination   4   regeneration

2   In this form of reproduction, what is true about
the offspring?
    1   a different type of organism will form
    2   daughter cell will be exactly like the parent
      cell
    3   daughter cell will be a different color from the parent cell
    4   daughter cell will be much taller than parent

3   Commercial apple growers usually start new trees by
    1   planting seeds   3   using the budding process
    2   planting bulbs   4   using grafting

4   A fisherman cuts up a live sponge and throws it back into the ocean.
What will most likely happen?
    1   a new form of life will develop
    2   a coral reef will form
    3   the pieces will die
    4   the sponge pieces will form new sponges

5   Which form of reproduction is
represented by this diagram?
    1   budding
    2   grafting
    3   spore formation
    4   layering

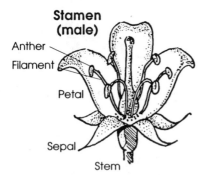

**Stamen
(male)**

Anther

Filament

Petal

Sepal

Stem

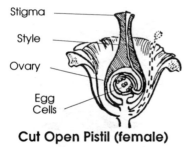

Stigma

Style

Ovary

Egg
Cells

Cut Open Pistil (female)

D. Sexual Reproduction

Sexual reproduction occurs when two different parents (male and female of the same species) produce an offspring. This produces variations.

Flowering plants reproduce sexually by flowers, pollination, and seeds.

The male part of the flower is the stamen. The stamen consists of the anther and filament. The female part is the pistil, consisting of the stigma, style, and ovary.

Sperm cells are located in pollen grains formed in the anther. Egg cells are produced in the ovary.

Pollen from one flower is transferred to the stigma of the same flower or another flower of the same species. This is called **pollination**. Sometimes insects or the wind help pollination to occur.

After pollination, a sperm enters the ovary and fertilizes the egg. The fertilized egg develops into a seed.

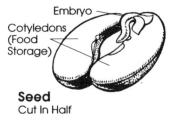

Embryo

Cotyledons
(Food
Storage)

Seed
Cut In Half

Each seed contains an embryo plant and a supply of food. In addition, some flowering plants produce fruit which aids in seed spreading. Fruit improves the new plant's chances for survival.

Fruit

Sexual reproduction in animals occurs by either external fertilization (such as frogs and most fish) or internal fertilization (such as birds and mammals).

E. Life Cycles

The life cycle of an organism is the series of changes it goes through. These changes occur in its development and in producing more of its kind.

Mammals, including man, have a simple life cycle. The mammal is born. After childhood, it enters a stage called **puberty**. Puberty is when the organism's body prepares for the process of reproduction. After puberty comes adulthood.

The life cycle of some animals is not as simple. The frog, for instance, goes through very dramatic changes during its life.

Life Cycle Of A Frog

In early spring the female frog deposits her eggs in a pond. The male frog helps squeeze the eggs out of the female. Then, he deposits the sperm over the eggs. The sperm swim to the eggs and fertilize them. This is an example of **external fertilization** in animals because the egg and sperm join *outside* of the female's body. The fertilized eggs hatch into tadpoles. They have gills and a fin-like tail. The tadpoles breathe underwater and behave like fish.

After a while, a jaw and legs develop. At the same time, the gills and tail disappear, and the adult toad or frog is formed. The adult now breathes through nostrils (lungs) out of the water. It now behaves like a land creature.

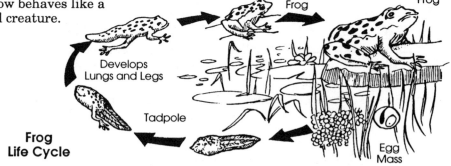

Young
Frog

Adult
Frog

Develops
Lungs and Legs

Tadpole

**Frog
Life Cycle**

Egg
Mass

Life Cycle Of A Beetle

After internal fertilization has occurred, the female flour beetle will deposit her eggs on a food source such as bread flour. In a couple of days, the eggs will hatch and small worm-like organisms appear. This is called the **larva** stage. The young will feed on the flour for a week or two. Then the larva will become inactive or **pupate**. During the pupa stage the insects are enclosed in a protective casing.

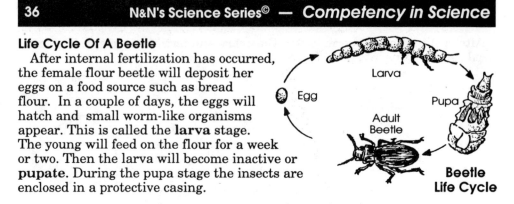

Beetle
Life Cycle

After several days they will change into adults. The beetles will mate a short time afterwards. The life cycle is complete and begins again.

Life Cycle Of A Flowering Plant

Sperm from the male structure of the plant enter the pistil. These sperm move down to the ovules (eggs), and fertilization takes place. A fertilized egg develops into an embryo. The outer covering of the ovule hardens into a protective covering called a seed coat. The ovule has now become a **seed**. Each seed contains the plant embryo and stored food. The stored food becomes the source of nutrients and energy for the germinating (beginning to grow) seed.

In some flowering plants, the ovary enlarges and becomes a **fruit**. Some fruits are good to eat (such as oranges, peaches, apples, tomatoes, and green beans). Others, like the fruits of maple and elm trees, are not.

When a seed is deposited, and if conditions are favorable, it will begin to **germinate** (start to grow). The life cycle of the plant begins all over again.

Questions

1 During the pupa stage an insect
   1 hibernates   3 sleeps
   2 changes its form   4 dies

2 Of the following animals, which has offspring that look completely different from the adult?
   1 snake   2 cow   3 eagle   4 butterfly

3 Flowering plants produce egg cells in the
   1 anther   2 ovary   3 stem   4 stigma

4 The process of transferring pollen from the stamen to the pistil is called
   1 fertilization   3 regeneration
   2 pollination   4 reproduction

5 An example of external fertilization would occur with
   1 horses   2 frogs   3 bees   4 eagles

F. Needs For Living Things

Even though living things are divided into different kingdoms, having many different characteristics and needs, almost all of them still have the same five basic needs:

> · Food
> · Water
> · Oxygen
> · Proper Temperature
> · Proper Environment

Food

All living things require food. Food provides the energy and raw materials for growth, repair, and all other life activities.

Plants

Plants make their own food through the process of **photosynthesis**. Green plants have a chemical substance called **chlorophyll**. Without chlorophyll, a plant cannot produce food. This is why only green plants can make their own food. Photosynthesis occurs when chlorophyll reacts with carbon dioxide, water, and sunlight. A plant takes in carbon dioxide from the air and obtains water from the soil.

The chlorophyll is found mainly in the leaves of the plant. Sunlight is absorbed by the chlorophyll and provides the energy needed for chemical change to take place. The end products of photosynthesis are a simple sugar (glucose), water, and oxygen. The sugar provides the energy (life process of respiration) needed for a plant to carry on its life functions. During respiration, the plant releases carbon dioxide into the atmosphere. Photosynthesis can be explained easily by this formula:

$$\text{Carbon Dioxide} + \text{Water} + \text{Sunlight} \xrightarrow{\text{Chlorophyll}} \text{Sugar} + \text{Oxygen} + \text{Water}$$

Photosynthesis makes green plants very important to nearly all life on Earth. Two reasons for this are:

1) Green plants produce their own food. Almost all other forms of life depend on the green plants for their own food needs.
2) During the process of photosynthesis, green plants take in carbon dioxide from the air and release oxygen. This is very important because oxygen is continually being removed from the environment by all forms of combustion (for example: fires, car engines, and furnaces). In addition, all plants and animals use this oxygen for their own energy needs (respiration).

Animals

Animals depend on green plants for food and oxygen. Since animals have to find their food, locomotion is very important to an animal's survival. The animals move from place to place to find food. Man is the only animal who has learned to grow his own food in one area.

Food is used by animals for three main purposes:
- to supply energy to carry on the life activities of the animal
- to build and repair tissue
- to function as body regulators

Food requirements can regulate an animal's activity. An animal eats more when the temperature gets colder. This provides more energy. Any extra food (stored as fat) acts as insulation to protect the animal from the cold.

Fungi

Some nongreen plants and Fungi, such as mushrooms, cannot produce their own food because they lack chlorophyll. These organisms, like animals, depend on other living things for food.

G. Nutrients In Food

Food provides energy and materials (nutrients) needed to build and repair body cells and tissues. These nutrients keep the systems of the organisms in balance (homeostasis).

Nutrients And Their Functions

Carbohydrates are made up of sugars and starches. Carbohydrates are the body's main source of energy. Fruits, honey, potatoes, bread, and cereal are foods rich in carbohydrates..

Fats are called the "stored energy foods." Fats also help keep the body warm, cushion joints, and protect nerves. Some foods that are high in fats include butter, oil, and peanuts.

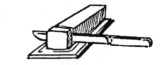

Proteins are found in many foods including meats, milk, eggs, and vegetables. They help to build and repair body parts.

Vitamins are necessary for normal growth, development, and functioning of the body. A well-balanced diet will provide you with all the vitamins your body needs.

 Minerals are found naturally on the Earth. They are necessary for the development of your bones and teeth and for cell growth. Minerals also aid in the repair of body parts and the regulation of body processes.

Water may be considered the most important nutrient. No organism can survive without water.

Water is important because it performs all of the following functions:

- makes up most of the blood

- moistens the lining of the lungs making it easier for oxygen to enter and carbon dioxide to leave

- helps remove cell wastes through exhalation, urination, and perspiration

- is the major part of perspiration (sweat) which cools the body

The Major Vitamins

VITAMIN	SOURCE	VALUE and FUNCTION
A	eggs, fruits, liver, green and yellow vegetables	necessary for normal growth, healthy eyes and skin
B_1 thiamine	whole-grains, seafood, milk, nuts, vegetables, poultry	helps release energy from foods, necessary for healthy nerve tissue, maintains appetite and metabolism
B_2 riboflavin	whole-grain cereals, milk, eggs, cheese, liver	helps maintain skin, eyes, and nerves, necessary for normal growth
B_{12}	meats, liver, whole-grains, milk, eggs	needed for proper development of red blood cells, helps keep the nervous system healthy
C ascorbic acid	vegetables, tomatoes, citrus fruits	keeps teeth, gums, and blood vessels healthy, helps with tissue repair
D	fruit, liver, milk, eggs	helps build strong bones and teeth
K	pork, liver, grains, green-leafy vegetables	aids in the clotting of blood
E	vegetables, milk, butter	protects cell membranes

The Major Minerals

MINERAL	SOURCE	VALUE and FUNCTION
Calcium	soybeans, eggs, milk, cheese	keeps teeth and bones healthy, needed for proper nerve function, necessary for blood clotting
Iron	eggs, beans, raisins, liver, leafy vegetables	forms part of the red blood cells, helps transport oxygen in the blood
Sodium	green & yellow vegetables, seafood, salt	controls water balance, needed for the normal action of nerves and muscles
Phosphorus	dairy products, eggs, beans, whole grains	maintains healthy teeth and bones
Potassium	green & yellow vegetables	promotes growth, keeps cells and blood healthy, controls heart activity, nervous system, and kidneys
Iodine	seafoods, iodized salts, onions	needed for normal cell metabolism, promotes growth

Questions

1   The vitamin needed for proper development of red blood cells is
   1 A   2 B2   3 B12   4 D

2   A child has soft, weak bones. His/her diet needs to be enriched with vitamin
   1 A   2 C   3 D   4 K

3   A person is about to have surgery. The doctor prescribes extra vitamin K before the operation. This is to help
   1 clot the blood   3 protect cell membranes
   2 maintain nerves   4 strengthen bones

4   Which two minerals are necessary to keep teeth and bones healthy?
   1 calcium and phosphorus   3 potassium and sodium
   2 iron and iodine   4 sodium and calcium

5   A doctor prescribes a diet with more eggs, beans, raisins, liver, and leafy vegetables. The student probably needs to improve the condition of her/his
   1 cell metabolism   3 teeth and bones
   2 red blood cells   4 water balance

Water

   Water is essential for life and is provided by the environment. The bodies of living things are from 65% to 95% water. Green plants use water for photosynthesis. All cells and living organisms need water to help transport materials.

Water is a reusable natural resource that is recycled. Water is both taken in and given off by organisms. The processes of respiration, secretion, and excretion help recycle water in the environment.

Humans have begun to misuse their water supply through pollution and wastefulness. Without proper conservation measures, the Earth's natural water supply will eventually be depleted.

Oxygen
All living things, including plants, must release energy from their food (respiration) as they carry on life activities. During respiration, most living things use oxygen and release carbon dioxide as a waste product. Some microbes (yeast) do not require oxygen for respiration.

Oxygen is obtained by most organisms either from the atmosphere (air) or from water. Many marine (sea) organisms are able to take out the oxygen that is dissolved in the water.

Proper Temperature
Most organisms cannot survive extremes in temperature. Each organism has its special temperature needs. All organisms have a temperature range that sets the limits of high and low temperatures. Beyond these temperature limits, organisms have difficulty surviving.

Proper Environment
All living things are in constant contact with their environment. An environment includes all the living (*biotic*) and nonliving (*abiotic*) things that affect the life of each organism within that environment. The amount of water, sunlight, temperature, certain gases, and minerals are some "nonliving conditions" that make up the type of environment within which an organism lives.

Questions

1 In order for photosynthesis to occur, plants need water, sunlight, chlorophyll, and
   1 oxygen   3 nitrogen
   2 carbon dioxide   4 sugar

2 A good source of carbohydrate is
   1 beans   2 red meat   3 bread   4 eggs

3 The five basic needs of living things are proper temperature, proper environment, food, water, and
   1 shelter   3 soil
   2 sunlight   4 oxygen

4 The major part of the body is made up of
   1 salts   2 minerals   3 water   4 air

5 Stored energy foods are
   1 fats   3 proteins
   2 carbohydrates   4 nutrients

II. Different Environments

The survival of an organism depends upon its ability to adjust to its environment. If the organism is unable to adapt to changing conditions, it must move to a more suitable place. If it is unable to adapt or find a satisfactory place to live, it will die.

A. Habitats

Each kind of organism is adapted to survive in a certain type of environment. Differences in the physical features of the Earth provide different environments or **habitats**. A habitat is a place where a plant or animal lives.

Water Habitat

Most water plants have no real roots. They are able to float near the surface to obtain their carbon dioxide and oxygen. Some water animals take their oxygen out of the water. Fish have gills that enable them to do this. Mammals, such as the whale, beaver, and seal, adjust by holding their breath for long periods of time.

In order to be better swimmers, aquatic animals have webbed feet or fins. They all have smooth, sleek water resistant bodies to enable them to move quickly in the water.

Soil Habitat

Worms and insects make up the bulk of the animal life in the soil. The worm's tube-like body helps it to burrow below the surface. Ants and other insects build small colonies underground by making tunnels.

These natural burrowers enrich the fertility of the soil by letting air and water drain into the ground. They also help in producing humus.

Air Habitat

Animals that spend most of their time in the air have wings to fly. Mosquitoes, bats, and birds all have an "airplane-like" structure.

Birds have hollow, air-filled bones to make them light. Feathers give their wings a large surface area. Insects also have light bodies with air tubes. Many insects have wings which enable them to fly.

Desert Habitat

Look at the cactus. How does the shape of its body help it to store water? Cacti have "needles" instead of leaves. The camel also has a special area for storing water. Why do desert animals need special water storage? Snakes and lizards are **nocturnal** animals. They are awake at night and sleep during the day. Why would being nocturnal be helpful in the desert?

Polar Habitat

Plants in the far north have a short growing season. During the long winter they are **dormant**. The exposed part appears to die. Life still exists in some roots. Often seeds remain dormant over winter and sprout in the spring. How would this affect the animals in the area?

During the short growing season, some animals, such as the arctic hare, store up food. This allows them to survive the winter when there is very little food to be found.

Arctic animals have adapted in other ways to survive the harsh climate. As compared to their "southern cousins," their fur grows much thicker and more body fat is stored. Why is this helpful?

Some arctic animals "sleep" during the coldest part of the winter. This is called **hibernating**. How would extra fat help them survive?

Forest Habitat

Why do trees grow tall in a forest? They have to compete for light. Where do you find mushrooms growing? Do they need sunlight in order to make food? Why not? How has the deer adapted to its environment? How might its long legs aid the deer in survival? Does the forest help protect the deer from predators? The slow-moving snail and turtle have adapted something else in order to protect themselves. What do you think that is?

In northern climates, birds have learned to **migrate**. They "fly south" in order to escape the poor weather conditions and lack of food during the winter months. The birds that migrate have not adapted physically to live in the same environment all year. Therefore, they must change their environment.

Natural Habitats

There are many different habitats. Each has its own specialized plants and animals. The plants and animals that live in a particular habitat are dependent upon the environmental factors in that habitat.

Questions

1 If an animal has a webbed foot, it most likely lives in what kind of habitat?
   1 terrestrial   2 air   3 desert   4 water

2 All of the following help an animal survive cold temperatures *except*
   1 hibernation   3 migration
   2 hollow bones   4 thicker fur

3 Most animals that live in soil are
   1 bats and worms   3 spiders and frogs
   2 gophers and moles   4 worms and insects

4 Water, soil, desert, polar, and air are particular habitats on Earth. They are the result of
   1 biotic factors in the environment
   2 communities of organisms
   3 the numerous populations of living things
   4 various physical features on the Earth's surface

5 When an animal hibernates, it is most likely
   1 escaping very cold weather   3 searching for food
   2 looking for water   4 seeking extra oxygen

III. Organisms And Their Environment

Living things are interdependent on one another and with their environment. This means that all organisms are somehow influenced by other living things and their surrounding environment.

A. Food Relationships

Food is necessary for all organisms to survive. Food (energy) is passed on from one organism to another forming a "food chain." Every plant, animal, protist, Monera, or fungus is part of a food chain.

Food Chain

Green plants are the *only* living organisms that can produce their own food. They are the *starting point* of any food chain. The food chain consists of:

Producers	Consumers	Decomposers

Producers are green plants. They produce glucose (simple sugar) and other nutrients which are needed by all other living organisms.

Consumers. All animals are consumers because they cannot make their own food. They are called **consumers** because they consume (eat) plants and other animals to survive.

Decomposers are the organisms that break down the remains of dead organisms. Certain bacteria are decomposers. Members of the Fungi kingdom (such as mushrooms, yeasts, and mold) are also decomposers. The job of a decomposer is just as important as the role of the producer and consumer in the food chain. Decomposers break down dead organisms into nutrients. These nutrients keep the soil fertile for the producers (green plants).

A Typical Food Chain Looks Like This:

green plant	→	**mouse**	→	**bacteria**
(producer)		(consumer)		(decomposer)

A food chain may also be illustrated by a pyramid shape. Producers, the largest group, are on the bottom and provide the consumers with their food source. Decomposers are the smallest group and recycle materials for the producers.

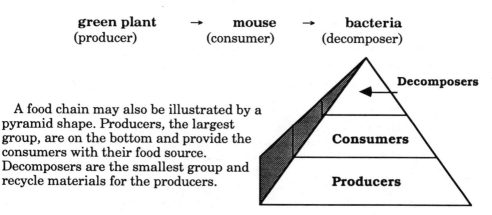

Some animals only eat plants, others prey on weaker animals for food. The animals that **prey** on other animals are called **predators**. A food chain could also look like this:

green plant	→	**mouse**	→	**snake**	→	**bacteria**
(producer)		(prey)		(predator)		(decomposer)

In this chain, the mouse is both a consumer and prey. There is a good chance that the mouse may be eaten by a larger organism. A **food chain** could be called an **energy chain**. First, green plants convert the Sun's energy to the energy in foods. Then, the consumers pass the energy on to other consumers and decomposers.

Food Webs

Sometimes food chains overlap each other. One organism (like the snake) can belong to two chains. It can be the predator; yet, it can also be preyed upon. For example, the snake may eat the mouse and then become the prey of an owl. Below is a typical **food web**. Identify the producers, consumers, predators, and decomposers in this food web.

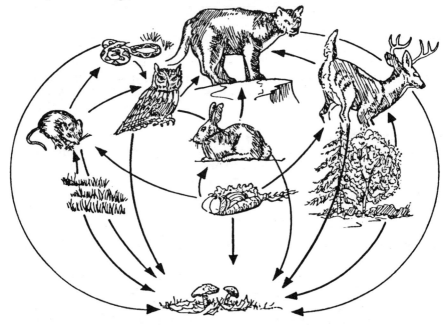

Animals' feeding habits help classify them. All animals that feed on other organisms, are called consumers, and may be grouped as:

> **Herbivores** — plant eaters (deer, rabbit, cow)
> **Carnivores** — meat eaters (lion, wolf)
> **Omnivores** — both plant and animal eaters (man)

Look back at the food web. Can you identify herbivores, carnivores, and omnivores? Are all of these groups represented in the food web?

Questions

1   The owls represented in the diagram are
    1   carnivores
    2   producers
    3   herbivores
    4   decomposers

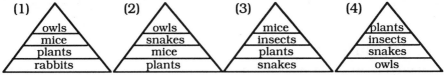

2   Which food pyramid best represents a food and energy relationship in the diagram above?

(1)
owls
mice
plants
rabbits

(2)
owls
snakes
mice
plants

(3)
mice
insects
plants
snakes

(4)
plants
insects
snakes
owls

Base your answers to questions 3 through 6 on the information below and on your knowledge of life science.

"A farmer planted corn in a field. At harvest time, he stored a great amount of corn in his corn cribs. The corn was needed to feed his live-stock during the winter. Several mice entered the corn cribs and ate some of the corn. The farmer's cat caught and ate some of the mice. After the cat died, bacteria broke down the substances in the cat's body. These useful materials were returned to the earth."

3   Which represents the food chain described above?
    1   cat → mouse → corn → bacteria
    2   bacteria → cat → mouse → corn
    3   corn → cat → mouse → bacteria
    4   corn → mouse → cat → bacteria

4   Which diagram best represents the food relationships in the paragraph?

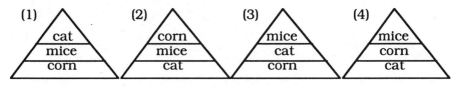

(1)
cat
mice
corn

(2)
corn
mice
cat

(3)
mice
cat
corn

(4)
mice
corn
cat

5   Which organisms could be the decomposers in this food chain?
    1   bacteria   3   algae
    2   protozoa   4   grasshoppers

6   The cat-mouse relationship could be described as
    1   predator - prey   3   producer - predator
    2   producer - consumer   4   herbivore - prey

7   The type of solid waste that is the least likely to be decomposed is
   1   paper   2   manure   3   wood   4   plastic

8   Which food chain is the correct order?
   1   mouse to seed to sparrow   3   banana to tiger to monkey
   2   earthworm to robin to frog   4   insect to toad to snake

9   Which of the following represents animals that eat both plants and other animals?
   1   herbivores   2   omnivores   3   carnivores   4   decomposers

10   Which is classified as a producer?
   1   tree   2   snake   3   lion   4   bacteria

B. Communities

All organisms of the same kind that are living in a certain place make up a **population**. All the interacting populations of a given area form a natural **community**. The interaction of a community with its environment is called an **ecosystem**.

Changes Over Time

Natural communities change over time. One community can be replaced by an entirely different community. Natural communities change in an orderly sequence of events. This is called **succession**. Succession is due to changes in the environment. When a balance is achieved, a new community is established.

Succession that begins with bare rock is called **primary succession**. The first stage of a forest is identified by lichens growing on rocks. These lichens decay and form humus (rich soil). Later, more complex plants such as shrubs and trees appear. Animals that live in each of the succession stages are dependent on the plants that live in that stage of succession.

Natural Community Succession

Primary   **Secondary (Changing)**   **Climax**

Destruction of a large land area might be due to either natural causes (such as floods, fires, and volcanoes) or human causes (such as strip mining and tree cutting). What will happen? New plant growth begins. With the appearance of plant life, the animals begin to return.

Secondary succession occurs when once uninhabitable land begins to support life again.

C. Energy Relationships

Energy usually enters a community during photosynthesis. Green plants use sunlight to produce energy for themselves. They store the rest as food. All the other organisms in the community use this energy produced by the green plants. When the plant is eaten by the consumer, the energy from the green plant is transferred to the consumer. The consumer now combines the food with oxygen. This process, known as **oxidation** or **respiration**, provides the energy for the consumer to carry on its life activities.

During photosynthesis, a plant produces simple sugar. Some plants combine molecules of sugar together to form starch. Oils and fats are also made. With the addition of other elements, proteins and vitamins are also made by plants.

The Energy Cycle

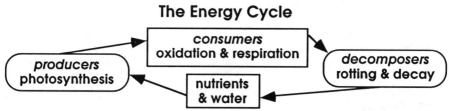

Certain bacteria and fungi called decomposers break down dead plants, animals, and garbage. This decaying changes the organisms back into nutrients to help fertilize the soil. Plants absorb elements from the soil. The bacteria help recycle the nutrients, keeping nature in balance. When nutrients are lacking in the soil, the soil can be fertilized artificially. Artificial fertilizers contain the elements nitrogen, phosphorus, and potassium. These are needed by the plants.

Recycling By Humans

Humans can take decaying plants and garbage and create a compost pile. A compost pile allows once living organisms to decay naturally into fertilizer. Then, the compost can be spread around living plants to provide the nutrients to help them grow better.

Questions

1 Primary succession begins with
   1   maple trees   3 lichens
   2   small animals   4 grass

2 All the organisms of the same kind living in a certain place make up a
   1   habitat   2 ecosystem   3 community   4 population

3 Energy continually enters a community during
   1   photosynthesis   3 succession
   2   recycling procedures   4 the water cycle

4 A forest fire completely destroys a large area of land. Which of the following organisms would most likely appear first?
   1   lichens   2 grasses   3 shrubs   4 small trees

5 The source of energy for an ecosystem is
   1   compost piles   3 decaying animals
   2   mature plants   4 sunlight

D. Balance Of Nature

The natural balance present in any ecosystem is the result of complex interactions. These interactions occur among community members. They also happen between the organisms and their environment.

Nature has provided organisms with a unique sense of survival. All living organisms have learned to adapt to their environments in order to survive.

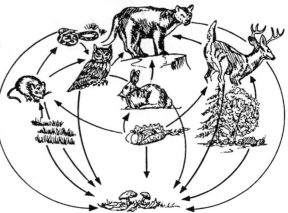

Again, look at this food web. The owl and the mountain lion may eat the rabbit. But, nature has provided the rabbit with a very fast rate of reproduction. The rapid reproduction of the rabbit insures that the species will not die out. This is called the **balance of nature**.

You should also note that members of a community interact in many ways to preserve the ecosystem's natural balance. Green plants are necessary to provide food for the animals (consumers). Some animals are predators. They rely on other animals for their food. The coyote eats the deer, and the bird eats the insect. The role of the predator is necessary. Predators insure that no one kind of animal (lets say the insect) becomes too abundant and overruns the community.

Bacteria also keep the community balanced. They break down dead plants and animals back into nutrients for the soil. Without these nutrients, the green plants would not be able to grow.

E. Disturbing The Environment

Natural balances may be disturbed in various ways, natural and human. Natural disturbances include floods, fires, disease, and severe climatic changes. Earthquakes and volcanoes also can drastically change an environment. An example of a natural disturbance of balance is the era of the dinosaurs. Dinosaurs roamed the Earth for a long time. Then for some reason, they became **extinct** (died out).

Man is the biggest contributor to the extinction of animals today. The construction of new homes, buildings, dams, and shopping malls has wiped out many natural habitats and the species living in them.

Hunting, fishing, industry, and pollution can also cause species to become extinct. Go to your library and find out about the plight of the American buffalo and the spotted owl.

Species that are in danger of becoming extinct are called **endangered species**. There are many groups of people today who try to save these animals from human carelessness.

Animals are not the only things that mankind has endangered. Soil, plants (grasses, shrubs, and trees), and fresh water are renewable resources which humans, through overuse, might use up.

Questions

1 The disturbance of the natural balance can cause an organism to
   1 become extinct
   2 gradually change its characteristics
   3 migrate
   4 all of the above

2 Which animals may have become extinct due to the loss of sunlight?
   1 polar bears   3 ground hogs
   2 golden eagles   4 dinosaurs

3 A fox catches and eats a field mouse. Besides getting food, the fox has helped nature by
   1 keeping the mouse population in check
   2 increasing the number of mice around
   3 saving the mouse from disease
   4 putting the mouse out of its misery

4 This diagram is of a typical ecosystem. All living things in this ecosystem interact with
   1 community members only
   2 community members and the environment
   3 members of their own population only
   4 the environment only

5 The main contributors to the endangerment and extinction of many animals today are
   1 natural disasters
   2 human beings
   3 animal predators
   4 diseases

IV. You, Society, And The Environment

Ecology is the study of the relationship of organisms and their environments. Ecologically speaking, the relationship that human beings have with their environment is generally *not* a good one.

The Earth's resources and recycling systems can support a limited number of people. Due to the rapid and large increase in people on the Earth, the natural resources have decreased. Man is faced with serious shortages of natural resources. Man's quality of life depends on these natural resources.

Soil, forests, water, and wildlife are renewable resources which humans, through overuse, may use up. Good conservation programs are the only way that man can guarantee his future on Earth. Each individual, as well as all of society, must do his/her part in order to conserve what resources we have.

Soil

Soil is a mixture of minerals, humus, air, water, and living organisms. The development of fertile soil requires a very long period of time. Soil is formed by the breaking up of rock into fine particles. When humus (decayed organisms) is mixed with these particles, a rich soil is made.

Causes of Soil Damage:

·   **Over-cropping** is the excessive planting of crops in the same area. The soil is not given a chance to become fertile again through natural or artificial processes.

·   **Leaching** is the dissolving of minerals out of soil by water. It is usually caused by flooding.

·   **Mismanagement** by land developers and urbanization is destroying prime agricultural land.

·   **Erosion** is caused mainly by wind and water. But, man can stop the loss of fertile land. He can use natural and chemical fertilizers, rotate crops, plant cover crops, and build terraces to prevent erosion. He must be careful when developing building sites.

Water

The water on Earth today has been here since the Earth was first formed. If this water is used up, there is no other source for it. However, the water cycle replenishes (recycles) the water used.

Human pollution of water from factories, oil spills, and man himself further decreases man's supply of clean water. Pollution also affects sea life which affects man in other ways (decrease in food supply).

Water conservation is accomplished through the use of reservoirs, pollution control, and purification processes.

Forests

Forests provide wood products and lumber, soil and water conservation, wildlife habitat, beauty, and recreation.

The greatest loss of forest resources is through fire, misuse, waste, insects, and disease. All of these are due directly, or indirectly, to human activity.

Conservation is achieved through fire protection and prevention, reforestation (tree replacement), selective cutting, and insect and disease control. Recycling of forest products, such as wood and paper, helps to cut back wasteful use of trees.

Wildlife

The wildlife resource is important for natural balance, food and clothing (wool and fur), insect control, recreation, and beauty.

Wildlife needs food and shelter in order to survive. Habitat improvement, restocking, game refuges, and environmental protection laws help to provide a natural balance on Earth.

Nonrenewable Resources

Minerals are nonrenewable resources which may eventually run out. Many minerals used by humans, however, can be recycled. Soda and beer cans, glass bottles, and some plastic containers are being recycled in some states by using a deposit system. Legislation makes this recycling possible.

Questions

1 The study of organisms and their environment is called
   1 botany   3 conservation
   2 ecology   4 paleontology

2 Which of the following can be recycled by man?
   1 newspapers   3 glass bottles
   2 aluminum cans   4 all of these products

3 Crop rotation helps to conserve
   1 forests   3 food
   2 water   4 soil

4 Forests are important to man because they are needed for
   1 building materials   3 recreation
   2 wildlife habitats   4 all of the above

5 Which of the following resources cannot be depleted through overuse?
   1 water   2 soil   3 oil   4 sunlight

Unit B — Living Systems:

Humans

Humans are the highest form of life on Earth. They share all the same life processes of the other organisms. Some of these processes are circulation, digestion, respiration, responsiveness, and reproduction.

The highly developed brain of humans makes them different from all other organisms. Human beings are able to "reason." No other living thing can do that. Humans need to use this reasoning power to care for their bodies.

Humans must eat the proper foods. By breathing properly, oxygen joins the food in the cells. The cells are then able to release the necessary energy to perform the activities of life.

Unit B describes how the human body works.

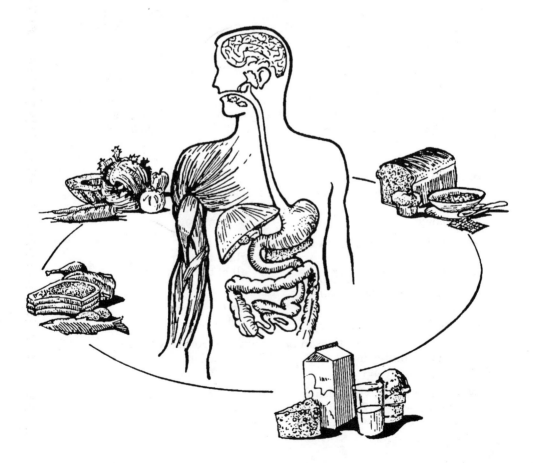

Concepts and Words To Be Understood

cartilage
cell
circulation

excretion
glands
hormone

reproduction
system
tissue

I. Body Organization

The human body is a complex organism composed of a variety of systems working together. Body systems are interdependent with one another. Each contributes to the operation of the system as a whole.

Cells Of The Body

In the human body, there are many different kinds of **cells**. Not only does each cell carry on its own life activities, but each one is also specialized. The cell performs a particular task enabling the organism to carry on its life activities.

The size, shape, and structure of the cell usually contributes to the function it performs.

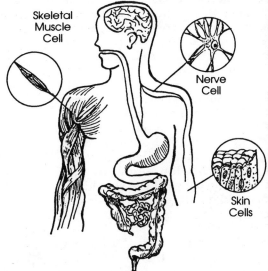

Skeletal Muscle Cell

Nerve Cell

Skin Cells

Tissues And Organs Of The Body

Tissues are a group of similar cells that perform the same function.

Organs are made up of either similar or dissimilar tissues that work together to do a particular activity. An example of an organ made of similar tissues is the stomach. An organ such as the eye is made of dissimilar tissues.

Organ Systems Of The Body

A **system** is a group of organs that act together. Systems perform certain functions such as digestion and circulation.

All the systems functioning together form an **organism**. The more complex the organism, the greater the differentiation (division of labor) between tissues and systems. This causes complex organisms to have a great dependence on their systems performing well with each other. Each organ system allows the human body to perform a particular life function.

Human Organization Summary:

Cells which act together are organized into tissues. Tissues which act together are organized into organs. Organs which act together are organized into systems. Finally, systems which act together are organized into a multicellular organism.

$$\text{Cells} \rightarrow \text{Tissues} \rightarrow \text{Organs} \rightarrow \text{Systems} \rightarrow \text{Organism}$$

II. Human Body Systems

A. Skeletal System

The 206 bones in the adult human skeleton give **form** and **support** to the body. They work together with the muscles to allow the body to **move**. They are also a **protection** for delicate body organs. In addition to **storing** minerals, the bone marrow found inside the bones supplies the blood stream with **red blood cells, white blood cells**, and small cell fragments called **platelets**.

The human skeleton is divided into two parts. The **axial skeleton** includes the bones of the skull, vertebrae, ribs, and sternum. The rest of the human skeleton is called the **appendicular skeleton** and includes the bones of the shoulders, arms, and hands and the pelvic girdle, legs, and feet.

Bones come in many shapes and sizes. Like a cell, the shape of the bone aids in the function it performs. Long bones are found in the arms and the legs. Long bones are lightweight and easy to move.

Bones of the hands and feet are small with many joints. This allows them to be more flexible with an ability to grip. The opposing thumbs and fingers of the hand make humans more advanced than many other animals.

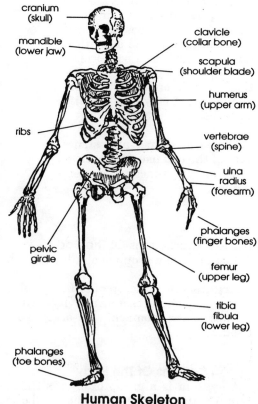

cranium (skull)

mandible (lower jaw)

clavicle (collar bone)

scapula (shoulder blade)

humerus (upper arm)

ribs

vertebrae (spine)

ulna radius (forearm)

phalanges (finger bones)

pelvic girdle

femur (upper leg)

tibia fibula (lower leg)

phalanges (toe bones)

Human Skeleton

Skeletal System Composition

The **skull** consists of the cranium (which covers and protects the brain), the bones of the face, and the jawbone.

The **spinal column** (also called the backbone). The top of the spinal column is attached to the skull. The bottom is attached to the **pelvis** (hip bones). It is made up of a line of bones called **vertebrae. Cartilage** is found between the vertebrae for flexibility and protection.

The **rib cage** is made up of the breastbone and twelve pairs of ribs. The ribs are attached to the spinal column in the back, and ten pairs are attached to the breastbone in the front. The rib cage protects the heart and lungs.

The **pelvis** (also called the hip bones) supports the upper part of the body and protects some organs in the lower abdomen.

The rest of the human skeleton is made up of bones which form the limbs. These are the bones of the legs, arms, feet, and hands.

Ligaments are strong, stringy bands that hold one bone to another. **Tendons** attach muscles to bones.

Cartilage is a tissue that is softer than bone but stronger than muscles. It is found at the ends of bones and at the joints between the vertebrae of the spine. It also attaches the ribs to the breastbone. Since cartilage is softer than bone, it gives flexibility to the spine, joints, and rib cage. This flexibility enables you to bend and twist your back. It also allows the chest area to expand and contract during breathing. Cartilage also provides rigidity to body areas that lack bones, such as the tip of the nose and the outer ear.

A **joint** is where two bones meet. Joints help the organism to bend and turn.

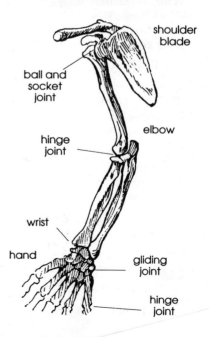

Movable Joints include:

- **Ball and socket joints** can move forward, back, and in circular motions (such as hips and shoulders).

- **Hinge joints** can move only back and forth (such as elbows, knees, and fingers).

- **Gliding joints** are found between the vertebrae of the spine and bones of the rib cage and palm area of the hand.

Immovable Or Fixed Joints do not move at all and are found only between the bones of the cranium (skull).

Skeletal System: Advances In Technology

Over the years, man has been able to repair or substitute for injured parts of his skeletal system. Early in human history, man used splints to set broken bones for healing. Wooden legs were used as a substitute for deformed or missing legs. Today, **prosthetics** (artificial limbs) enable doctors to repair broken bones with lightweight plastic parts. Doctors can also use metal and plastics to create workable joints and artificial feet, hands, arms, and/or legs for people who have lost that body part.

Questions

1 A group of specialized tissues performing one main function is known as
1 an organ
2 a cell
3 an organism
4 a system

2 Which order of organization is correct?
1 Cells → organs → tissues → systems → organism
2 Organs → tissues → cells → organism → systems
3 Cells → tissues → organs → systems → organism
4 Tissues → cells → organs → systems → organism

3 What part of the skeletal system connects bones with muscle?
1 cartilage
2 tendons
3 ligaments
4 vertebrae

4 Which joint has the greatest range of movement?
1 ball and socket
2 hinge
3 immovable
4 gliding

5 What is formed where the end of one bone meets the end of one or more other bones?
1 a joint
2 a socket
3 a pivot
4 a ligament

6 The heart is protected by what part of the skeletal system?
1 pelvis   2 rib cage   3 skull   4 joints

7 Which of the following is not a function of the skeletal system?
1 protection
2 support
3 repair
4 movement

8 Cartilage is found
1 at the end of bones
2 attached to the rib cage
3 between vertebrae
4 all of the above

9 The number of bones in the human skeleton is
1 53   2 112   3 206   4 600

10 The brain is almost completely surrounded by bone. This is because the brain
1 is connected by tendons
2 is made up of muscle cells
3 moves from one place to another
4 is delicate and needs protection

B. Muscular System

Our flesh is made up of more than 600 skeletal muscles plus fat. The flesh lies beneath the skin covering. Muscles have the power of contraction. They help the body to move in cooperation with the skeletal system. Tendons are tough, stringy bands that attach the muscles to the bones. The muscular system is also a protective covering for the organs. Fat is stored food that helps keep the body warm and cushioned from shock.

Muscles need a large supply of blood. This is because they require very large amounts of energy-supplying nutrients and oxygen.

There are three kinds of muscles. They are named according to their function and shape.

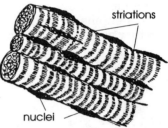

Voluntary muscles or **striated muscles** are long and slender. They are sometimes called skeletal muscles because they are attached to the bones. You are able to control these muscles (when you see an object, you pick it up, but only if you want to).

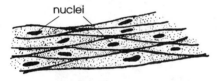

Involuntary muscles or **smooth muscles** are short and slender. You cannot control these muscles. They help to perform functions such as digestion and circulation. They are found usually in a "wrapped" position. This enables them to "squeeze." Squeezing is needed to push down food, transport blood, push out air, and secrete waste materials.

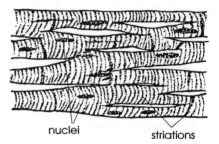

Cardiac muscle is found only in the heart. It is the strongest muscle in the body. Its structure is similar to both striated and smooth muscle cells, but it is an involuntary muscle. You cannot stop your heartbeat just like you cannot stop your food from being digested.

Questions

1. What type of muscle is used for "squeezing" in the internal organs?
   1. striated   2. skeletal   3. smooth   4. voluntary

2. When cardiac arrest occurs, what organ stops?
   1. intestines   2. brain   3. lungs   4. heart

3. Blood circulating through the veins is controlled by which type of muscle?
   1. striated   3. involuntary
   2. voluntary   4. circulatory

4   Cardiac muscle is found in the
   1 legs   2 intestines   3 brain   4 heart

5   Muscles can cause bones to move because they are able to
   1 contract   3 get longer
   2 grow fast   4 make blood

C. Nervous System

All living things respond to environmental **stimuli** (a change). The nervous system, along with the skeletal and muscular systems, enables you to **respond** to changes about you.

The nervous system consists of the **brain**, **sense organs**, and the **nerve cells** (neurons) of the spinal, sensory, and motor nerves. The nervous system, together with the endocrine system, controls the activities of the body.

Brain

A human brain is the most highly developed brain in the animal kingdom.   This gives humans a greater ability to think, reason, and create. The brain has three areas that control voluntary and involuntary movement.

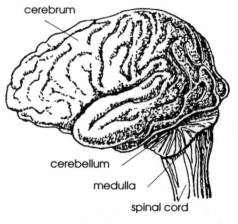

Human Brain
(side view)

The **cerebrum** controls thinking, memory, and senses. The senses include seeing, smelling, touching, hearing, and tasting. The cerebrum receives all messages from sense organs and responds to them.

The **cerebellum** controls muscle movement (coordination), and it also helps you to keep your balance.

The **medulla oblongata** controls the movement of internal organs and systems that require automatic action for survival (such as rate of heartbeat, breathing, and digestion).

Spinal Cord

The spinal cord, together with the brain, makes up the **central nervous system**. The brain sends signals or **impulses** to the spinal cord. The spinal cord relays these messages to other body structures. These impulses cause the involuntary and voluntary reactions of the body.

Spinal Cord Reflex Action

The spinal cord is also responsible for many reflex actions. A **reflex action** is automatic and protects the body.

The brain does not control most body reflex movements. Only after the response occurs does the knowledge of what happened register.

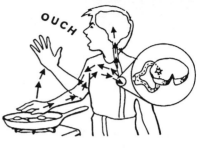

1) Boy touches hot pan.
2) A receptor sends an impulse to the spinal cord.
3) The spinal cord sends a message to the arm muscles to contract, lifting the hand.
4) A message also goes to the brain - "OUCH!"

Spinal Reflex Pathway

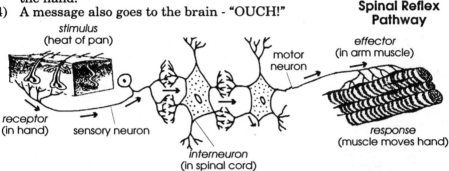

stimulus
(heat of pan)

motor neuron

effector
(in arm muscle)

receptor
(in hand)   sensory neuron

response
(muscle moves hand)

interneuron
(in spinal cord)

Neurons

Neurons are the nerve cells of the body. They are arranged so that they can carry **impulses** or messages in one direction only.

Neuron
(motor neuron)

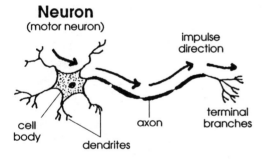

impulse direction

terminal branches

cell body

axon

dendrites

Motor nerves transmit messages from the brain and spinal cord to the muscles. This enables the body to move and causes glands to secrete.

Sensory nerves pick up messages from the sense organs and transmit them to the spinal cord or brain.

Associative nerve cells (also called interneurons) are found in the brain and spinal cord. They connect sensory and motor nerves.

The Learning Process

All learning processes are based on our ability to perceive or understand sensations. Sensations are the messages we pick up from the environment. Our senses of sight, smell, hearing, taste, and touch provide us with information about our surroundings.

Whenever we respond to a stimulus, it is an experience. Our brain records and our memory remembers these experiences. This helps us to act accordingly if the same situation should arise again. In order to learn new things, we must relate these things to previous experiences.

Reasoning is the power of understanding. Our brain takes our past experiences and makes sense out of new ideas, thoughts, and stimuli. Reasoning helps us to make mental judgments between two or more concepts.

Behavior
Behavior is the external action of an organism.

Inborn Behavior. Every animal is born with certain inherited behavior traits. These actions function automatically and help protect the animal. Simple reflex actions are inborn reactions which are *unlearned*. All animals, regardless of intelligence, have **instincts** that allow them to obtain food, breathe, reproduce, care for young, and move away from fires.

Acquired Behavior. Acquired behavior is *learned* behavior. Our voluntary acts are willful and are based on previous experiences.

Conditioning is a technique used to modify or change behavior to a desired response. For example: A boy wants to teach his dog to sit. Each time the boy pushes his dog into a sitting position, he says "sit." He then rewards the dog with a treat. The dog responds favorably due to the treat stimulus. So after repeated tries, when the boy says, "sit," the dog automatically does it. After a while, the treat can be dropped, and only the "sit" stimulus is needed.

Habits are responses to stimuli which become automatic. This is a result of constant repetition. Habits may be helpful or harmful.

Nervous And Muscular Systems:
Advances In Technology
Due to an injury to the nervous system or a disease, some people have trouble moving. The muscles or the nerves that control them are damaged. Operations sometime help in repairing the damage. When operations are not possible, crutches and wheelchairs help to increase the mobility of the injured person. Computers are also being used to help individuals who have problems with writing and/or speaking.

Questions
1   Nerves carrying messages of touch, taste, and smell to the brain are
   1   reflexes   3   sensory nerves
   2   stimuli   4   motor nerves

2   When a reflex occurs, what part of the nervous system controls the response?
   1   the brain   3   an impulse
   2   the spinal cord   4   sensory neurons

3   A change in the environment that causes the human nervous system to react is called
   1   a response   2   a stimulus   3   an effector   4   an impulse

4 The part of the brain that controls breathing and circulation is the
1 cerebrum   3 medulla oblongata
2 cerebellum   4 spinal cord

5 If your muscle coordination or balance is off, due to a blow to the head, you most likely injured the
1 cerebrum   3 medulla oblongata
2 cerebellum   4 spinal cord

6 An example of inborn behavior is
1 walking   2 talking   3 blinking   4 standing

7 An automatic response to a repeated stimulus is called
1 an impulse   3 a sensation
2 a message   4 a habit

8 Sensory nerves are found
1 in the brain   3 in muscles
2 in bones   4 all over the body

9 Conditioning is used to change or modify
1 memory   2 impulses   3 behavior   4 nerve cells

10 Which of the following cell structures is best adapted to carry messages from the brain?

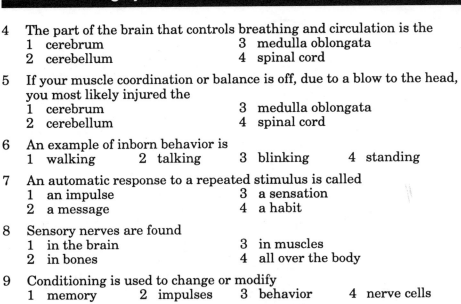

1 smooth   2 skin cell   3 neuron   4 skeletal
    muscle   muscle

D. Digestive System

The digestive system consists of the **mouth, esophagus, stomach, small intestine,** and **large intestine.** The liver and pancreas are **accessory organs.** They help in digesting foods. Digested food is needed to produce the energy that carries on life functions.

The Digestive Process

The process of digestion is as follows:

1. The **mouth** breaks down and softens the food (mechanical or physical digestion). **Saliva** contains an **enzyme** or protein that helps break starch molecules into simple sugar (chemical digestion).

• The **teeth** cut, tear, chop, and grind food. Teeth are useful in mechanical digestion to break large food pieces into smaller pieces. This increases their surface area for chemical digestion.

• **Saliva** moistens the food to make it easier to swallow. It helps to change starch into sugar. Besides mixing food, the **tongue** helps to push the food back into the throat (pharynx) for swallowing.

Human Digestive System

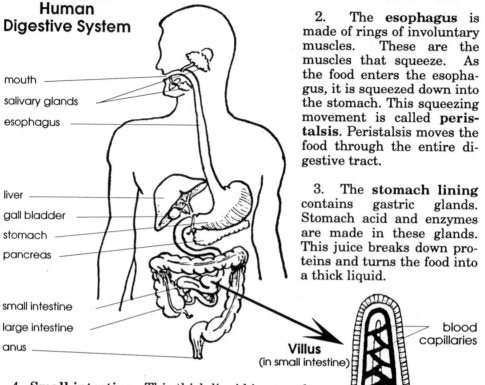

mouth
salivary glands
esophagus

liver
gall bladder
stomach
pancreas

small intestine
large intestine
anus

Villus
(in small intestine)

blood capillaries

lacteal

2.   The **esophagus** is made of rings of involuntary muscles.   These are the muscles that squeeze.   As the food enters the esophagus, it is squeezed down into the stomach. This squeezing movement is called **peristalsis**. Peristalsis moves the food through the entire digestive tract.

3.   The **stomach lining** contains gastric glands. Stomach acid and enzymes are made in these glands. This juice breaks down proteins and turns the food into a thick liquid.

4. **Small intestine.** This thick liquid is passed on into the **small intestine.** Here digestive juices from the **liver** and **pancreas** break it down further into a thick watery form. Digestion is now completed. The dissolved food passes through the walls of the small intestine into the bloodstream through small finger-like projections called **villi**.

5. **Large intestine.** Undigested and indigestible materials are pushed into the **large intestine.** These wastes (feces) move automatically through the large intestine and are eliminated from the body. In addition, the large intestine removes water from the wastes and returns the water to the body.

Pollution And Digestion Problems

Many harmful substances find their way from the environment into the human digestive system. Chemicals and harmful organisms may enter through the drinking of polluted water. The Safe Drinking Water Act of 1974 gives the U.S. Government the power to set drinking water standards. Some countries do not have such standards. Can you understand why Americans do not drink tap water in some foreign countries?

Harmful toxic chemicals are sometimes eaten. Pesticides and strong fertilizers are used on farms for better food production. The Food and Drug Administration (FDA) and the Environmental Protection Agency (EPA) protect consumers from eating poisons in their normal diets.

Digestive System: Advances In Technology

Artificial teeth have been around for a long time to aid in digestion. Even our first president, George Washington, is known to have used "wooden false teeth." False teeth today are made of ceramic materials. These materials make the false teeth look and feel more natural.

Besides new teeth, modern science can help with many problems in the stomach and intestines. A build up of stomach acid causes discomfort. Medicines, such as antacids that absorb excess acid, help to make you feel better.

Cancer can damage many parts of the digestive system. Operations to remove the cancerous growth can be performed in most cases. Chemotherapy (the use of drugs to arrest cancer growth) also may be used.

E. Excretory System

The excretory system removes (excretes) wastes from the blood and, eventually, the body. Besides the solid wastes (feces) stored in the **large intestine**, the human body gets rid of wastes made by body cells through the kidneys, lungs, liver, and skin.

The **kidneys** filter the waste from the bloodstream. These wastes are stored in the urinary bladder as urine. Eventually, urine is removed from the body.

The kidneys have another very important job. They control the water and the mineral balance in the body. The kidneys balance the levels of sugar, water, and minerals in the bloodstream.

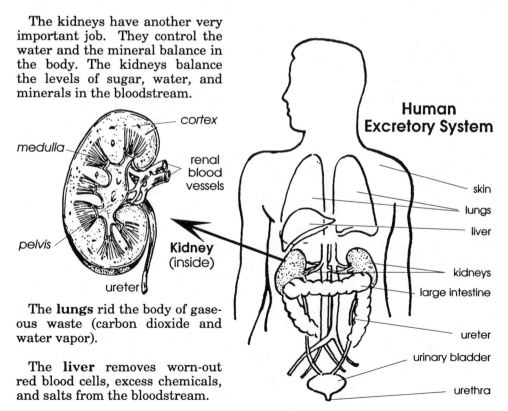

cortex

medulla

renal blood vessels

pelvis

Kidney (inside)

ureter

Human Excretory System

skin

lungs

liver

kidneys

large intestine

ureter

urinary bladder

urethra

The **lungs** rid the body of gaseous waste (carbon dioxide and water vapor).

The **liver** removes worn-out red blood cells, excess chemicals, and salts from the bloodstream.

Skin. Perspiration is one way the body protects itself. When the body overheats, the sweat glands lower body temperature. As perspiration pours onto the skin, it has a cooling effect when it evaporates.

Excretory System: Advances In Technology

A malfunctioning kidney can cause great pain and even death to an individual. A kidney transplant can give a person a new lease on life. However, donated organs are in great demand and short supply. Most people with kidney problems today depend on an artificial kidney machine. A person's blood passes through the machine so that the waste products can be filtered out. This process is called **dialysis.**

Questions

1   In humans, food passes from the mouth into the stomach through
   1   the esophagus   3   the small intestine
   2   the large intestine   4   the liver

2   Which organ filters the blood and makes urine for excretion?
   1   liver   2   lung   3   kidney   4   stomach

3   A body structure that aids in the process of *ingestion* is the
   1   intestine   2   stomach   3   esophagus   4   tongue

4   Which organ excretes water and helps maintain a normal body temperature?
   1   skin   2   kidney   3   lung   4   liver

5.   The main function of the human digestive system is to
   1   break down food   3   make minerals
   2   add vitamins to food   4   excrete carbon dioxide

6.   In humans, most digested food is absorbed through the
   1   stomach   3   small intestine
   2   esophagus   4   large intestine

7.   Why do most people with a malfunctioning kidney have to get dialysis treatments instead of having a kidney transplant?
   1   transplant kidneys are too large
   2   kidneys cannot be transplanted
   3   the transplant is too painful
   4   organs are in short supply

8.   Where in the digestive system does an enzyme begin the breakdown of starch into sugar?
   1   mouth   3   esophagus
   2   stomach   4   small intestine

9.   Which government agency protects consumers from eating foods with harmful chemicals in them?
   1   Urban Coalition   3   Environmental Protection Agency
   2   United States Senate   4   Federal Bureau of Investigation

10.   Without which of the following body parts could a human survive?
   1   heart   2   liver   3   teeth   4   kidneys

F. Circulatory System

The circulatory system is the transportation system of the body. It carries digested food, water, and oxygen to all body cells. At the cells, it exchanges these materials for carbon dioxide and other wastes.

Material Exchange

Diffusion. All small particles (molecules) are in constant motion. This allows materials to go into the spaces between other materials and cells.

Generally, molecules move from an area where there are more of them (high concentration) to an area where there are fewer of them (lower concentration). This is called **diffusion**.

The movement continues until there is an equal number of molecules in each area (equilibrium).

Osmosis is a special type of diffusion which takes place when water moves through a semipermeable membrane such as the cell membranes.

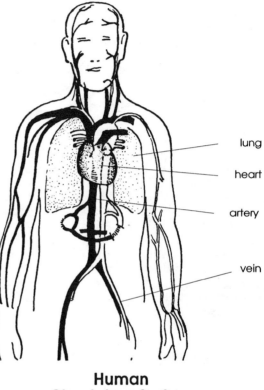

lung

heart

artery

vein

**Human
Circulatory System**

Circulatory Organ Functions

The human circulatory system consists of the heart, blood, arteries, veins, capillaries, lymph, and lymph vessels. The following are the structures and functions of the circulatory organs:

1. The **heart** is a pump that keeps the blood moving throughout the body. The heart consists of four (4) chambers. It is also divided into two (2) sides, the right side and the left side. Blood from the veins enters the heart in the right upper chamber and then passes down into the right lower chamber. A valve snaps shut to prevent the blood from flowing backwards.

The blood is then pumped out of the heart to the lungs. Another heart valve snaps shut so the blood cannot flow back into the heart. At the lungs, the blood cells get rid of carbon dioxide and pick up oxygen. When the blood absorbs a large amount of oxygen, it turns bright red in color.

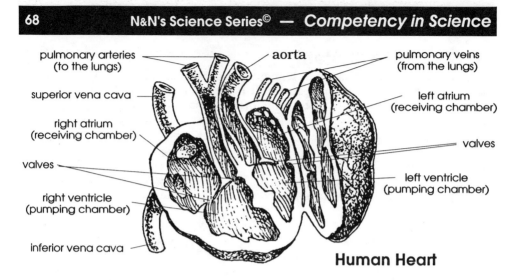

pulmonary arteries
(to the lungs)

aorta

pulmonary veins
(from the lungs)

superior vena cava

left atrium
(receiving chamber)

right atrium
(receiving chamber)

valves

valves

left ventricle
(pumping chamber)

right ventricle
(pumping chamber)

inferior vena cava

Human Heart

From the lungs, the oxygenated blood returns to the heart and enters the top left chamber. It then moves through another valve down into the bottom left chamber and is pumped out to the arteries. Another valve snaps shut to prevent the oxygen-filled blood from flowing backwards. The *snapping closed* of these pairs of valves in the heart causes the "thump thump" ("lubb - dub") sound of the heartbeat.

The heart pumps three to four liters (five to eight quarts) of blood through the arteries of the body each minute. This blood leaves the heart through the **aorta**, the body's largest artery. The process of the blood leaving the heart through the arteries and returning back to the heart through the veins is called **systemic** or **system circulation**.

Pulmonary Circulation is the process in which blood flows from the heart to the lungs and back to the heart again.

2. **Arteries** carry blood away from the heart to the capillaries (remember "A" for artery, aorta, and away). Arteries are large, strong, and thick. This allows arteries to withstand the spurts of high pressure produced by the heart. All arteries (except the pulmonary artery) carry oxygenated blood.

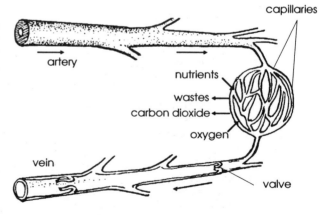

capillaries

artery

nutrients

wastes

carbon dioxide

oxygen

vein

valve

3. **Veins** carry the blood from the capillaries back to the heart. Veins have valves which do not allow the blood to flow backward. In the veins, the blood flows towards the heart under very low pressure. All veins (except the pulmonary vein) carry blood which is low in oxygen.

4. The **capillaries** are tiny blood vessels that connect the arteries to the veins. They surround all body cells. It is here that the exchange of food, oxygen, and water is made for carbon dioxide and wastes.

5. **Lymph vessels** carry a fluid called **lymph**. Lymph moves through a system of tubes from the body parts back into the bloodstream. The lymph helps to remove wastes and disease causing microörganisms from the body.

Blood

The blood is a **tissue** that is composed of a fluid called plasma and cells. The blood cells include red blood cells, white blood cells, and platelets.

Plasma is mostly water and contains dissolved nutrients, wastes, salts, gases, and chemical regulators (hormones). Plasma carries these things to and from the body cells.

Blood cells make up the "solid" part of the blood.

· **Red blood cells** (RBC's or erythrocytes) carry oxygen to the body cells. They are the smallest cells in the body. There are about five million in just one drop of blood.

· **White blood cells** (WBC's or leucocytes) fight infection, make antibodies, and protect the body from diseases. There are several kinds of white blood cells. White blood cells seek out and destroy foreign particles such as bacteria and viruses.

Platelets are very small cell parts (fragments) that help the blood to clot. The clotting of blood stops bleeding.

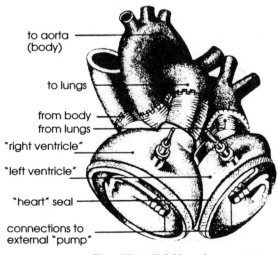

to aorta (body)

to lungs

from body
from lungs

"right ventricle"

"left ventricle"

"heart" seal

connections to external "pump"

The "Jarvik" Heart

Circulatory System: Advances In Technology

Blood transfusions (giving a person's blood to another person) have been around for many years. Both transplants of actual and artificial hearts (like the Jarvik VII) are relatively new. Not all patients who receive a new heart transplant survive. But, newer technology provides better chances. Plastic tubing is also being used to substitute for damaged veins and arteries.

Questions

1 Which sequence indicates the correct path of blood through the heart?
   1 left side of heart, to lungs, to right side of heart, to the body
   2 lungs, to right side of heart, to left side of heart, to the body
   3 right side of heart, to left side of heart, to lungs, to the body
   4 right side of heart, to lungs, to left side of heart, to the body

2 Blood leaves the heart and is pumped to the body through the
   1 pulmonary arteries   3 aorta
   2 vena cavas   4 pulmonary veins

3 Which blood vessels carry blood away from the heart?
   1 arteries   2 veins   3 capillaries   4 alveoli

4 Jarvik VII is the name of an artificial
   1 lung   2 kidney   3 brain   4 heart

5 Which cells carry oxygen?
   1 red blood cells   3 platelets
   2 white blood cells   4 muscle cells

6 Which blood cells help blood to clot?
   1 plasma   3 red blood cells
   2 platelets   4 white blood cells

7 Your heart pumps blood to the
   1 brain, only   3 lungs, only
   2 lower part of the body, only 4 all parts of the body

8 The blood carries
   1 only oxygen and carbon dioxide
   2 only wastes
   3 only food and water
   4 everything that the body cell needs to maintain life

9 Veins
   1 carry blood to the heart
   2 carry oxygen rich blood
   3 do not carry blood
   4 carry blood away from the heart

10 The right ventricle pumps blood to the lungs. This blood is high in
   1 lymph   3 oxygen
   2 plasma   4 carbon dioxide

G. Respiratory System

Respiration is the release of energy from the oxidation of food within an organism's cells. During this process, most organisms (plants and animals) use oxygen and give off carbon dioxide and water as wastes.

The respiratory system consists of the nose, trachea (windpipe), bronchial tubes, lungs, and the diaphragm. This system provides for the exchange of oxygen and carbon dioxide between the external environment and the body's cells.

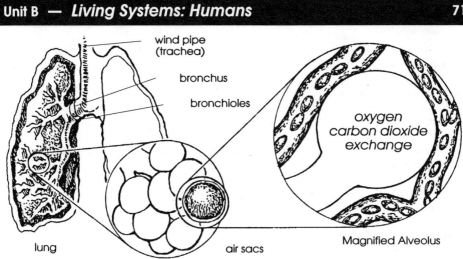

wind pipe (trachea)

bronchus

bronchioles

oxygen carbon dioxide exchange

lung

air sacs

Magnified Alveolus

Gas Exchange Between The Lungs And Blood
Carbon dioxide waste, which makes the blood very dark in color, is carried from the heart into the lungs. Inside the lungs are tiny air sacs (alveoli). These air sacs are full of oxygen that the body has just inhaled. Capillaries surround each air sac. Oxygen moves from the air sacs into the capillaries. Carbon dioxide moves from the capillaries into the air sacs. Then, the carbon dioxide is exhaled through the nose. The oxygen rich blood is now bright red in color.

Gas Exchange Between The Blood And Body Cells
The arteries carry the oxygen rich blood to all body cells. Once again, the blood enters tiny blood vessels called capillaries. Capillaries surround all cells and exchange the blood's oxygen for carbon dioxide waste. The blood, now with a high level of carbon dioxide, returns to the heart. The heart pumps the blood to the lungs for carbon dioxide excretion.

Process Of Breathing
1. The **nose** is the first struc-ture in the breathing process.

Air enters the nose through two openings called **nostrils**. **Mucus** lines the inside of the nose and nasal passages. This mucus traps dust and bacteria.

Cilia (tiny hairs) inside the nose filter the air. Also, the nose warms the air before it enters the lungs.

2. The **trachea** or windpipe connects the nose to the bronchi.

Human Respiratory System

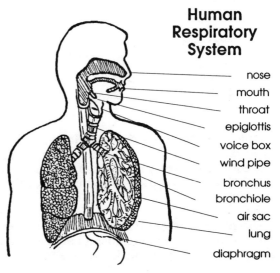

nose
mouth
throat
epiglottis
voice box
wind pipe
bronchus
bronchiole
air sac
lung
diaphragm

The **larynx** (Adam's Apple) or voice box contains the vocal cords. It is located at the top of the trachea.

The **epiglottis** is a flap of cartilage located at the back of the throat and above the windpipe. While eating, the epiglottis closes over the opening to the trachea to prevent food and liquids from entering.

3. **Bronchi.** The trachea divides into two tubes called the **bronchi or bronchial tubes.** These tubes go into each lung.

4. The **lungs** are two spongy organs. The bronchial tubes branch off into smaller tubes called **bronchioles.** At the end of each bronchiole is a balloon-like structure called an **alveolus** (air sac). It is here that carbon dioxide and oxygen are exchanged.

Breathing

Inhalation. The **diaphragm** moves down, creating a vacuum in the chest, and air enters the body. The air sacs inside the lungs fill and pass the oxygen out into the blood cells.

Exhalation. The diaphragm moves up, squeezing the unused air and carbon dioxide out of the lungs. The air moves back up through the bronchial tubes, windpipe, and out through the nose.

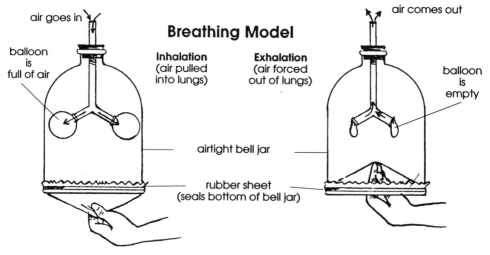

air goes in

Breathing Model

air comes out

balloon is full of air

Inhalation (air pulled into lungs)

Exhalation (air forced out of lungs)

balloon is empty

airtight bell jar

rubber sheet (seals bottom of bell jar)

Respiratory System: Advances In Technology

Diseases, such as asthma and bronchitis, inhibit an individual from breathing normally. **Antihistamines** are chemicals that help break up the "stuffiness" that causes poor breathing. Antihistamines come in pill or aerosol (spray) forms.

Oxygen masks and tents provide temporary relief for breathing problems. They also enable man to spend long periods of time underwater or in a spaceship, by carrying the air in storage tanks.

The Environment And Your Lungs

Pollutants and contaminants in the air are produced by natural and man-made processes. Examples of natural pollutants are smoke from fires, pollen from plants, and dirt and dust carried by the wind.

Man has lived with these natural pollutants for centuries. Only people with **allergies** (sensitivity to certain particles like pollen) were disturbed.

Today there are many more types of pollutants that man has to worry about. These contaminants are the results of man's advances in the field of technology. Some examples are:

car exhausts	**aerosol sprays**	**factory smoke**

These pollutants endanger the health of people, especially those who live in city areas. Air pollution, including smoking, causes such lung diseases as pneumonia, bronchitis, asthma, emphysema, and lung cancer.

Questions

1   Compared to inhaled air, exhaled air contains
    1   more oxygen
    2   more carbon dioxide
    3   more oxygen and carbon dioxide
    4   the same level of oxygen and carbon dioxide

2   In which region (shown in the diagram) does oxygen enter the blood?
    1   A
    2   B
    3   C
    4   D

3   When a person runs upstairs, the increased heartbeat supplies muscle cells with more
    1   oxygen   2   vitamins   3   proteins   4   minerals

4   Which factor would directly interfere with the normal functioning of the structures shown in the diagram of an air sac?
    1   diet (food)   3   drinking alcohol
    2   smoking   4   diabetes

5   The diaphragm moves down during
    1   inhalation
    2   exhalation
    3   both inhalation and exhalation
    4   neither inhalation nor exhalation

H. Endocrine System

The endocrine system is composed of **hormone-secreting glands**. These glands produce powerful chemical substances. The chemical substances work together with the nervous system to coordinate and control the body processes.

Hormones are chemical substances that affect or control the activity of some body organ or tissue. They are secreted directly into the blood from their glands. For this reason, these glands are sometimes called "ductless" glands.

Human Endocrine System

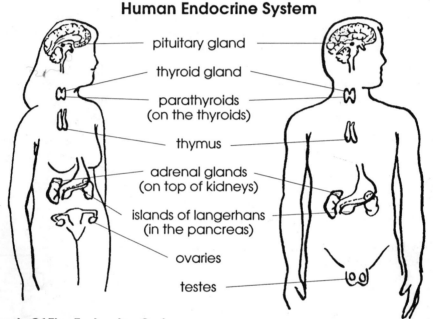

- pituitary gland
- thyroid gland
- parathyroids (on the thyroids)
- thymus
- adrenal glands (on top of kidneys)
- islands of langerhans (in the pancreas)
- ovaries
- testes

Glands Of The Endocrine System

Pituitary Gland (Master Gland). Located under the brain, the pituitary gland produces hormones that control the production of all other hormones. If this gland is not working properly, the other endocrine glands do not work correctly either. For example, some dwarfs and/or giants are the result of a malfunctioning pituitary gland.

Thyroid Gland. Located in the neck, it regulates the body's work pace (rate of metabolism). Too much hormone causes <u>hyper</u>activity (excessive movement). Too little causes <u>hypo</u>activity (less than normal movement) and obesity (overweight).

Attached to the thyroid gland are tiny **parathyroid glands** that regulate the calcium levels in the body. This is important for nerve function, blood clotting, and the proper growth of teeth and bones.

Adrenal Glands. Located on top of the kidneys, the adrenal glands produce the "Fright/Flight" hormone, **adrenaline**. Adrenaline causes the body functions to speed up in frightening situations. For example, suppose you were walking alone late at night on a dark street and heard a frightening sound. Your heartbeat and breathing rate would increase. You could begin to perspire. Your muscle reactions would increase. You would be more aware of your surroundings and might begin to walk faster.

Pancreas. The Islands of Langerhans found in the **pancreas** produce **insulin**. Insulin is needed to maintain the level of sugar in the body. If there is too little or no insulin being produced, the person is a **diabetic**. Diabetics must be careful of their diet. Some diabetics must take medication or injections of insulin to control their diabetes.

Adrenaline - "Super Drug"
Have you ever heard of a mother, after seeing her baby trapped under a car, lifting the car to save her baby?

Reproductive Glands. In males, they are the **testes** found in the scrotum. In females, they are the **ovaries** located in the abdominal cavity. They produce sex hormones that enable the human body to undergo a physical change called **puberty**. Puberty in boys develops facial hair, larger muscles, a deeper voice, and the production of sperm. Puberty in girls produces breasts, wider hips, the development of mature eggs by the ovaries, and menstruation.

Endocrine System: Advances In Technology
Today doctors can control many human problems that are caused by a gland that is not working properly. They administer hormones through injections or medicines. These liquids or pills help the gland to work properly. Sometimes they do the job of the gland, such as insulin does for diabetics.

Questions
1   The gland that controls all other glands is the
   1 thyroid   3 pancreas
   2 adrenal   4 pituitary

2   Diabetes occurs when which gland malfunctions?
   1 pancreas   2 adrenal   3 thyroid   4 pituitary

3   What condition may increase the flow of adrenaline?
   1 relaxation   3 ingestion
   2 circulation   4 stress

4   A malfunctioning thyroid gland could cause
   1 fertility   2 sterility   3 obesity   4 asthma

5   Testosterone is the male hormone produced by the
   1 thyroid   3 testes
   2 pancreas   4 adrenal

I. Reproductive System

The human reproductive system provides for the formation and development of offspring.

Male Reproductive System

The male reproductive system consists of the testes, penis, and sperm ducts. The basic function of each part of the system follows:

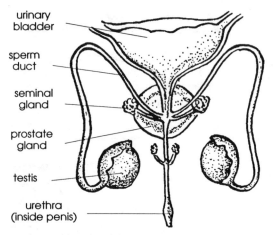

- urinary bladder
- sperm duct
- seminal gland
- prostate gland
- testis
- urethra (inside penis)

The **testes** are two enclosed glands found suspended from the body behind the penis. The testes produce male sex cells called sperm.

The **sperm ducts** are small tubes that carry the sperm into the penis.

The **penis** is the male sex organ through which the sperm are transferred to the female (into the vagina).

Female Reproductive System

The female reproductive system consists of ovaries (the sex organs), oviducts, uterus, vagina, and mammary glands. The basic function of each part of the system is as follows:

The **ovaries** produce female sex cells (eggs) around once a month.

The egg travels down a tube called the **oviduct** (Fallopian tube) into the **uterus** (womb).

The **vagina** is the female body organ where the male sperm is deposited.

In order for fertilization to take place, a sperm must travel up into the oviduct and join with an egg.

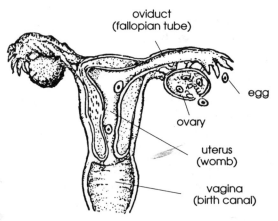

- oviduct (fallopian tube)
- egg
- ovary
- uterus (womb)
- vagina (birth canal)

If the egg is fertilized, the cell moves into the uterus and begins splitting and growing into a *fetus*. Under normal conditions, the fetus will eventually pass through the vagina to the outside of the mother's body. The baby is born.

The **mammary glands** are located in the female breasts. They produce milk following pregnancy. The milk provides nourishment for the newborn infant.

Characteristics And Chromosomes

Sexual reproduction carries **genes** from both the male and female to the baby by the union of the egg and sperm cells. Genes, which are found in the **chromosomes**, permit characteristics to be passed from the parents to their offspring. The sperm cell has 23 chromosomes, and the egg cell has 23.

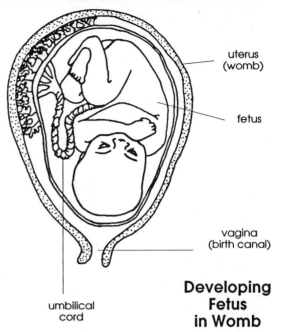

uterus (womb)

fetus

vagina (birth canal)

umbilical cord

Developing Fetus in Womb

The fertilized egg cell (zygote) receives 23 from each parent for a total of 46 chromosomes. This is the number necessary for human life to begin. Since the child gets half of its genes from each of the parents, the child is a combination of characteristics. Therefore, the offspring may be similar or much different from either parent.

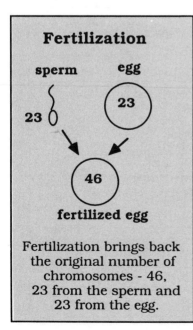

Fertilization

sperm   egg

23   23

46

fertilized egg

Fertilization brings back the original number of chromosomes - 46, 23 from the sperm and 23 from the egg.

Reproductive System: Advances In Technology

This system, unlike other systems, may malfunction and not necessarily affect a person's survival.

Today, modern science can aid in helping a pregnancy to occur or preventing a pregnancy from occurring. This is done through operations or medications.

Artificial insemination and in-vitro fertilization (commonly called the "test tube baby" procedure) can improve the chances for pregnancy to occur.

Artificial insemination is used widely on farms to impregnate cows. This allows for an abundance of beef calves produced for market and the production of milk on the dairy farm.

Use the chart below for a review of the human body systems and the major body organs and their activities.

Human Systems Review Chart

System	Major Organs	Major Activities
Skeletal	206 body bones	Provides body framework (shape); Produces blood cells; Supports, protects, and allows movement.
Muscular	About 400 skeletal muscles (that is, biceps, triceps working in pairs); About 200 involuntary muscles	Produces movement (along with the skeletal system); Determines body shapes and contours.
Nervous	Brain, spinal cord, nerves, and sense organs	Regulates most body activities; Collects information about everything going on around the body; Thinking and Memory.
Digestive	Mouth, esophagus, stomach, small intestine, large intestine, liver, and pancreas	Physical and chemical breakdown of food; Absorption of nutrients into the blood; Removal of wastes and reabsorption of water.
Excretory	Kidneys, skin, lungs, and large intestine	Removal of wastes, including solids, liquids, and gases.
Circulatory	Heart, arteries, veins, and capillaries	Transportation of blood, including food, oxygen, hormones, and wastes; Helps regulate body temperature and life functions.
Respiratory	Nose, throat, voice box, windpipe, lungs, and diaphragm	Exchanges carbon dioxide and oxygen in the lungs; Provides oxygen for cellular respiration (energy production in the cells).
Endocrine	Ductless glands: pituitary, parathyroid, thyroid, adrenal, testes, ovaries, and pancreas	Works with nervous system to regulate all life activities; Effects are very strong and usually last for a long time.
Repro-ductive	Female: ovaries, vagina, uterus, and oviducts Male: testes, prostate and seminal glands, and penis	Produces eggs and hormones that control female characteristics; Provides location for pregnancy; Produces sperm, fluids, and hormones that control male characteristics

Questions

1 The sex cell of a female animal is called
 1 an egg 2 a sperm 3 a zygote 4 a baby

2 The joining of a sperm cell with an egg cell is called
 1 puberty 2 fertilization 3 respiration 4 gestation

3 Which of the following is a sign of puberty (choose from the list below)?

a. growth	c. mammary glands
b. menstruation	d. facial hair

 1 a and b 3 b, c, and d
 2 a, b, and c 4 all of the above

4 The number of chromosomes found in most human cells is
 1 72 2 64 3 46 4 23

5 Which of the following cells are made by the male in testes?
 1 sperm cell 2 skin cell 3 brain cell 4 blood cell

6 Which of the following female glands produce milk for a newborn?
 1 ovaries 2 uterus 3 vagina 4 mammary

7 Puberty is part of the life cycle of
 1 human females only 3 human females and males
 2 humans males only 4 all plants

8 Which of the following processes *cannot* fertilize a human egg cell?
 1 internal fertilization 3 artificial insemination
 2 regeneration 4 in-vitro fertilization

9 If the mother has green eyes and the father has brown eyes, their son
 may have hazel eyes. This is true because the son received his genes for
 eye color from
 1 just his father 3 both his father and mother
 2 his mother, only 4 neither his father nor his mother

10 A newly born baby is called
 1 a fetus 2 an egg 3 a zygote 4 an infant

Directions for questions 11 through 15:
Match the following systems (1, 2, 3, or 4) with the statements below. (Any
choice may be used more than once.)

1 Circulatory System	3 Endocrine System
2 Digestive System	4 Nervous System

11 ___ Main function is to break large food into small nutrients.
12 ___ Transports nutrients, respiratory gases, and wastes.
13 ___ Uses hormones to coordinate and control other body systems.
14 ___ Uses ductless glands and the circulatory system to carry its chemicals
 to various parts of the body.
15 ___ Includes the brain, spinal cord, and neurons. It allows for rapid responses to stimuli.

Unit C — Living Systems:

Microörganisms

The smallest living organism is a "single cell." Microscopes are needed to see most single cells. With the invention of the microscope, scientists were able to see things that they had never seen before.

One-cell organisms, like bacteria and amoeba, were seen for the first time. Their life cycles were studied. With further research, scientists learned what caused certain diseases. They also found out what made bread rise, flavored some cheese, and spoiled foods.

In more recent times, the electron microscope gave scientists a chance to study viruses. Viruses are strange. They are clearly not plant, animal, or protist.

Unit C tells how cells work and what they do.

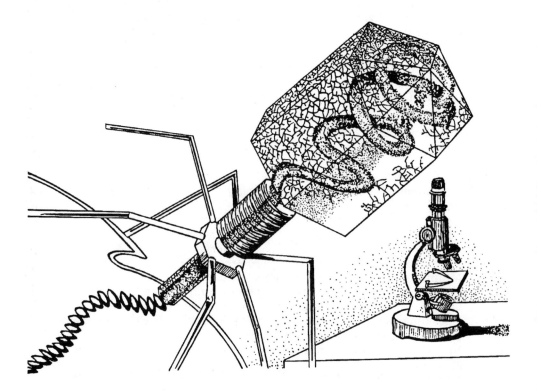

Concepts and Words To Be Understood

bacteria	meiosis	organelle
deficiency	microörganism	pasteurization
disinfect	microscope	pathogenic
fertilization	mitosis	porous
genetics	mitosis	porous
genetics	mutation	sterilization
infection		virus

I. Cells

A cell is the basic unit of structure and function of all living organisms. Each cell carries on all the life activities that a whole organism can do. These activities are growth, respiration, ingestion, secretion, sensitivity (response to stimuli), locomotion, excretion, digestion, death, and reproduction.

Cells may also be *specialized* to perform a specific job within an organism. For example, red blood cells transport oxygen and a small amount of carbon dioxide, bone cells aid in support, muscle cells contract and move bones at joints, and nerve cells pick up sensations and carry them to the brain.

Some organisms, such as bacteria or paramecia, consist of a single cell. They are called *one-cell* organisms. Some organisms have only two cell layers, such as, jellyfish and sponge. Organisms, such as humans, are complex because they consist of many specialized cells.

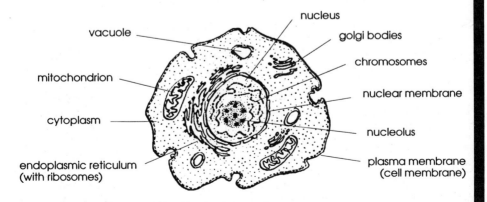

The Main Structures of the Generalized Animal Cell

Cells can only be produced by other living cells. This is known as the **Cell Theory**. They are composed of **protoplasm**, a jelly-like mass made up of proteins, carbohydrates, fats, water, and salts. Each cell contains various structures that carry on all the life functions.

A. Parts Of A Cell

Plasma Membrane

The **plasma membrane** (also called cell membrane) is a covering of the entire cell. It holds the cell's contents inside and keeps the cell's shape. The membrane is **porous**. It regulates (selects) the exchange of materials (such as food, water, oxygen, and wastes) into and out of the cell.

Nucleus

The **nucleus** is a small, dark body that is the cell's "brain." The nucleus controls cell division, growth, and all other cell activities.

The **nuclear membrane** is a protective double skin-like covering around the nucleus. It functions like the plasma (cell) membrane.

Chromosomes are long thread-like bodies made up of nucleic acid and protein. They are found in each cell's nucleus. They control cell division which is necessary for growth and reproduction. Each species of plant and animal has a definite number of chromosomes. For example, humans have 46, fruit flies have 8, dogs have 78, and a garden pea has 14.

1) A **gene** is a specific area on a chromosome. It determines a particular characteristic. There are at least 2 genes for each characteristic. With sexual reproduction, the genes may differ causing variations.

2) **DNA** (deoxyribonucleic acid) is the molecule inside the chromosomes that carries genetic information and makes cell reproduction possible. The Watson-Crick Model of DNA, known as the "double helix," is the best explanation of the structure of DNA.

3) **RNA** (ribonucleic acid) is similar to DNA in chemical makeup. RNA works with DNA in carrying out the instructions of the genetic code. It is also responsible for directing protein synthesis (manufacturing) in the cell.

The **nucleolus** is a small round body found inside the nucleus. It is where ribosomal RNA is formed.

double helix

DNA

Cytoplasm

Cytoplasm is mostly water (jelly-like) and contains the "living material" of a cell. Inside the cytoplasm are important structures (organelles) that carry out the life functions of the cell.

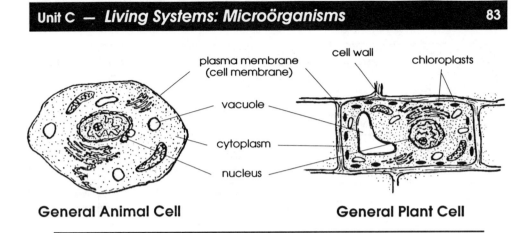

General Animal Cell   **General Plant Cell**

Other Cell Parts Within The cytoplasm

Vacuoles are empty areas used for storage of food, water, and/or wastes.

The **respiratory center** (mitochondrion) supplies the cell with energy (ATP) by the oxidation of food molecules.

Circulation centers, called E.R. (Endoplasmic Reticulum), transport materials throughout the cell often from the nucleus. Endoplasmic reticulum is also involved as an "assembly line" for the production of proteins at the ribosomes.

The **ribosomes** are located along the endoplasmic reticulum. They produce enzymes and other proteins from amino acids.

Golgi bodies secrete carbohydrates (cellulose in plants) and protein containing materials like **mucus** (in animals).

The **centrosome** is *only* found in animal cells and plays an important role in animal cell division (mitosis).

B. Special Plant Cell Characteristics

Plant cells are similar to animal cells and contain most of the same structures. However, there are two major differences.

Chloroplasts are structures that contain chlorophyll, a green substance necessary for photosynthesis. **Photosynthesis** is the method by which green plants make food. They are able to take water and carbon dioxide and convert them into simple sugar (food). This is done with the help of the energy supplied by sunlight.

The **cell wall** is a thick layer of "nonliving" material which surrounds the cell membrane. This wall gives the plant cell its box-like shape. It is porous and provides support and protection to the plant cell. The cell wall is made up of cellulose, a carbohydrate made by the plant. When you eat celery, you may get "strings" stuck between your teeth. The "strings" are cellulose threads.

Organelle	Plant	Animal	Organelle	Plant	Animal
Plasma Membrane	√	√	Endoplasmic Reticulum	√	√
Cytoplasm	√	√	Golgi	√	√
Nucleus	√	√	Vacuoles	√	√
Chromosomes	√	√	Centrosome		√
Mitochondria	√	√	Chloroplasts	√	
Ribosomes	√	√	Cell Wall	√	

Comparison of Plant and Animal Cell Organelles (√ = present)

Questions

1   The basic unit of every living organism is the
   1 system   2 organ   3 tissue   4 cell

Questions 2-4 are based on this diagram of a typical animal cell.

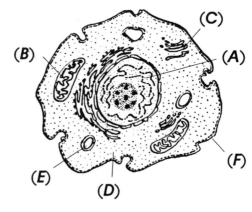

2   The part of the cell that controls the cell activities is represented by
   1 A
   2 B
   3 C
   4 D

3   "F" represents the cell part that
   1 stores food and/or wastes
   2 releases energy from food
   3 controls what goes in and out of cell
   4 makes proteins

4   Chromosomes would be found in what part?
   1 A
   2 B
   3 D
   4 E

5   Structures present in plant cells but *not* in animal cells are
   1 cell membrane and nucleus
   2 cell wall and chloroplasts
   3 chloroplasts and nucleus
   4 cytoplasm and cell wall

II. Cell Division

Cell division is the reproductive process of a cell. The cell divides itself into two equal parts. When this happens, each new cell may grow to full size and divide again. This process is necessary for growth, repair, and reproduction of cells. Cell division occurs in two ways:

A. Mitosis

This kind of cell division is used for growth and repair. It involves both the equal division of the nuclear material (chromosomes) and cytoplasm (cell contents). A cell enlarges and then splits into two **identical** daughter cells. The diagram at the right shows the stages of mitosis.

Mitosis is used by all cells to *exactly duplicate themselves* for growth and to replace worn out or dead cells. Plant cell mitosis is similar to animal cell mitosis. The animal plasma (cell) membrane "pinches" together to form two daughter cells. In the plant cell, a cell plate is made which divides the cell into two daughter cells.

Mitosis (cell reproduction) is basic to the continuity of life. A fertilized egg divides many times, over and over again, until an adult organism is formed. Mitosis is also the process that may produce identical twins.

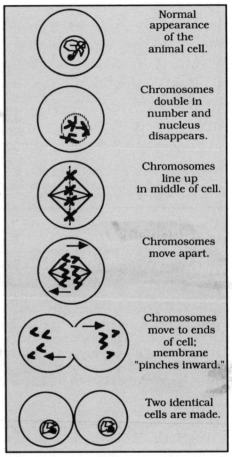

Normal appearance of the animal cell.

Chromosomes double in number and nucleus disappears.

Chromosomes line up in middle of cell.

Chromosomes move apart.

Chromosomes move to ends of cell; membrane "pinches inward."

Two identical cells are made.

B. Meiosis

Meiosis occurs *only* in the ovaries and testes. This cell division involves the production of reproductive cells (gametes). A male reproductive cell splits into four gametes (sperm). A female reproductive cell splits into one gamete (egg) and three "nonfertile" cells. These new cells contain only one half the chromosomes needed to carry on life. When an egg cell is fertilized by a sperm cell, it completes the needed number of chromosomes to begin life functions. This fertilized egg is called the zygote.

Half the chromosomes are from the female and the other half are from the male. This permits *variations* to occur from generation to generation. Further differences can occur during meiosis by crossing-over, a process that swaps genes on similar chromosomes.

Summary of Meiosis and Fertilization

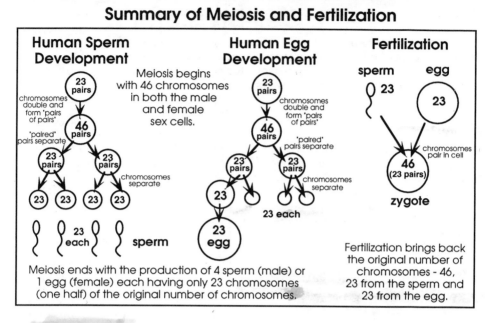

Human Sperm Development

23 pairs

chromosomes double and form "pairs of pairs"

46 pairs

"paired" pairs separate

23 pairs   23 pairs

chromosomes separate

23   23   23   23

23 each   **sperm**

Human Egg Development

Meiosis begins with 46 chromosomes in both the male and female sex cells.

23 pairs

chromosomes double and form "pairs of pairs"

46 pairs

"paired" pairs separate

23 pairs   23 pairs

chromosomes separate

23

23 each

23 **egg**

Fertilization

sperm   egg

23   23

chromosomes pair in cell

46 (23 pairs)

zygote

Fertilization brings back the original number of chromosomes - 46, 23 from the sperm and 23 from the egg.

Meiosis ends with the production of 4 sperm (male) or 1 egg (female) each having only 23 chromosomes (one half) of the original number of chromosomes.

C. Variations

Sexual reproduction leads to the possibility of *variation* in the next generation. The fertilized cell receives half of its chromosomes from the female parent and half from the male parent. The offspring will most likely have a blend of the characteristics of both parents. This is called **variation**.

Sometimes a sudden change to the genetic material will occur. The chemical makeup of a gene or the number of chromosomes in the cell may change. When reproduction occurs, this change will be passed on to the offspring. This is called a **mutation**.

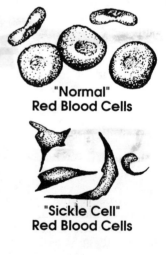

"Normal" Red Blood Cells

Mutations may increase or decrease a cell's ability to adapt to its environment. Some insects have become resistant to certain insecticides through mutations. In this case, mutations improved the insects' chances for survival. However, some mutations, like sickle cell anemia, can be deadly to the organism.

"Sickle Cell" Red Blood Cells

Mutations can also be helpful. Farmers use mutations of crop plants and farm animals to increase food supplies and improve variations.

Mutations are also used to aid in the raising and breeding of domesticated animals (for example, the hornless Hereford cattle). A good example of a useful mutation is the improvement made in the size, disease resistance, and "ear" production of corn.

The genetic makeup of an organism is called its **genotype**. What the organism looks like or behaves like is called its **phenotype**. The genotype of an organism cannot always be determined by its physical characteristics. Therefore, "what you see may not be what you get."

Questions

1   The cell in the diagram is going through a process that indicates it is a
    1   nerve cell
    2   brain cell
    3   blood cell
    4   sex cell

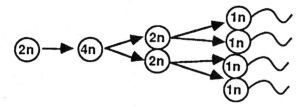

2   When the chemical makeup of a gene is changed, the result will be a
    1   variation   3   mutation
    2   blend   4   new organism

3   How many chromosomes does a human body cell have?
    1   32   2   46   3   54   4   64

4   A parent amoeba (one-cell animal) is about to reproduce by asexual reproduction. The offspring will
    1   have half the number of chromosomes as the parent
    2   have twice as many chromosomes as the parent
    3   be exactly like the parent
    4   contain chlorophyll

5   Variation in the next generation is possible in which type of reproduction?
    1   grafting   3   sexual
    2   budding   4   regeneration

III. Microscopic World

A **microörganism** (microbe) is too small to be seen with the naked eye. A compound microscope enables us to view microörganisms and their behavior.

Microscope Study

The **compound microscope** is the type of microscope found in the high school biology laboratory. It uses ordinary light.

The compound microscope has two types of lenses (ocular and objective) to magnify the specimen. This combination can increase the visual size (image) of the specimen up to 1,000 times its actual size.

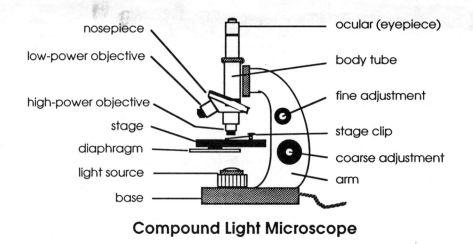

Compound Light Microscope

Magnification is determined by:

Magnification of the Ocular Lens (eyepiece)	X	Magnification of the Objective Lens	=	Total Magnification
10X	x	30X	=	300X

When using the compound microscope, there are several things to keep in mind:

a) When an object is viewed through the microscope, *it appears upside down and backwards* from the position in which it was mounted on the slide.

Therefore, in order to observe an area to the right of the field of vision, the student must move the slide to the left.

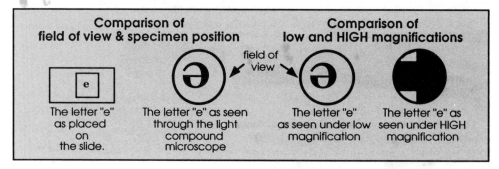

b) To observe the *greatest amount of the specimen* in the field of view, the student must *use the lowest power* possible.

c) *As the magnification is increased, the field of view is reduced.* The student will see less of the specimen. Because the object appears darker with increased magnification, the student may have to increase the amount of light hitting the slide specimen. This is done by changing the diaphragm setting.

d) When focusing, move the body tube (magnification objective) or the stage (location of the slide) *as close together as possible without touching.* Use the coarse adjustment to focus the specimen under low power only. The stage and objective should move apart. *Be careful not to bring the objective and slide together.* This could cause damage to either or both the objective and the slide specimen.

Staining Techniques

Many parts of the cell are colorless and are hard to distinguish from other cell parts. Stains have been developed to add color to certain **organelles**. This makes them easier to study under the compound microscope. Some examples of stains include Lugol's Iodine and Methylene Blue. A drop of iodine solution on a slide of cheek cells makes the nuclei easier to see.

Questions

Base your answers to questions 1 through 8 on the diagram which represents a compound light microscope.

1 Which parts should be used to carry the microscope?
  1 1 and 5
  2 1 and 13
  3 2 and 6
  4 8 and 11

2 Which parts of the microscope contain the lenses?
  1 1, 2, and 3
  2 1, 3, and 7
  3 3, 5, and 6
  4 1, 4, and 5

3 On which part of the microscope should a slide be placed?
  1 1   2 5   3 7   4 9

4 Which part regulates the amount of light passing through the stage?
  1 6   2 11   3 12   4 13

5 The magnification of the microscope is based on the magnifying power of the objective lens and
  1 1   2 2   3 3   4 4

6 When the microscope is switched from low power to high power, the object will appear
  1 larger   3 smaller
  2 upside down   4 brighter

7   A slide in focus on the stage is moved to the right. As observed through
    the eyepiece, the slide will appear to move to the
    1 right   3 top
    2 left   4 bottom

8   Which is the fine adjustment control on the microscope?
    1 4   2 7   3 12   4 none is correct

9   When a microscope is switched from low to high power, most of the time
    you must also
    1 change the slide   3 stain the slide
    2 increase the amount of light 4 decrease the amount of light

10 A household liquid that can be used as a stain for slides is
    1 alcohol   3 iodine
    2 pen ink   4 ammonia

IV. Microbes

A. Nonpathogenic - Helpful Microbes

Pathogenic means "disease causing," and is associated with microörganisms. **Nonpathogenic** microbes, therefore, do not cause disease and
are helpful to man.

There are untold numbers of microörganisms in existence, but only about
5% of them seem to be harmful. The rest are vital to the balance of nature.
Without these helpful microörganisms, decay would not occur, wine would
not be made, and many foods would be tasteless. The following examples of
microbes show how microörganisms help us every day of our lives.

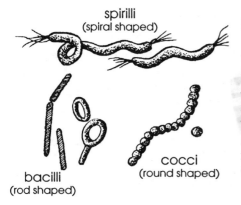

spirilli
(spiral shaped)

bacilli
(rod shaped)

cocci
(round shaped)

Bacteria

Bacteria are the simplest, the oldest, and the most abundant one-cell
group of organisms in the world. They
are named for their shapes: rod shaped
bacteria are called bacilli; round bacteria are called cocci; and spiral shaped
bacteria are called spirilli. Although
some bacteria are helpful, many bacteria cause disease and may be deadly to
other living things.

Anaerobic bacteria are microörganisms that are able to live without oxygen. These microbes live deep in the soil and digest waste materials. Methane gas is given off in the process, and may be recovered and burned as fuel.

Aerobic bacteria are microörganisms that need oxygen to survive. After anaerobic bacteria have decomposed the waste material, the waste is exposed to air where the aerobic bacteria add oxygen to it. This changes the waste into inorganic compounds such as carbon dioxide, sulfates, and water.

Soil
The microörganisms found in soil help fertilize the soil so that plants can grow better. Soil microbes include bacteria, molds, protozoa, algae, and some yeasts.

Soil is vital to the life cycles of nearly all organisms. It is important that society protect its soil resources and the microörganisms that live in it. Without these soil microbes, dead material would not be decayed or broken down. The decayed matter, called **humus**, replenishes the minerals and nutrients that were taken out of the soil by growing plants.

Sewage Treatment
The decay of once living matter helps to rid the Earth of some of its sewage (waste). The value of sewage treatment is to change **organic** materials (living or once living matter) into **inorganic** materials (not living matter). These materials can then be used as plant fertilizer.

Foods
Many foods such as bread, cheese, yogurt, and wine are created by microörganisms reacting with certain other foods.

Some foods produced through the action of microörganisms :

> grapes + microörganisms = wine
> milk + microörganisms = yogurt
> dough + microörganisms (yeast) = bread

Yeasts are used to ferment sugars and produce alcoholic beverages. Wine is made from fermented fruit juices. Beer is made from fermented grains. Also, yeast is used in baking to produce carbon dioxide. The carbon dioxide puts the tiny holes in the bread and makes the bread rise.

Molds are used in the production of various kinds of cheese such as roquefort and blue cheese.

Bacteria is used to prepare foods such as sauerkraut, yogurt, cottage cheese, and butter.

Questions

1 A science student observes clumps of rod-shaped organisms with a microscope. They are probably
    1 bacteria   3 fungi
    2 molds   4 yeasts

2 The flavor of blue cheese results from the action of certain
    1 yeasts   3 molds
    2 viruses   4 bacteria

3 Sewage treatment plants are able to change
    1 aerobic bacteria to anaerobic bacteria
    2 humus into soil
    3 molds into bacteria and yeasts
    4 organic matter into inorganic materials

4 Approximately what percentage of microörganisms are helpful to mankind?
    1 5%   2 50%   3 95%   4 100%

5 Necessary microbes found in soil are
    1 bacteria and molds   3 tree roots and dead leaves
    2 gophers and spiders   4 worms and insects

B. Pathogenic - Harmful Microbes

Like other organisms, microörganisms need nutrients to live. Some get their nutrients by eating other cells of living organisms. When this occurs, the internal environment of the organism is disturbed. This disturbance by a microörganism is called a **disease.**

Common Diseases Caused by Microörganisms:

Virus   — AIDS, cold, flu, measles, herpes
Bacteria — syphilis, tuberculosis, typhoid fever, gonorrhea
Protozoa — malaria
Fungi   — athlete's foot, ringworm

Diseases may be classified as infectious and noninfectious.

Infectious Diseases. Many infectious diseases are caused by microscopic organisms. They are usually spread from one organism to another. Infectious diseases can be spread in three different ways:

· **By air** — cold, flu, measles, and chicken pox (the disease is spread by a cough or sneeze).

· **By water** — dysentery and typhoid fever (drinking the water in which the microörganisms live may give you the disease).

- **By contact** — ringworm, athlete's foot, malaria (mosquito bite), gonorrhea, herpes, syphilis, and AIDS (body fluid exchange or sexual contact).

Noninfectious Diseases are not spread like the infectious diseases, but are caused by such factors as:

- **Deficiencies** in diet
- **Malfunctioning endocrine glands**
- **Allergies** to foreign substances
- **Malfunctioning organs**
- **Diseases** caused by chemicals introduced into the environment

Examples of Noninfectious Diseases:

Anorexia	— poor or little nourishment
Rickets	— lack of Vitamin D
Obesity	— underactive thyroid gland
Hives	— allergies to certain foods
Hay fever	— allergy to ragweed
Diabetes	— lack of insulin production in pancreas
Lung cancer	— excessive smoke inhalation

C. Control Of Microörganisms

To prevent infection, contamination, and spoilage, harmful microbes must be controlled. This can be done by removing them, killing them, or by stopping their growth.

Viruses present a special problem. Viruses have been included here as microörganisms. However, scientists have not been able to agree whether or not a virus is an "actual living" organism.

Some feel that it is only a molecule because it has no cell parts and does not grow or reproduce on its own. It can only reproduce when it is inside of another living organism, such as a body cell. For this reason viruses are very hard to control or destroy.

Ways Of Controlling Microbes

Sterilization and disinfecting kill harmful microbes. Pasteurization, canning, refrigeration, and freezing inhibit (stop) the growth of microbes.

1. **Sterilization** is a process of destroying living microörganisms by using high heat or chemical action.

2. **A disinfectant** is a substance, such as alcohol, hydrogen peroxide, or iodine, that destroys bacteria.

3. **Pasteurization** is a method of inhibiting the growth of bacteria in a liquid (such as milk) by heating it at a high temperature for at least 30 minutes.

4. **Canning** is the process of preserving food by heating the food and sealing the container (can or jar) airtight.

5. **Drying** is the removal of moisture which is necessary for the microbes to grow. This will stop the growth but not destroy the organisms.

6. **Preservatives** prevent the breakdown of a food by bacteria.
   - **Salt curing** is done by adding salt to foods. When the salt content is very high, it destroys the microörganisms.
   - **Pickling** is adding an acid like vinegar to foods. This preserves the food because the microbes cannot live in high acid concentrations.
   - **Sugaring** (adding sugar to foods) lowers the amount of available moisture for the microbes. As in drying, the microbes cannot grow but are not killed.
   - **Smoking** helps destroy microbe growth. This process is done by using the smoke from burning wood. An example of smoking is "hickory smoked" bacon.

7. **Ultraviolet Radiation.** The ultraviolet rays found in sunlight are very effective in killing many spore forming bacteria. Ultraviolet radiation even kills bacteria which are not destroyed by boiling. Ultraviolet lamps are also used to give people tans. However, over-exposure to ultraviolet rays can cause skin cancer. If not properly shielded from the eyes, these rays can do serious damage to the retinas of the eyes.

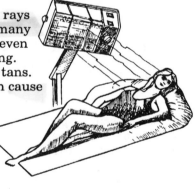

8. **Refrigeration.** Lowering the temperature of food to about 4°C stops the growth of microörganisms but does not kill them.

9. **Freezing** is a method of preserving things, even the microbes. It does not kill them but does stop the growth. Remember: Do not refreeze thawed (once frozen) foods.

Product Safety. In order to produce and sell safe products, many food industries maintain their own laboratories to test their products. Federal, State, and local health departments check to see that certain standards are maintained. These standards are established by law to protect the public.

Questions

1 Insulin helps to control which of the following diseases?
   1 rickets   3 cancer
   2 hemophilia   4 diabetes

2 An example of an infectious disease is
   1 rickets   2 measles   3 cancer   4 hay fever

3 A process for killing bacteria in food with heat so that the food will not spoil is
   1 immunizing   3 culturing
   2 disinfecting   4 pasteurizing

4 Chemicals such as alcohol, hydrogen peroxide, and iodine are known as
   1 disinfectants   3 vaccines
   2 antibiotics   4 fungus

5 A person who is sensitive to a specific substance is said to be
   1 mutant   3 resistant
   2 abnormal   4 allergic

6 Which of the following noninfectious diseases would a person have if they had very poor or little nourishment?
   1 rickets   2 anorexia   3 obesity   4 diabetes

7 A microörganism that causes illness is
   1 a virus   3 a protozoa
   2 a bacteria   4 all of these may cause illness

8 Bacteria that are inhaled may irritate which of the following systems?
   1 respiratory   3 skeletal
   2 endocrine   4 circulatory

9 What method is used to slow down the growth of bacteria?
   1 disinfecting   3 sterilization
   2 pasteurization   4 vaporization

10 Infection after surgery has been greatly reduced in modern medicine due to the use of
   1 disinfectants   3 ultraviolet radiation
   2 pasteurization   4 preservatives

D. Human Defenses Against Disease

The human body has many natural as well as artificial defenses to fight disease.

Natural Defenses

1. **Skin.** The skin acts as a protective covering to keep out germs and bacteria. By simple soap and water washing, the microbes are removed.

2. **Mucus.** Lining the inside of the nose and throat is a thick liquid called mucus. Mucus traps dust, dirt, germs, and bacteria. This prevents them from entering the body as we breathe. In the respiratory, urinary, and digestive tracts, mucus traps invading organisms. Mucus is very important to our "first line" of defense against sickness.

3. **Hydrochloric acid** in the stomach inhibits microbes which enter this portion of the body.

4. **Stomach acid.** The acid found inside the stomach helps to destroy harmful microörganisms that may be ingested.

5. **Blood system.** The blood contains white blood cells that fight germs. It also produces **antibodies**. Antibodies are produced only after the disease enters the body.

Antibodies may be considered our "second line" of defense against illness and infection.

For example, once you contract the measles, your body makes antibodies against this disease. You are usually protected from this disease thereafter. This type of protection against disease is called **immunity**.

6. **Cilia** (tiny hairs) line the nasal passages and respiratory tract. Cilia trap harmful particles and clean the air when inhaled.

7. **Tears** wash away microbes that enter the eyes.

Questions

1 The moist lining inside your nose and throat that traps dust particles and microörganisms is called the
   1 mucous membrane   3 cell membrane
   2 nuclear membrane   4 humor

2 Immunity best helps to
   1 digest foods   3 carry on reproduction
   2 fight disease   4 preserve food

3 Immunity is a type of body protection produced by antibodies. Within which body part would you most likely find antibodies?
   1 the stomach   3 the nasal passages
   2 the blood stream   4 the skin

4 Disease germs and bacteria are kept *outside* the body by
   1 antibodies   3 stomach acid
   2 lymph   4 unbroken skin

5 The body's natural defenses against disease include
   1 cocaine, opium, marijuana
   2 methiolate, surgery, alcohol
   3 skin, mucus, antibodies
   4 warm clothing, good shoes, sunglasses

Area 2
Earth Sciences

- **The Changing Surface**
  - **Weather and Climate**
    - **Astronomy**

Unit D — Earth Sciences:

The Earth's Changing Surface

The one thing that is "constant" about the Earth's surface is that it is "always changing." Volcanoes and earthquakes can push up the land to form mountains. Weathering and erosion tear them down. This process takes a long time, but it happens.

Geologic research shows us that the ocean basins have landforms just like those on dry land. Mountains, valleys, and plateaus have been found under water. Islands are often the tops of the ocean's mountains.

Fossils have been used to piece together a history of the Earth. Complete dinosaur skeletons have been found. Why dinosaurs became extinct still puzzles scientists.

The forces of nature that shape the Earth's surface are described in Unit D.

Concepts and Words To Be Understood

breakage	erosion	mineral
carbonate	fracture	nonrenewable resource
cleavage	fragment	ore
constructive force	hardness	organic
crust	inorganic	streak
crystal	luster	vulcanism
destructive force	magma	weathering

I. Earth's Surface

A. Surface Features

The surface of the Earth is constantly going through changes. These changes are a result of two forces that work against each other.

• The **destructional force** includes weathering and erosion. This destructional force wears down and removes land features that already exist.

• The **constructional force** builds up the Earth's surface. This constructional force builds up the Earth's surface by raising the crust and forming new landforms.

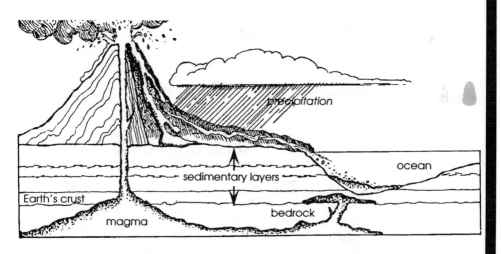

Constructional and Destructional Forces at Work on the Earth

B. Rock Fragments And Bedrock

When the forces of nature break down bedrock, rock **fragments** are formed. The remains of plant and animal life left in the ground to decay are known as **organic materials**. These organic materials, called **humus**, are mixed with the tiny rock fragments. **Soil** is the combination of the humus and the tiny rock fragments.

C. Minerals

A **mineral** can be defined as a naturally occurring element or inorganic (nonliving) compound. An **inorganic compound** is a substance that has never been alive and does not contain a combination of the elements carbon and hydrogen. For example, common table salt (NaCl - sodium chloride) is an *inorganic* compound. But, simple sugar ($C_6H_{12}O_6$ - glucose) contains both carbon and hydrogen. Sugar is an *organic* compound.

An **element** is the simplest form of a substance. It cannot be broken down any further. Of all the elements found in the solid part of the Earth's crust, eight of them make up 98% of the Earth's crust.

These eight elements (from the most abundant to least abundant) are: *oxygen, silicon, aluminum, iron, calcium, sodium, potassium, and magnesium.*

Mineral Formation

Most minerals are formed far below the Earth's surface. Magma is the hot, molten rock inside the Earth. When magma breaks through the surface of the Earth, it is called **lava**. There are three ways in which minerals form:

- **Cooling and Hardening of Magma.** Minerals can form as magma cools and hardens. Quick cooling causes small crystals to form. If the magma cools slowly, the crystals have a longer time to form. This causes larger crystals to form.

- **Evaporation of Bodies of Water.** Dissolved minerals such as rock salt, gypsum, and borax form when the water evaporates. These minerals either fall out of solution or are deposited.

- **Chemical Weathering (Reactions).** Chemical weathering of rock can produce new minerals. One example of this is the changing of feldspar into clay.

General Characteristics of Minerals
Natural Substance
Nonliving (Inorganic) Substance
Solid Substance
Pure Element or Combination of Elements (Compound)
Fixed Atomic Pattern
Definite Shape

Identification

There are over two thousand minerals. All of these minerals have characteristics which can help them be identified easily.

Properties Of Minerals

Minerals are elements or compounds that have physical and/or chemical properties. A physical property can be seen or observed easily. A chemical property is the way a mineral can change when it reacts with other elements or compounds.

1. Physical Properties

Hardness. How a mineral resists scratching is called **hardness.** To help decide how hard a mineral is, Mohs' Scale of Hardness is used.

A mineral can be scratched by any other mineral that has a higher number on the Mohs' Scale. For example, gypsum (2) can only scratch talc (1). But, gypsum can be scratched by all other minerals above it. Quartz (7) *can* scratch talc (1), gypsum (2), calcite (3), fluorite (4), apatite (5), and feldspar (6). But, quartz *cannot* scratch topaz (8), corundum (9), or diamond (10).

Moh's Scale of Mineral Hardness
1 – talc
2 – gypsum
3 – calcite
4 – fluorite
5 – apatite
6 – feldspar
7 – quartz
8 – topaz
9 – corundum
10 – diamond

Breakage. A mineral can be identified easily by how it breaks. Sometimes, a mineral breaks in a definite direction along a smooth surface. This break is called a **cleavage.** Some minerals have one, two, three, four, or six directions of cleavage.

A mineral cleaves because of areas of weakness in the structure of the mineral itself. When a mineral breaks along an uneven surface, it is called a **fracture.**

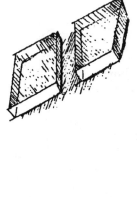

Three Examples of Cleavage:
Crystals of Quartz (left), **Halite** (center), and **Mica** (right).

Streak. A streak is the color of a fine powder of a mineral when it is rubbed against a hard surface. Usually a streak plate (unglazed porcelain) is used to see the color of a mineral's powder. Sometimes the color of the streak is different from the surface color of a mineral.

A streak is helpful in identifying some minerals. When you use a "lead" pencil, a black streak of graphite is left on paper.

bright

Luster. A mineral can be identified by its luster. How a mineral reflects light from its surface is its **luster**. A mineral can have a metallic or a nonmetallic luster. If the mineral reflects light (for example, the surface of a metal), it has a metallic luster.

dull

Luster should be determined from a freshly broken surface. A nonmetallic luster can include dull or earthy, pearly, waxy, greasy, glassy, and diamond-like, or brilliant.

Color. A mineral can be identified by its color. The color should be observed from a fresh surface. Some colors are easy to recognize. Sulfur has a yellow to bright yellow color.

A mineral like quartz can have many colors. These colors are caused by many different impurities. Therefore, color alone may be a poor way to identify some minerals.

Crystal Form. A mineral can be identified by different geometric shapes (crystal form). A crystal shape depends on how the particles that make up the crystal are arranged.

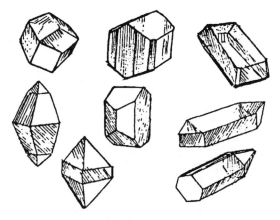

Density. Minerals can be identified by their density. Density refers to the number of particles in a specific space. The **specific gravity** of a mineral is the weight of a mineral sample in air compared to its weight in water.

2. Chemical Properties

A mineral can be identified by its chemical properties. **A chemical property** of a mineral is the way it changes, reacts, or behaves with other elements or compounds.

Acid Test. A mineral is a carbonate (contains carbon and oxygen) if it produces bubbles of carbon dioxide when a dilute acid is placed in contact with the mineral. Calcite and limestone are examples of carbonates.

Economic Uses Of Minerals

Minerals, for the most part, are nonrenewable resources. This means that once they are used up, there will be no more. **Ores** are mineral resources that can be mined. This mining can be done for a profit (to make money). Some examples of minerals that can be mined are gold, silver, bauxite (source of aluminum), and hematite (source of iron). Other minerals have special properties that make them valuable or useful. Some useful minerals are halite, gypsum, talc, and sulfur.

A gem or gemstone is a certain mineral that has beauty and value, such as rubies, emeralds, and diamonds.

Our nation's future existence and standard of living depend on the wise use of these mineral resources. How well a nation survives may be determined by the variety and availability of its natural resources.

Questions

1 An example of a destructive force is
   1 crustal movement   3 erosion
   2 volcanism   4 mountain building

2 An example of a constructional force is
   1 weathering   3 erosion
   2 volcanism   4 running water

3 A mixture of weathered rock fragments and organic material is called
   1 bedrock   2 soil   3 crust   4 magma

4 Which of the following is *not* a way in which minerals form?
   1 cooling of magma   3 evaporation of water
   2 adding acid to carbonate   4 chemical reaction

5 How many of the Earth's most abundant elements form the most common minerals in the Earth's crust?
   1 six   2 eight   3 ten   4 twelve

6 Which element is the most abundant in the Earth's crust?
   1 oxygen   2 mercury   3 krypton   4 uranium

7 A poor way to identify a mineral is by its
   1 hardness   2 luster   3 streak   4 color

8   Some minerals that were once in solution in oceans and lakes are listed
    below. Which one does *not* belong?
    1 quartz   2 gypsum   3 borax   4 rock salt

9   The color of the fine powder that is produced when a mineral is rubbed
    against an unglazed piece of porcelain is called its
    1 color   2 hardness   3 luster   4 streak

10 The mineral apatite cannot scratch
    1 quartz   2 talc   3 calcite   4 fluorite

11 A piece of unglazed porcelain has a hardness of 6.5. Which mineral will
    leave a streak on it?
    1 corundum   2 calcite   3 diamond   4 topaz

12 The ability of a mineral to resist scratching is called
    1 breakage   2 hardness   3 streak   4 luster

13 Larger crystals tend to form when
    1 erosion exposes domes   3 magma cools slowly
    2 magnesium settles   4 magma cools quickly

14 To identify minerals, you should *not* use color since minerals may have
    many
    1 shapes   2 impurities   3 lusters   4 crystal forms

15 A mineral can be identified by different geometric shapes called
    1 hardness   2 crystals   3 density   4 luster

D. Rocks

The crust of the Earth is made up of rocks which are naturally occurring
substances. These substances are made up of one or more minerals. Rocks
are classified according to how they formed.

Igneous Rocks

Igneous rocks form through the cooling and hardening of hot, molten material. Hardening below the surface of the Earth forms intrusive rocks. When
liquid rock hardens above the surface, it is called extrusive rock (lava rock).

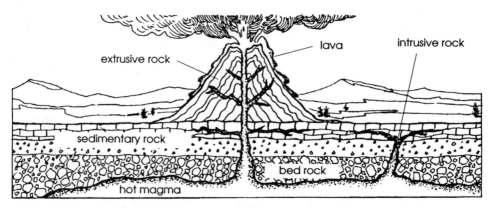

Igneous Rock Formation Through Heating and Cooling

Igneous means "formed from fire," but fire is not involved in the formation of these rocks. Some examples are obsidian, pumice, basalt, and granite. Granite is the major rock found in the Earth's crust beneath the continents. Basalt forms the Palisades along the Hudson River and much of the Hawaiian Islands.

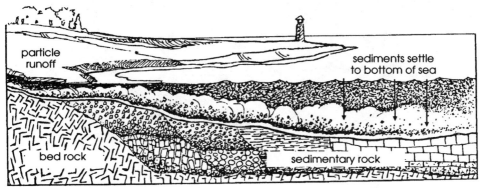

Sedimentary Rocks

Most sedimentary rocks are made of small pieces of rock (**fragments**) that have been broken away from other rocks. Rock fragments (sediments) are then carried by water, wind, or ice (a glacier) to new locations. These locations can be in rivers, oceans, or new places on land. Some of these rock fragments are then cemented together. A few examples of sedimentary rocks are sandstone, shale, limestone, and conglomerate. The rock form at the brink of Niagara Falls is limestone.

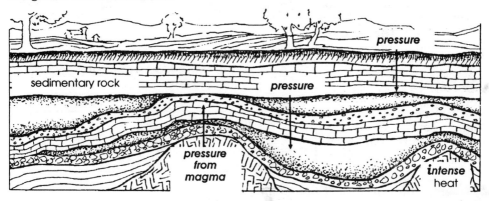

Metamorphic Rocks

Metamorphic rocks are formed when igneous, sedimentary, or other metamorphic rocks are changed. This change can be brought about by heat, pressure, chemical action, or any combination of these. Vermont has vast formations of marble. Visit a marble quarry sometime.

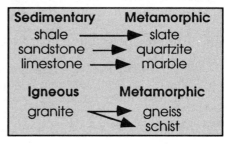

Sedimentary	Metamorphic
shale ⟶	slate
sandstone ⟶	quartzite
limestone ⟶	marble
Igneous	**Metamorphic**
granite ⟶	gneiss
	schist

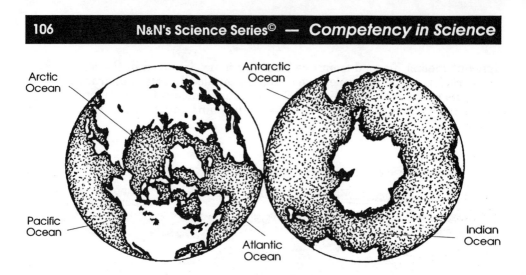

E. Oceans

The Earth is covered by about 75% water. There are five major oceans on Earth: Pacific, Atlantic, Indian, Arctic, and Antarctic Oceans.

Ocean Floor Shape

The ocean floor has features that are much like those formed on the continents. Many underwater mountains, valleys, plains, and plateaus have been located and mapped.

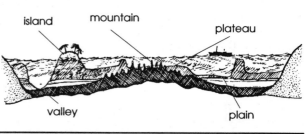

Sea Water

Sea water contains much more than just water. There are many kinds of salts and gases dissolved in sea water.

| The Three Most Abundant Salts and Gases in Sea Water ||
Salts	Gases
sodium chloride magnesium chloride magnesium sulfate	nitrogen oxygen carbon dioxide

Economic Importance Of The Oceans

The oceans can be looked upon as a great reservoir of water. This reservoir can benefit the whole human race in many ways:

- The ocean contains a major source of food for the Earth.
- The ocean serves as a way to help modify temperatures. This helps keep coastal land warmer in the winter and cooler in the summer.
- The ocean is a great source of minerals. Most of these minerals have washed off the land.
- Ocean water may be desalted and serve as a source of fresh water. This water can then be used for agricultural or domestic purposes.

Questions

1 Igneous rocks form from
   1 other sediment   3 heat and pressure
   2 the cooling of magma or lava   4 chemical action

2 Which rock listed below is a sedimentary rock?
   1 slate   2 marble   3 sandstone   4 granite

3 An example of a metamorphic rock is
   1 conglomerate   3 shale
   2 slate   4 lava rock

4 The type of rock that forms from heat, pressure, or chemical action is
   1 igneous   3 metamorphic
   2 sedimentary   4 extrusive

5 Which type of rock is made up of fragments cemented together?
   1 sedimentary   3 metamorphic
   2 igneous   4 granite

6 About how much of the Earth is covered with water?
   1 25%   2 50%   3 75%   4 81%

7 Earth's five major oceans are the Pacific, Arctic, Antarctic,
   1 Hudson and Atlantic   3 Indian and Hudson
   2 Indian and Atlantic   4 Gulf Stream and Hudson

8 The most abundant gases that are dissolved in ocean water are carbon dioxide, nitrogen, and
   1 fluorine   2 helium   3 hydrogen   4 oxygen

9 Rocks are classified according to
   1 the way they form   3 their size and shape
   2 their mineral content   4 their weight

10 Sodium chloride and magnesium sulfate are
   1 gases found in sea water
   2 rocks formed around volcanoes
   3 intrusive rocks
   4 salts found in sea water

Concepts and Words to be Understood

biological weathering	glacier	water table
chemical weathering	ground water	waves
physical weathering	soil	wind

II. Surface Changes

The Earth is constantly changing. The two forces creating this change are at odds with each other. The destructional forces are constantly wearing down the Earth. At the same time, the constructional forces are constantly building up the Earth.

A. Destructional Forces

Destructional forces are always working to break down and move materials away from the continents (land). This is done in many ways.

Weathering

Rocks that are at, or near, the Earth's surface are always exposed to the atmosphere. This is the reason for the term weathering. The atmosphere and all of its conditions are working to crumble and break down the rocks. This weathering can be physical, chemical, or biological. Because of weathering, rock fragments are produced on the Earth's surface. The continued weathering of these rock fragments can produce soil. Soil is very necessary to agriculture.

1. Physical Weathering

Physical weathering takes place when rock is broken down without any change in its chemical make up.

Freezing is one kind of physical weathering. The cracks in rocks can fill up with water. If the temperature drops below freezing, the water will turn to ice. Freezing causes the water to expand. This cracks the rocks even more.

**Physical Weathering
Through Freezing Water**

Expansion and contraction are also types of physical weathering. Rocks contain many different kinds of minerals. Great differences in temperatures can cause these minerals to expand (get larger) and contract (get smaller) at different rates. The different rates cause the minerals to break apart. In the illustration below, note that the rocks crack due to the change in temperature between the heat of summer and the freezing of winter.

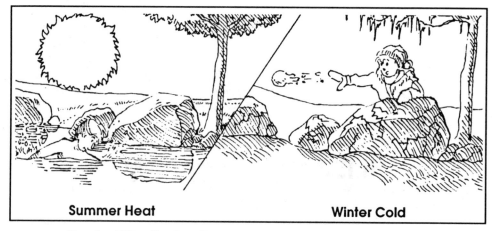

Summer Heat   **Winter Cold**

Physical Weathering Through Expansion and Contraction

2. Chemical Weathering
Chemical weathering takes place when there is a breakdown in the chemical make up of the rock. There are four different ways in which chemical weathering can take place.

Oxidation. Oxygen combines with some other minerals when they are wet. This forms new compounds that are less able to hold the rock together; so, it breaks apart.

Solutions. Water can dissolve (break down and hold in solution) some minerals in rocks and form a solution.

Carbon dioxide. There is carbon dioxide present in the air. Water joins together with some carbon dioxide forming a weak carbonic acid. This acid reacts with many rocks to form soluble materials. This chemical change causes the formation of limestone caves. Examples of such caves are Carlsbad Caverns (New Mexico), Luray Caverns (Virginia), Howe Caverns (New York) and Mammoth Cave (Kentucky).

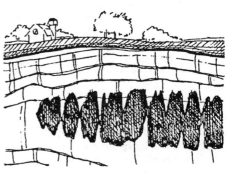
Chemical Weathering Through Action Of Acid And Water

Decaying animal and vegetable matter. Decaying animal and plant matter (organic material) make acids. These acids can dissolve minerals in some rocks and cause others to crumble and fall apart.

3. Biological Weathering
Biological weathering involves the action of living things in breaking down rocks. One way is the action of roots. This is called **wedge work of roots**. The force of roots is strong enough to crack roads and sidewalks and clog sewer pipes. The action of **lichen and moss** is another form of biological weathering. Some of these organisms grow on rocks and split their surfaces.

Biological Weathering Through Action Of A Living Tree

Factors That Influence Weathering
Weathering depends on many factors. For example:

1) The **physical and chemical properties of the rocks**.

2) The **climate area** in which the rocks are located. The greatest rate of weathering takes place in areas that have a moist climate with hot summers and cold winters.

3) The **amount of rock surface exposed to the elements**.

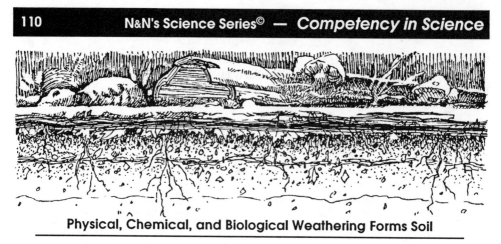

Physical, Chemical, and Biological Weathering Forms Soil

Soil

Soil is formed when rock fragments are broken down by the slow processes of physical and chemical weathering. Living organisms also play their roles in soil formation. For example, the earthworm digs into the soil leaving spaces or holes. These holes allow air and water to enter. The depth of the soil depends on how far down the living things go.

The **composition of soil** is varied. The main parts of soil are: water, minerals, and organic materials. Air and living organisms are also present in soil.

Questions

1   A "falling rock zone" in winter is most likely the result of which type of weathering?
    1   physical   2   chemical   3   biological   4   none of these

2   The type of weathering listed below that is *not* a type of chemical weathering is
    1   decaying animal and plant matter
    2   water forming with carbon dioxide
    3   oxygen combining with minerals when wet
    4   wedge work or roots

3   The main parts of soil are organic materials, water, and
    1   boulders   2   lakes   3   minerals   4   mountains

4   Which of the following is *not* a factor that influences weathering?
    1   physical properties of rocks   3   rock exposure
    2   chemical properties of rocks   4   longitude

5   Rocks and boulders heat up when the Sun shines on them. When the Sun sets, which part of the rocks and boulders cools first?
    1   inside   3   all parts cool evenly
    2   outside   4   no parts will cool down

6   Caverns, such as Mammoth Cave in Kentucky were formed when
    1   tree roots broke the rock
    2   freezing water pushed the rocks apart
    3   carbonic acid dissolved the limestone
    4   prehistoric animals built underground dens to hibernate in

7   Water may be considered a *strange* substance. It contracts when cooled until it reaches 4°C. At this temperature, it begins to expand. This explains why
   1   roots growing in the cracks of rocks can break the rock apart
   2   carbon dioxide and water can dissolve rock
   3   oxygen joins with hydrogen and forms water
   4   freezing water in cracks can break up the rock

8   Lichens and mosses are a part of which type of weathering?
   1   physical   2   chemical   3   biological   4   none of these

9   When there is a change in the chemical composition of rock, the type of weathering is most likely
   1   chemical   2   biological   3   physical   4   none of these

10 Earthworms are important for soil formation because they
   1   eat everything that they can and clean the soil
   2   dig holes to let water and air enter the soil
   3   have a slow reproduction rate
   4   provide food for robins

Erosion
Erosion is a destructive force. **Erosion** can be defined as a wearing away of the surface of the Earth by water, wind, and ice.

Ground Water
Ground water is that part of rainfall that sinks into the ground. Ground water can cause erosion below the surface of the Earth.

**Destructive Forces
Causing Erosion**

As ground water moves slowly into the the ground, it can dissolve minerals. A chemical solution forms. Carbon dioxide combines with ground water. This forms a type of **carbonic acid.** The carbonic acid can dissolve the limestone in the bedrock and form caves.

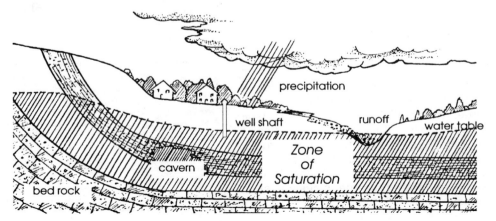

Gravity moves ground water through porous rocks to the lowest levels of the land. Then, the water moves towards streams, lakes, and oceans.

Ground water is one of man's most important natural resources. Many people depend on ground water for their drinking water. Water wells are drilled into the water table. The **water table** is the top of the *Zone of Saturation*. In many areas of the United States, the water table is dropping. Some wells "dry up." Where possible, wells are drilled deeper to obtain more fresh water.

Running Water

Running water causes most of the erosion on the Earth's surface. The Catskill Mountains of New York and the Grand Canyon in Arizona were formed by running water. Water flows from the higher to lower elevations. This running water carries and moves rock materials and particles. These materials and particles are deposited (dropped) at the lower levels when the water flow slows down.

When running water flows into a stream, it wears away the loose earth over which it moves. The particles that are carried by the stream rub against each other (friction) and erode more particles. Over a long period of time, the erosion causes stream beds to become longer and wider. A valley forms.

Land erosion by running water can be slowed down by planting trees, shrubs, and grass. It is important to slow down this erosional process.

Wind

Wind can erode the land by carrying away loose particles of soil and rock. These particles carried by wind can act as an **abrasive force** by scratching and breaking up solid rock. Wind also moves materials from one place and deposits them in another place. In this way, "dunes" are formed.

Glaciers

A **glacier** is a large mass of ice that is moving or has moved at one time. It forms from the recrystallization of snow. Glaciers move because of gravity. They can move a few inches to a few feet each day. As a glacier moves, it carries rock fragments that cut away and erode the surface over which it passes.

Ice Age

The glaciers of the Ice Age acted as an erosional force. The ice advanced and then retreated. It was moving materials constantly from one place and depositing them at another place. Many landforms found in the northern parts of North America are the direct result of the movement of glaciers.

The last Ice Age retreated from our continent about 10,000 years ago. The Great Lakes were "carved out" by the action of glaciers. So were the Finger Lakes of upper New York State and many lakes found in Minnesota and Wisconsin.. Long Island (near New York City) was deposited from materials eroded by glacial action.

Waves And Shore Currents

Erosion can be caused by a large lake's or ocean's waves. These waves are produced by wind blowing over the surface of the water. As the waves and shore currents move, they erode the shoreline. These loosened materials are moved from the shore and deposited somewhere else.

Questions

1   Which force causes ground water to move into the ground?
    1   wedge work   3   weathering
    2   gravity   4   expansion and contraction

2   Planting an adequate amount of plant life
    1   can slow down erosion by running water.
    2   can speed up erosion by running water.
    3   will not make a difference in erosion by running water.
    4   will build up the water table.

3   Which of the following is an important erosional agent?
    1   volcano   3   longitude
    2   water   4   bedrock

4   Much of the topography of New York State and Wisconsin is a result of erosion by
    1   wind   3   ground water
    2   glacial action   4   ocean waves

5. The erosion of a shoreline is mainly due to
    1   movement of a glacier
    2   running water from streams
    3   waves produced by wind
    4   overflow from the water table

6   Carbon dioxide dissolved in ground water is the probable cause of the formation of
    1   Carlsbad Caverns   3   Lake Michigan
    2   Grand Canyon   4   Mississippi River

7   Suppose that carbonic acid in ground water formed a cave far below the Earth's surface. The cave was most likely formed in what type of rock?

1   granite   3   sandstone
2   limestone   4   shale

8   The wearing away of the Earth's surface by water, wind, and ice is

1   volcanism   3   ground water
2   streams   4   erosion

9   Lake Superior and Lake Erie are land features formed by

1   the action of waves   3   the movement of rivers
2   glacial erosion   4   the runoff from Niagara Falls

10 Particles carried by wind and water erode surfaces. This happens because the particles bump into and rub against other fragments. This contact is called

1   chemical weathering   3   friction
2   biological weathering   4   fragmentation

Concepts and Words to be Understood

continental drift	faults	plate tectonics
convection currents	mid-ocean ridge	plateaus
faulting	plains	vulcanism

B. Constructional Forces

Destructional forces are constantly wearing away the surface of the Earth. At the same time, there are forces that are working to build up the surface. These building forces are called **constructional forces**. Forces beneath the surface of the Earth can cause the Earth's crust to move.

Earth Movements

There is evidence that the crust has risen and the sea has receded many times in the past. Changes are happening today that can be observed. These changes are clues to what may have happened in the past.

One indication that the crust has changed is the way mountains have formed. Many mountains contain horizontal layers of sedimentary rock. (Remember that all sedimentary rocks were originally formed under water.) The layers have been folded, tilted, and broken. Strong forces must have acted on the rock.

Evidence of Earth Movement

Earthquake and volcano zones are found with uplifted areas that are bordered by faults. Volcanic activity has formed mountains and islands. This offers evidence that forces are at work below the Earth's surface (Note the following map of Earthquake and Volcano Zones of the World).

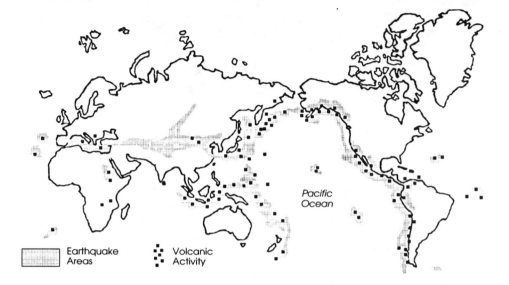

Earthquake and Volcano Zones of the World

Other evidence that points to crustal movement is the location of fossils of marine animals. Marine animals are organisms that live, or once lived, in seawater. Such fossils have been found high above sea level. These marine fossils must have been deposited in the past on the bottom of seas or oceans. Uplifting caused the sea floor to become parts of higher elevations.

Possible Causes
1. Continental Drift Theory

The present day continents may have once been part of one large landmass. Scientists believe that the continents have drifted to their present positions.

The shape of the continents suggests this possibility. They appear to fit together like pieces in a jigsaw puzzle. The rock layers of Europe and North America, as well as Africa and South America, are similar and seem to match.

2. Ocean Floor Spreading

Scientists believe that lava oozes from valleys found in the mid-ocean ridges of the Atlantic Ocean. The lava solidifies (cools and hardens). This hardened igneous rock pushes the crust (ocean floor) on both sides of the ridge in opposite directions.

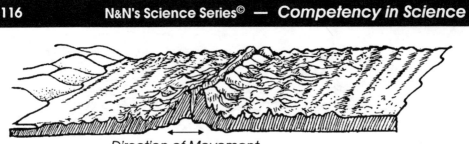

Direction of Movement

The Movement of the Mid-Atlantic Ocean Ridge

3. Plate Tectonics Theory

The crust of the Earth seems to be made up of several large plates (sections). The plates seem to "float" on the hot liquid (magma) of the mantle (the layer below the Earth's crust). Differences in the temperatures of gases and liquids produce **convection currents** in the liquid magma.

The plates may move in different directions. There is great pressure when the plates are pushed together. This pressure could create the folding and faulting of mountains, earthquake zones, and areas of volcanic activity.

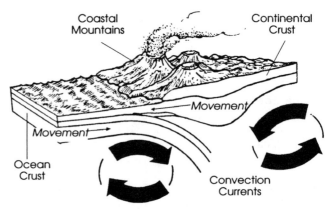

As the crust moves, it creates a lateral (sideways) pressure. This lateral pressure causes the folding of the rock layers. If the pressure is sudden, faulting (fracture or break) may develop causing the displacement (movement) of bedrock.

Earthquakes are caused when the rock layers move suddenly. Movement inside the Earth's crust causes earthquakes. The internal pressures put great stress on the crust. This stress can push the crust together or pull it apart. Either way, vibrations are sent out in all directions. Rock layers can break under this pressure and move in different directions.

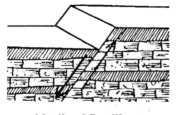

Vertical Faulting

Movement occurs along a **fault line**. The San Andreas Fault in California is one of the best known and most widely studied fault lines. This part of California is located in an area of high earthquake activity. Several times in the recent past, there has been movement at the San Andreas Fault. Movement along the fault line has been both sideways (horizontal) and up and down (vertical).

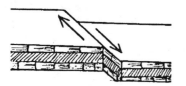

Horizontal Faulting

Thrust Faulting

Questions

1 The plate tectonic theory could explain all of the following *except*
  1 earthquake zones
  2 volcanic zones
  3 why mountains may contain horizontal layers of sedimentary rock
  4 folding and faulting of mountains

2 Three possible causes for the movement of the Earth's crust are all of the following *except* the
  1 continental drift theory   3 mid-ocean floor spreading theory
  2 compression theory   4 plate tectonics theory

3 Seafloor spreading may be caused by a type of current that causes molten rock to move through cracks in the ocean ridges. This current is called a
  1 rolling current   3 moving current
  2 rising current   4 convection current

4 Mid-ocean ridges form where the ocean floor is
  1 spreading   2 sinking   3 contracting   4 none of these

5 A sudden movement in surface rock layers could cause a (an)
  1 earthquake   3 flood plain
  2 dome mountain   4 sedimentary rock

Major Landforms

The constructional forces of the Earth can develop major landforms on land and under bodies of water. Some of these landforms are **plains**, **plateaus**, and **mountains**.

• **Plains** are broad, flat surfaces of horizontal rock layers found at low elevations (levels). Plains can form from:

  • the uplifting of continental shelves producing coastal plains (Atlantic Plains Region of the Southeastern United States - parts of Georgia, North and South Carolina, and Florida),

  • river deposits producing flood plains (Mississippi River Delta near New Orleans),

  • glacier deposits producing outwash plains and till plains (Long Island, New York),

  • uplifting of the crust or the draining away of a lake producing a lake plain (Erie - Ontario Low Lands of New York State), and

- lava coming out of cracks and spreading over a large area producing lava plains (for example, the "Pineapple Valley," Hawaii).

- **Plateaus** have undisturbed horizontal bedrock at high elevations. This elevation can be a thousand feet or more above sea level. Plateaus can form as a result of faulting. Plateaus can also form from lava flows. The lava piles up and produces a higher area than a lava plain. The Columbia Plateau in Washington, Oregon, and Idaho is the largest lava plateau in the world.

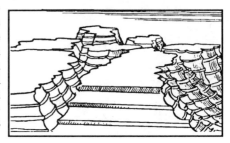

- **Mountains** are huge masses of rock that have been pushed up to higher elevations. There are four ways in which mountains can form. These mountains are named by the way they form:

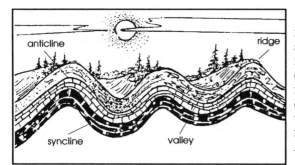

1) A **folded mountain** forms when lateral (from the sides) pressures push the crust into a wave-like form. Upfolds called **anticlines** and downfolds called **synclines** are created which make hills and valleys. This up and down formation can be seen in the Appalachian Mountains.

2) **Block** or **fault block mountains** form when the folding of the crust produces breaks or faults. These faults are pushed up higher than the other rock layers. One example is the Grand Teton Range in Wyoming.

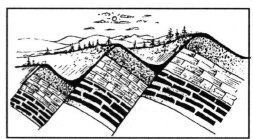

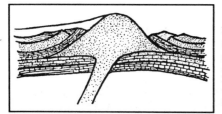

3) A **dome mountain** forms when magma moves into rock layers below the surface of the Earth and forms a large dome. The rock layers erode away, exposing the dome-shaped mountain. The Black Hills in South Dakota are examples of dome mountains.

4) **Volcanic mountains** form because of the buildup of lava and other volcanic materials. These volcanic materials come from erupting volcanoes. This can be seen in the Hawaiian Islands, which are still building in this way.

Shield **Cinder** **Composite**

Vulcanism

Vulcanism causes changes of the Earth's surface. Vulcanism is the movement of the molten rock at, or near, the Earth's surface. If the magma finds a weak spot, it can cause a volcanic eruption. Each eruption of lava builds up the volcanic cone.

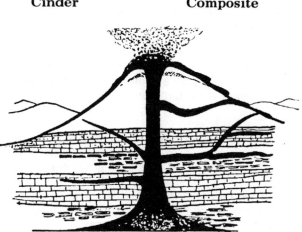

How many formations can you name?

Questions

1   Folded mountains are one type of mountain. They are formed by
   1   earthquakes   3   oceans
   2   lateral pressure   4   volcanoes

2   Anticlines would be found in what type of mountains?
   1   dome   2   fault block   3   folded   4   volcanic

3   The major difference between plains and plateaus is that
   1   plains are higher than plateaus
   2   plateaus are higher than plains
   3   there is more water on plateaus
   4   glaciers formed the plateaus

4   A cone is most likely to be formed near a (an)
   1   dome mountain   3   plain
   2   anticline   4   volcano

5   Magma moving into and/or pushing up rock layers below the Earth's surface can cause
   1   block mountains   3   dome mountains
   2   cinder cones   4   synclines and anticlines

III. Age Of The Earth

Concepts and Words to be Understood

Law of Superposition	extinct	geologic history
Condensation Hypothesis	climate	deposition
Tidal Hypothesis	fossil	relative age
radioactive dating	era	

A. Rock Record

Written records have been kept for only the last few thousand years. Scientists are interested in knowing what geological events took place before written records.

Geologists study rocks to gather data about their composition (make up), where they are found, and what fossils they contain. This information gives us clues to the Earth's geologic history. Changes that are now occurring may be clues as to what happened in the past.

Fossil Content

Fossils are the remains of plants and animals that lived in the past. The fossils were buried in mud, sand, frozen ground, or other materials. These fossils are often found in sedimentary rock.

In order for an organism to be preserved, it had to have hard body parts. These parts were then buried immediately. In this way, the parts were not exposed to the air and did not decay.

Fossils can tell us whether the Earth's surface has changed over a long period of time. Fossils of organisms that lived in the sea are now found on dry land. This discovery indicates that the land was underwater in the past. Sometimes fossils are found of organisms that no longer exist (extinct) on the Earth today. Fossils have been found that were formed in areas where the climates are unlike the present day climates. These fossils "tell" scientists that life and landforms have changed.

Fossils can tell about past climates. Coal forms in warm, moist, swampy areas. Coal has been found in some eastern and western states. Those areas were probably warm, moist, and swampy at one time. Greenland, a "frozen country," has fossils of large tropical palm trees. This indicates that the climate of Greenland has changed.

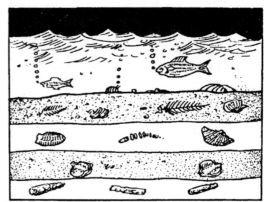

Age Of Sedimentary Layers

The position of sedimentary rock layers can help to determine the relative age of these layers (strata). The oldest rock layer is normally on the bottom.

The layer found on top is the youngest or the most recent one to form. This is known as the **Law of Superposition.** The Law of Superposition helps to piece together the history of the Earth.

Youngest Rocks

Oldest Rocks

Evidence in the rock record indicates that there must have been much up-lifting of the crust. Also, there must have been long periods of erosion and deposition. Most of the rocks formed in the first two billion years of the Earth's history have been worn away, buried, or greatly changed.

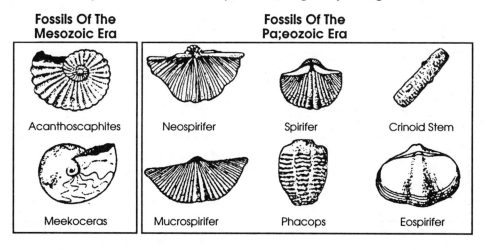

Fossils Of The Mesozoic Era

Acanthoscaphites

Meekoceras

Fossils Of The Pa;eozoic Era

Neospirifer

Spirifer

Crinoid Stem

Mucrospirifer

Phacops

Eospirifer

B. Earth's History

Age of the Earth. It is estimated that the age of the Earth is about five billion years old.

Earth's Beginning

It is not certain how the Earth was formed. There are two main hypotheses (educated guesses) that attempt to explain the formation of the Earth. One is the **tidal hypothesis.** This states that a star passed close to the Sun and pulled gaseous material away from the Sun. The gaseous material then formed the planets.

Another explanation for the formation of the Earth and other planets is the **condensation hypothesis.** This states that the Sun and the planets formed when a huge mass of rotating gas condensed (contracted and became smaller).

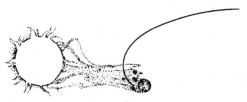

Geologic History

The history of the Earth covers a long period of time. The time has been divided into four eras (long period of deposition). Each era is separated from the others by mountain building processes.

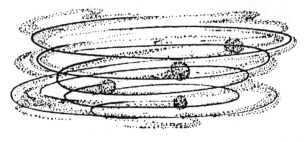

The life forms differ for each era. Also, there appears to have been major climatic changes that occurred between each era. Since climatic changes occurred, many species could not survive the changes and died out. Some adapted to the changes and survived to continue the evolutionary process.

Geologic Era	Beginning About	Ending About	Important Life Forms	Changes That Occurred
Cenozoic recent life	75 million years ago	25 million years to present	Cattle, modern horse, apes and monkeys, and flowering and modern plants dominate Earth.	Ice Age, Alps and Himalayan Mountains formed.
Mesozoic	200 million years ago	155 million years	Dinosaurs dominate Earth - then become extinct. 1st mammals, birds, and flowering plants	Rocky Mountains and Sierra Nevada Mountains formed.
Paleozoic	550 million years ago	350 million years	Fish, amphibians (early land animals), early forms of reptiles, insects, shelled sea animals (Trilobites), early land plants turn into thick forest-like swamps.	Coal begins to form along with other fossil fuels.
Pre-Paleozoic	4.5 billion years ago	4 billion years	Only very simple sea life exists (worms, jellyfish, sponges, and one-celled plants and animals).	Volcanic and earthquake eactivity dominate Earth crust changes. Adirondack Mountains are formed, and mineral ores are deposited.

Questions

1   Preserved remains of plants and animals or traces of their life are called
   1 fossils   3 periods
   2 remains   4 icebergs

2   The type of rock in which most fossils are found is called
   1 igneous   3 sedimentary
   2 metamorphic   4 granite

3   The age of the Earth is about
   1 5 million years old   3 5 trillion years old
   2 5 billion years old   4 5 thousand years old

4   The Law of Superposition states that
   1 the youngest rocks are on the bottom and oldest on top
   2 all layers were formed at the same time
   3 the oldest rocks are normally on the bottom and youngest on top
   4 the oldest rocks are on the bottom and the youngest are in the middle

5   Fossils can often indicate the
   1 temperature under which they formed.
   2 development of life and how long the organism lived.
   3 development of life, climates of the past, and conditions in which they
      were formed.
   4 environment the organism was in and its reproductive cycle.

6   During which geologic era did dinosaurs dominate the Earth and become
   extinct
   1 Cenozoic   3 Paleozoic
   2 Mesozoic   4 PrePaleozoic

7   A fairly accurate age of a rock can be obtained by using
   1 a calendar
   2 the Geologic History Chart
   3 the tidal hypothesis
   4 radioactive dating

8   In which era did our coal deposits begin to form?
   1 PrePaleozoic   3 Mesozoic
   2 Paleozoic   4 Cenozoic

9   The Law of Superposition can be compared to
   1 rows of peas and corn in the garden
   2 flowing water in a river
   3 piling up of daily newspapers
   4 billboards along highways

10 The "Tidal Hypothesis" suggests that the gases that may have formed the
   Earth came from
   1 the Sun   3 the Moon
   2 outer space   4 another planet

Unit E — Earth Sciences:

Weather and Climate

    Weather affects everyone in some way every day. Decisions are made daily to deal with weather conditions. Too much rain or not enough rain can ruin farm crops. Homes and other property can be destroyed by hurricanes and tornadoes. A day at the beach is more fun when the sun shines. A "snow day" is an unexpected day off from school.

    Meteorologists collect weather factors using many different instruments. Weather balloons can go places the weatherman cannot. Satellites are being used to follow fronts across the Earth's surface. Using all this information, weather forecasts are made. These predictions help us to plan our daily activities.

    General weather conditions over a long period of time produce different climates.

    This relationship is presented in Unit E.

Concepts and Words To Be Understood

acid rain	High pressure area	precipitation
air mass	Low pressure area	stationary front
atmosphere	maritime air mass	synoptic weather map
cold front	meteorologist	tropical air mass
condensation	occluded front	warm front
continental air mass	polar air mass	weather
forecast	pollutants	wind

I. Earth's Weather

The Earth is surrounded by layers of air called the **atmosphere**. The atmosphere is made up of a mixture of gases and some very small amounts of solid and liquid particles. The conditions that affect the atmosphere determine the **weather**.

A. Weather

Weather is a condition of the atmosphere that is affected by temperature, amount of moisture, wind, and pressure. These conditions are always changing. Local weather deals with the short term condition of the atmosphere. Local weather is affected by general or broad scale weather systems. The main reason for the changing weather is unequal heating and energy distribution in the atmosphere.

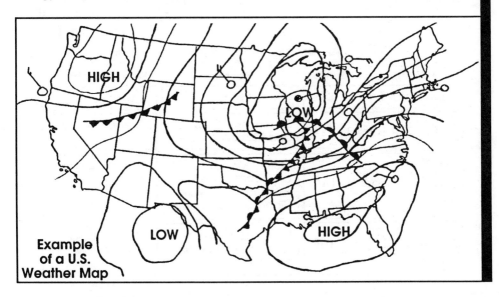

HIGH

LOW

LOW

HIGH

Example of a U.S. Weather Map

B. Weather Features

Air Masses

Our weather is determined mainly by large sections of air called **air mass-es.** *An air mass has the same moisture and temperature characteristics as the surface over which it forms.*

Air masses form when the air remains over a large surface for several days. The formation of these air masses usually occurs over land (**continental**) or water (**maritime**) and in cold (**polar**) or warm (**tropical**) regions.

The air masses are named according to where they form. If the temperature of the air mass is colder than the surface temperature below it, the air mass is called a cold air mass. If the temperature of the air mass is warmer than the surface temperature below it, then it is identified as a warm air mass.

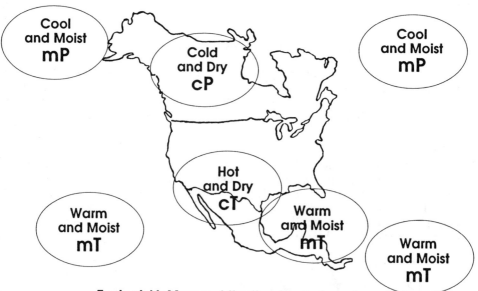

Typical Air Masses Affecting North America

Name	Symbol	Source	Typical Weather
Continental polar	**cP**	Canada	Clear, cold, dry
Continental tropical	**cT**	Southwestern U.S. and Mexico	Clear, hot, dry
Maritime tropical	**mT**	Gulf of Mexico and Caribbean Atlantic and Pacific Oceans near Equator	Cloudy, warm, rain, thunderstorms
Maritime polar	**mP**	Pacific and Atlantic Oceans near polar regions	Cloudy, cold, rain, or snow

In the United States, air masses generally move from west to east. In the winter, the Northeast is affected mainly by continental polar (**cP**) air masses. In the summer, the Northeast is affected mainly by maritime tropical (**mT**) air masses. These air masses have a definite effect on local weather. Which air masses most affect the weather where you live?

High Pressure Areas

The Earth's surface is not heated equally. Cool air sinks because it is heavier than warmer air. This forms a **high pressure area**. *The air flows outward from the center towards an area with lower air pressure.*

This air is affected by the Earth's rotation. The Earth's spinning causes the air to move in a *clockwise direction* in the northern hemisphere. Surface air pressure is usually highest in the center of the air mass. The center is represented on weather maps by the symbol "**H.**" High pressure areas generally bring cool, fair weather to regions.

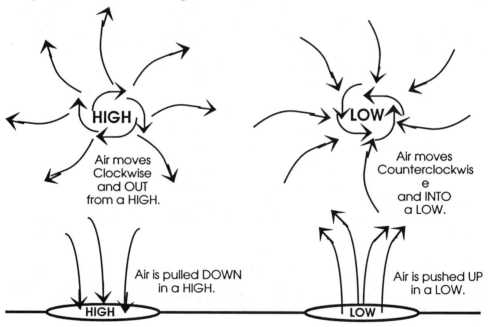

Low Pressure Areas

A **low pressure area** forms in an area where warm air is less dense and is rising. This less dense, rising air creates a low pressure area. As the air rises, it is cooled by expansion. Generally, cloudy or stormy weather is produced. *The air in a low pressure area moves inward toward the center* and is affected by the Earth's rotation.

This air movement results in a counterclockwise circulation in the northern hemisphere. Lows that are marked on weather maps indicate the center of low pressure. They are represented by the symbol "**L.**" Lows which may form along fronts produce the major storm systems.

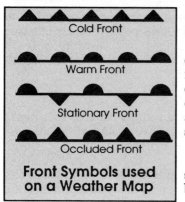

Front Symbols used on a Weather Map

Fronts

When air masses come in direct contact with one another, a boundary results. This boundary is called a **front**. Sudden changes in the weather usually occur along a front. The kind of front depends on the motion of the air in the different air masses. As these fronts move, there is often some form of **precipitation** along the front.

There are four kinds of fronts: **cold, warm, stationary, and occluded fronts**. Each front brings its own kind of weather change.

1) A **warm front** is produced when warm air is moving into colder air ahead of it. The warmer air moves up and over the colder air. A gentle slope is created. This causes the warmer air to rise and become cooled. The water vapor in the air *condenses* to form large clouds usually resulting in steady precipitation.

2) A **cold front** is produced when a cold air mass pushes under a warmer air mass. This causes the warmer air to rise. The cold dense air pushes the less dense air out of the way quickly. As the warmer air rises, it cools. The water vapor condenses to form clouds. The usual type of cloud formed is a cumulonimbus (thunderstorm) cloud. Rain that is produced is usually violent, covers a small area, and lasts a very short time.

3) A **stationary front** is the boundary between a cold air mass and a warm air mass that is not moving. This produces a gentle slope over the cold air mass like a warm front. It usually produces the same kind of weather as a warm front and may last for several days.

4) An **occluded front** is a front formed when a warm air mass comes between two cold air masses. The warm air mass is raised up by the cold air mass coming in behind it. This creates a mixture of weather produced by both warm and cold fronts. When the occluded front passes, there is usually no change in the temperature. The reason for this is a cold air mass is replaced by another cold air mass.

Questions

1   The layer of the air that surrounds the Earth is called the
   1   weather   2   circulation   3   atmosphere   4   hydrosphere

2   Conditions that affect the atmosphere determine the
   1   climate   3   weather
   2   time of day   4   darkness of night

3   Large bodies of air that determine much of our weather are called
   1   wind   2   clouds   3   air masses   4   atmosphere

4   As air masses move over the surface of the Earth, the conditions they change are
   1   local weather   3   day and night
   2   seasons   4   climate

5   An air mass that forms over northern Canada would be called a
   1   maritime polar   3   maritime tropical
   2   continental tropical   4   continental polar

6   An air mass is over the Gulf of Mexico for several days and begins to move northeast. This air mass is identified as
   1   mP   2   cP   3   mT   4   cT

7   High pressure areas generally result in weather that is
   1   stormy   3   unpredictable
   2   fair and clear   4   changeable

8   Low pressure areas usually bring weather that is
   1   stormy and cloudy   3   unpredictable
   2   fair and clear   4   the same

9   The boundary between two air masses is called a
   1   air mass   2   front   3   storm   4   fence

10   The term below that is *not* the name of a front is
   1   warm   2   cold   3   occluded   4   continental

11   Warm air rising, condensation forming thunderclouds, and short violent rain storms describes what kind of front?
   1   warm   2   cold   3   stationary   4   occluded

12   Warm air moves up and over cooler air to produce large cloud coverage. There is rain for a long period of time. These conditions indicate which type of front?
   1   warm   2   cold   3   stationary   4   occluded

13   An air mass moving toward the Northeast United States from the Gulf of Mexico will bring weather that is
   1   cold and moist   3   cold and dry
   2   warm and dry   4   warm and moist

14   Air masses take on characteristics of the surface below them. The two main characteristics are
   1   wind and temperature   3   moisture and temperature
   2   wind and moisture   4   temperature and pressure

15   Weather is a condition of the atmosphere that is affected by temperature, moisture, wind, and
   1   climate   3   change in seasons
   2   pressure   4   less daylight

C. Local Weather

Broad-scale weather systems cause atmospheric conditions that determine the weather that is experienced locally. These broad-scale systems change the daily and seasonal weather.

Local Weather Elements

Weather can be studied by collecting data on some weather elements. Some of these elements are:

Desert
(Very Low Humidity)

Jungle
(Very High Humidity)

1) **Atmospheric Pressure.** The pressure of the air is determined by the weight of the air above the surface. Air pressure and the way it changes (rising, falling, or remaining steady) are important ways of telling the passing of broad-scale weather systems (Highs and Lows).

2) **Air Temperatures** indicate the amount of heat energy in the air. Thermometers measure air temperature.

3) **Water Vapor (Humidity).** The amount of water vapor in the air varies. There is less in the air over a desert than there is over a tropical forest. The ability of the air to hold water vapor decreases as the temperature decreases.

4) **Wind** is the horizontal movement of air as it moves over the Earth's surface. Wind is measured and named in terms of its speed and the direction from which it is blowing. At the right, are the symbols used on a weather map to show wind speed in knots.

	calm	
1-2		28-32
3-7		33-37
8-12		38-42
13-17		43-47
18-22		48-52
23-27		53-57

5) **Clouds** are described in terms of up and down and sideways development. Also considered are the heights above ground level and the amount of cloud cover. The three basic types of clouds are **cirrus**, **cumulus**, and **stratus**.

6) **Solar radiation** refers to the amount of the Sun's energy (in the form of waves) that travels through space and reaches the Earth.

7) **Precipitation** refers to all types of moisture that fall from the atmosphere. The forms of precipitation are **rain, snow, hail,** and **sleet**.

Symbol		Symbol	
●	Rain	✳	Snow
══	Fog	△	Hail
▽	Showers	◗	Drizzle
⌐	Thunder-Storms	◭	Sleet

**Precipitation Symbols
Used on
a Weather Map**

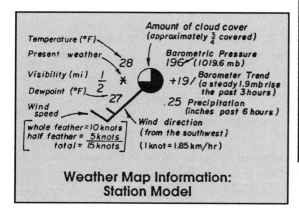

**Weather Map Information:
Station Model**

D. Weather Forecasting

The goal of weather forecasting is to make an accurate prediction of future weather. A **meteorologist** studies and forecasts the weather. Information is needed to do this. The kind of information collected is the air temperature, air pressure, direction and speed of the wind, humidity, kinds of precipitation, and the cloud cover. In addition to this, meteorologists have information from radar, computers, and weather satellites to help improve weather forecasting.

Weather tends to change slowly. High pressure areas are large and tend to be slow moving and slow in changing. Because of this, sudden changes in the weather are the exception, not the rule.

Weather forecasting is helpful to many in many ways. Knowing the future weather helps farmers know when to plant, care for, and harvest their crops.

Towns or cities can prepare for floods or heavy snowfalls. Power companies are able to prepare for extra energy if a long hot or cold spell is expected.

People can be warned of dangers like tornadoes, hurricanes, or thunder and lightning storms.

Forecasts can even help people each day. Predictions let them know what the daily weather will be so that they can act accordingly. Airports, trucking companies, road departments, as well as businesses, benefit from knowing the weather forecast ahead of time.

Questions

1   In addition to atmospheric pressure, air temperature, humidity, and clouds, the one below that is *not* a weather element is
   1 wind   3 ground water
   2 precipitation   4 solar radiation

2   The one that is *not* a tendency of air pressure is
   1 steady   2 not steady   3 rising   4 falling

3   Air temperature indicates the amount of heat energy in the air. Temperature is measured with a
   1 barometer   3 weather vane
   2 thermometer   4 rain gauge

4   The amount of water vapor in the air refers to the
   1 wind   2 pressure   3 humidity   4 temperature

5   Horizontal movement of air is called
   1 wind   2 pressure   3 humidity   4 temperature

6   Wind generally moves from an area of
   1 low pressure to an area of high pressure.
   2 high pressure to an area of low pressure.
   3 high pressure to an area of high pressure.
   4 low pressure to an area of low pressure.

7   The one below that is *not* a basic type of cloud is
   1 cirrus   2 stratus   3 tornado   4 cumulus

8   Which of the following is *not* a form of precipitation?
   1 snow   2 sleet   3 dew   4 hail

9   The Sun's energy that travels through space in the form of waves and reaches Earth is called
   1 prickly heat   3 solar radiation
   2 solar flares   4 Sun heating

10 A person who studies and predicts the weather is called a
   1 geologist   2 botanist   3 zoologist   4 meteorologist

11 Wind is named by the
   1 speed and direction it is moving to
   2 direction it is moving
   3 speed with which it moves
   4 speed and direction it is coming from

12 Weather usually changes slowly because high pressure areas are large and slow moving. Because of this, sudden weather changes
   1 happen all the time   3 are the exception, not the rule
   2 never happen   4 are the rule, not the exception

13 Which of the following has helped improve weather forecasting?
  1 hydrometer   3 weather satellites
  2 rain gauge   4 magnetic compass

14 Weather forecasting is
  1 very helpful   3 never right
  2 of no use   4 not reliable

15 The passing of a High or a Low indicates that there will be a change in
  1 air pressure   3 scenery
  2 seasons   4 solar radiation

II. Earth's Atmosphere

Substances found in the atmosphere as a result of human activity and natural events can have bad effects. They can damage humans, animals, vegetation, and nonliving objects.

A. Air Pollution And Contamination

Air **pollutants** usually include undesirable gases, liquids, and solid particles. One of the most severe effects of air pollutants is the making of acid rain. **Acid rain** is a weak acid precipitation produced by the dissolving of gaseous pollutants.

Natural contaminants in air include pollen, dust, volcanic ash, and smoke from forest fires. Volcanic ash that is put into the atmosphere after a major volcanic eruption can reduce the amount of sunlight reaching the Earth's surface. This can lower the air temperature and change climates. The action of Mt. St. Helens' eruption in 1986 is a good example of this.

B. Energy And Motion

The Sun is the primary source of energy for the Earth. The Sun's energy is not distributed equally on the Earth. The Sun shines directly on some areas (at or near the equator) and indirectly on other areas (near the North and South Poles). Unequal heating of the Earth's surface results. This produces a movement of air that flows from an area of high pressure to an area of low pressure. Weather is produced by unequal heating and distribution of energy in the atmosphere. The cooler air (High pressure areas) is more dense than the warmer air (Low pressure areas). Because of this, warm air rises and cool air sinks. This produces the High and Low pressure areas.

The highs and lows that dominate the weather in the United States, generally move from north to south. Because of the Earth's rotation, the major motion of these pressure areas is from **west to east**. It is this general west to east motion that brings most weather patterns to the Northeastern and Eastern portions of the United States.

Questions

1 Pollution in the atmosphere affects humans and all of the following except
   1 animals   3 vegetation
   2 earthquakes   4 buildings and statues

2 Most of the weather systems that affect New York, New Jersey, and Pennsylvania generally move from
   1 east to west   3 north to south
   2 west to east   4 south to north

3 Natural contaminants include combustion products from forest fires and all of the following except
   1 oxygen   3 dust
   2 pollen   4 volcanic ash

4 The primary source of energy in the atmosphere is
   1 the wind   3 the Sun
   2 precipitation   4 air masses

5 The unequal heating and distribution of energy in the atmosphere produces
   1 pollution   3 tides
   2 weather   4 day and night

6 Cold air is more dense than warm air. The statement that is true is
   1 warm air sinks and cold air rises
   2 warm air and cold air rise
   3 cold air sinks and warm air rises
   4 cold air and warm air sink

7 The effects of volcanic action on weather and climate were studied when
   1 Mt. St. Helens erupted
   2 the ocean tides changed
   3 there was a lunar eclipse
   4 the earthquake hit Mexico City

8 Gaseous pollutants in the atmosphere produce
   1 acid rain   3 a change in seasons
   2 high relative humidity   4 volcanic dust

9 Because the Earth rotates, high and low pressure areas move over North America from
   1 north to south   3 east to west
   2 south to north   4 west to east

10 Undesirable solids, liquids, and gases in the air are called
    1 clouds   3 storms
    2 pollutants   4 all answers are correct

Concepts and Words To Be Understood

absolute humidity	fog	transpiration
cloud	humidity	water cycle
condensation	relative humidity	weather warning
dew	saturated	weather watch
evaporation	sublimation	wind chill

C. Water In The Atmosphere

Water is constantly moving into the atmosphere, within the atmosphere, and from the atmosphere. This constant movement is of great importance to weather and climate. There are many ways that water enters and leaves the atmosphere.

Water Cycle

The water on the Earth is constantly evaporating and entering the atmosphere. Transpiration also puts water vapor in the atmosphere. The water vapor is constantly condensing into many forms of precipitation. Then, it falls back to Earth again. This constant transfer of water as a liquid, gas, and solid between the atmosphere and the Earth is called the **water cycle**.

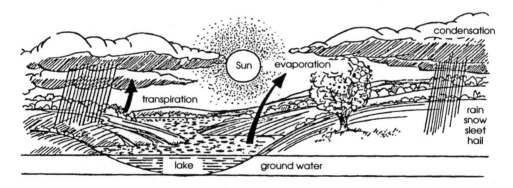

Evaporation and Transpiration in the Water Cycle

Evaporation And Transpiration

Evaporation is a change from a liquid state to the gaseous state. The process of evaporation can be affected by several conditions or factors:

- amount of water vapor in the air
- wind
- heat or temperature
- surface area

Transpiration is the process by which excess water enters the atmosphere from the leaves of plants and other living organisms. The excess water leaves the organisms in the form of water vapor.

Humidity

Humidity is the amount of water vapor in the air. **Absolute humidity** is the amount of water vapor in the air at a given or certain temperature. **Relative humidity** is the amount of water vapor in the air at a certain temperature as compared to the maximum amount the air can hold at that temperature.

Warm air can hold more water vapor than cool air. When the air is **saturated**, it is holding as much water vapor as it can. The level of saturation changes as the temperature changes.

Condensation

Water vapor leaves the atmosphere in several ways. **Condensation** is a process by which water vapor (gas) changes to a liquid. In order for this process to occur, tiny particles called nuclei are needed around which the water vapor can form. These particles are called condensation nuclei. They can be salt crystals, smoke particles, microscopic particles of sand or soil, or drops of sulfuric acid. When the proper amounts of water vapor and condensation nuclei are in the atmosphere, water vapor condenses if cooled enough.

Clouds And Fog

Clouds and fog form when the water in saturated air condenses on condensation nuclei (for example, dust particles). This forms tiny water particles that float in the air. Fog is a cloud that touches the ground. Clouds form into three basic types: **cirrus, cumulus,** and **stratus clouds.**

Cirrus Clouds

Cumulus Clouds

Stratus Clouds

• **Cirrus clouds** are the highest clouds in the atmosphere and are usually made up of ice crystals.

• **Cumulus clouds** have flat bottoms and high tops. Usually, cumulus clouds are associated with fair weather. Under certain conditions they can form into a very high dark cloud that can produce thunderstorms.

• **Stratus clouds** are layered close to the Earth and cover the whole sky. Stratus clouds are usually associated with weather that is "rainy."

Cloud Combinations. If a cloud has characteristics of two clouds, it is given a two part name like stratocumulus or cirrostratus. Sometimes the prefix "alto" meaning "high" or "nimbus (nimbo)" meaning "rain" are attached to a type of cloud to describe it. Altostratus (high stratus), nimbostratus (rain clouds), and cumulonimbus (thunderhead) are some examples of these clouds.

Dew And Frost
When water vapor forms directly on the surface of an object, dew or frost is made. **Dew** is formed by the condensation of water vapor from the air directly onto objects. **Frost** is made by the sublimation (gas to solid) of water vapor directly onto objects.

Precipitation
When cloud particles become very large, they can form into different kinds of precipitation. **Precipitation** usually refers to forms of moisture that fall from clouds. These forms include rain, snow, hail, and sleet.

- **Rain** is the liquid form of water that falls from clouds.

- **Snow** is a solid crystal form of water.

- **Sleet** is falling rain that freezes before it hits the ground.

- **Hail** usually forms in the summertime in association with thunderstorms.

Hail Formation. The currents or drafts within a thunderhead move the raindrops through a layer of air that is below freezing. This causes the raindrops to receive a coating of ice around them. As these drops move through a warmer layer, they are coated with water. These drops continue to circulate within the thunderhead and receive many coatings. Eventually, the coated raindrops become too heavy to remain in the cloud and fall as hail.

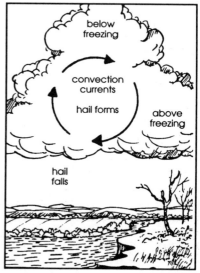

Questions

1   When water vapor changes to a liquid, the process is called
   1 sublimation   3 condensation
   2 evaporation   4 transpiration

2   The clouds that are usually associated with fair weather are
   1 cirrus   2 cumulus   3 altostratus   4 stratus

3   When frost forms directly from water vapor onto an object, the process is called
   1 sublimation   3 condensation
   2 evaporation   4 transpiration

4   Water vapor mainly enters the atmosphere through the two processes called
   1 condensation and transpiration
   2 sublimation and evaporation
   3 evaporation and transpiration
   4 sublimation and condensation

5   Dew forms onto objects through the process of
   1 transpiration   3 evaporation
   2 condensation   4 sublimation

6   The constant transfer of water between the atmosphere and Earth is called
   1 the water cycle   3 wind
   2 precipitation   4 transpiration

7   The amount of water vapor in the air, as well as the heat, surface area, wind, and saturation all affect the process of
   1 condensation   3 evaporation
   2 freezing   4 sublimation

8   The process by which plants and other living organisms give off water vapor into the air is called
   1 condensation   3 evaporation
   2 transpiration   4 sublimation

9   When air is holding as much water vapor as it can at a certain temperature, then the air is said to be
   1 very heavy   2 very dry   3 saturated   4 polluted

10 The form of precipitation that leaves the cloud as rain and freezes before reaching the surface of the Earth is
   1 hail   2 rain   3 sleet   4 snow

III. Hazardous Weather

Hazardous weather conditions can threaten life and property. People need to be aware of possible hazardous weather conditions. This information allows them to prepare for, and respond to, these conditions. This saves lives and property. Hazardous weather conditions include thunderstorms, tornadoes, hurricanes, and winter storms.

Thunderstorms

Thunderstorms may happen along fronts, near mountain barriers, and within air masses. They happen when warm, humid air is forced upward and meets with cool downdrafts. Thunderstorms may last only a few hours, but many thunderstorms can occur within the same day. Lightning always comes with thunderstorms. Lightning is a very large electrical discharge produced during a thunderstorm.

When lightning passes through the air, a sound is heard. This sound is produced by the rapid heating and expansion of the air creating something like a vacuum. The cold air rushing back into this space sets up a shock wave. This is called **thunder**.

Lightning is a major killer. Here are some safety rules to follow when lightning threatens:

- **Stay indoors and away from open doors and windows, stoves, metal pipes, sinks, plugged-in electrical appliances, and telephones.**

- **Get inside an enclosed, all-metal vehicle.**

- **Get out of the water, off beaches, and off small boats.**

- **Never stand under a tree.**

- **If caught in an open field, lie flat on the ground.**

Tornadoes

Tornadoes are small, violently rotating local winds. Generally, they are associated with severe thunderstorms. They strike with very little warning, do not last long, and cause much damage, even death. Tornadoes have a narrow funnel-shape cloud that looks black. When the bottom of the funnel-shape reaches the ground, it moves in an unpredictable route destroying everything in its path.

In the comic books, Superman was described as, "...faster than a speeding bullet, more powerful than a locomotive..." Perhaps Superman should have been compared to a tornado. The power, strength, and speed of a tornado should not be underestimated!

Tornadoes can move with a speed of anywhere from 42 to 66 kilometers (25 to 40 miles) per hour. The air speed within the funnel can reach up to 833 kilometers (500 miles) per hour. The tornado sounds like a roaring train and often brings heavy rains, thunder, and lightning.

Tornadoes have occurred all over the United States and at all times of the year. They occur most often during the spring in the warm part of the day. Usually this happens between noon and midnight. The pressure is very low inside the funnel. Because of this, buildings seem to "explode." The pressure inside the building is very high compared to the very low pressure inside the funnel of the tornado causing the walls to blow apart.

Here are some safety rules:

- **Act quickly! Your *immediate* action can save your life.**

- **Stay away from windows, doors, and outside walls. Protect your head.**

- **Go to a cellar (basement) or to an interior part of the lowest building level closets, bathrooms, or interior halls. Get under something sturdy and cover your head.**

- **In large buildings, go to predesignated (preassigned) shelter areas or to interior hallways on the lowest floor.**

- **If in a mobile home or vehicle, leave it and go to a substantial shelter. If none is available, lie flat in the nearest ditch or gully with your hands shielding your head.**

Hurricanes

Hurricanes are huge whirling storms with high winds and heavy rains. A hurricane often causes widespread flooding and great damage. Hurricanes tend to form over ocean surfaces during the warmest part of the year. They usually will form during the months of August through October.

Hurricanes are towering wall clouds surrounding a calm **eye**. The clouds around the eye can be moving at a speed of 250 kilometers (150 miles) an hour. The diameter of a hurricane can be around 500 kilometers (300 miles). The eye is usually around 20 to 25 kilometers (12 to 15 miles) in diameter. Within the eye, the sky is clear and the winds are calm.

Compared to other storms, the hurricane moves slowly, even though the winds are moving fast. Over water, the hurricane moves fairly fast. If it reaches land, it loses its force and slows down. Hurricanes that affect the Atlantic coastal states, from the Carolinas to New England, generally move in a northeasterly direction from the tropics where they form.

Here are some safety precautions that should be taken to prevent injury in the event that a hurricane threatens:

- *Hurricane watches* **are issued for coastal areas where there is a threat of hurricane conditions within 24 to 36 hours.** *Hurricane warnings* **are issued when the hurricane conditions are expected in 24 hours or less. Action to protect life and property should begin immediately when a warning is issued.**

- **Persons living in low lying coastal areas which could be subjected to the storm should evacuate (leave) threatened areas. Anyone living in flood prone areas should seek shelter at higher levels or elevation.**

- **Property should be prepared for the effects of high winds and flying debris. Board, shutter, or tape windows.**

- **Nonperishable food, water, medicines, flashlights, and the like should be acquired and safely stored for emergency use.**

- **Stay indoors during the hurricane.**

Winter Storms

Winter storms include such factors as snow, low temperatures, wind, freezing rain, or drizzle. Any one, or any combination of factors, can be hazardous.

Ice Storms

Freezing rain is precipitation that freezes when it hits exposed surfaces that are below freezing.

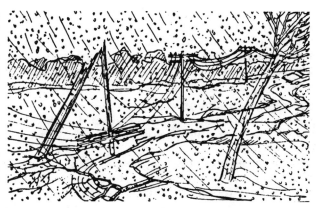

A build up of ice can cause slippery roads, fallen electrical wires, and broken tree branches. Any outdoor travel should be avoided during an ice storm because of slippery surfaces and falling wires.

Blizzards

A **blizzard** is a severe weather condition. In such a storm, low temperatures and strong winds bring blowing and drifting snow. Travel is nearly impossible because the blowing snow reduces visibility. Persons stranded in vehicles during blizzards should not attempt to walk to shelters or open areas.

Snowstorms And Windstorms

Heavy snowfall can happen any time during the fall, winter, and spring. The damage from extremely strong winds can disrupt a community for days. People should be prepared to spend several days without having to buy fresh food, fuel, and medicines.

Areas to the east of Lakes Erie and Ontario are subjected to "lake-effect" snowstorms. In these "snow belts" several feet of snow can collect within hours. Residents and travelers should be prepared for these local, sometimes sudden, storms.

Winter Storm Safety Precautions:

- **Prepare for winter storms by getting in supplies of food, heating fuel, batteries, medicines, and other necessities.**

- **During and after storms, dress warmly, avoid travel, and do not overextend yourself. Heart attacks are a major cause of death during and after winter storms.**

- **Wear protective clothing: coats, scarves, gloves or mittens, boots, and hoods. Remember that wind as well as temperature affects the rate at which the human body loses heat, especially from the head. The combined effect of temperatures and wind is called *wind chill*.**

Warning Systems

A **weather watch** indicates that the hazardous weather conditions described **may** occur. A **weather warning** indicates that the hazardous conditions are either about to happen, or are presently happening.

Summer Heat Waves

Heat waves are periods of uncomfortably hot and humid weather. They usually occur during the summer and may last a day or even several weeks.

Heat waves can result in heat exhaustion and/or death for very young, old, or ill people. The systems of the body must work hard during a heat wave. Normal body temperature must be maintained.

People should slow down, dress for summer, take in fewer calories, and drink plenty of water. They should also increase salt intake according to personal needs, and, if possible, spend their time in a cooler environment. A cooler environment can be an air-conditioned room, a cellar, or a cool bath.

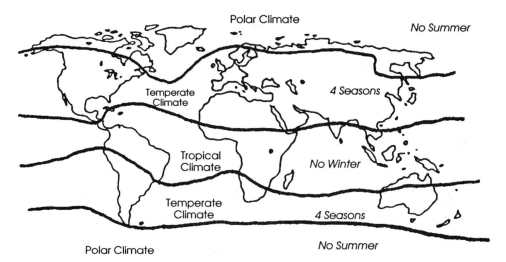

Major Climates Of The World

IV. Climate

The climate of a region or place describes its average characteristic weather from season to season and from year to year. Climate is like the history of weather. It can be described by factors like air temperature, wind, humidity, rainfall, snow, ice, and radiation over a long period of time.

The climate pattern of an area involves several factors. These factors include latitude, altitude, closeness to bodies of water, prevailing winds, and ocean currents.

In the Great Lakes' states such as, Illinois, Michigan, and Indiana, the climate varies with their location related to the lakes. Generally, their climate is considered to be humid continental with moderate rainfall, hot summers, and cold winters.

The economic development of an area is influenced by its climate. Whether or not an area can be developed agriculturally can depend on the climate.

How much energy is used can depend on the climate of an area.

Questions

1   You are told to stay indoors and away from open doors and windows, stoves, metal pipes, sinks, plugged-in appliances, and telephones. Probably, you are, or will be soon, experiencing a
1   thunderstorm   3   hurricane
2   tornado   4   blizzard

2   Small violently rotating local winds that can come with thunderstorms are called
1   heat waves   3   hurricanes
2   tornadoes   4   blizzards

3   You should not stay inside a mobile home when which kind of storm is coming?
1   thunderstorm   3   tornado
2   winter storm   4   blizzard

4   A huge whirling storm with high winds and torrential rains is called a
1   thunderstorm   3   tornado
2   hurricane   4   blizzard

5   A hurricane warning is given when hurricane conditions are expected in
1   two weeks   3   36 - 48 hours
2   12 - 24 hours   4   7 days

6   Which of these weather conditions is not associated with slippery roads, fallen electrical wires, and broken tree branches?
1   blizzard   3   windstorm
2   ice storm   4   heat wave

7   The climate of states around the Great Lakes is considered to be
1   humid marine   3   humid continental
2   dry continental   4   no answer here is correct

8   A house could "explode" during a tornado because of
1   higher pressure inside and lower pressure outside
2   lower pressure inside and higher pressure outside
3   the pressures inside and outside being the same
4   pressure has nothing to do with the "explosion"

9   During a heat wave, it would be wise to
1   dress warmly   3   play strenuous games
2   eat large meals   4   drink lots of water

10 Which violent storm is the largest and usually produces the greatest amount of damage to a wide area?
1   hurricane   3   tornado
2   thunderstorm   4   blizzard

Notes

Unit F — Earth Sciences:

Astronomy

The Earth is one of nine planets that revolve around the Sun. The Moon is a natural satellite that revolves around the Earth. The relationship of the Earth to the Sun, other stars, Moon, and the heavenly bodies is the study of astronomy.

When Galileo first saw the Moon through his telescope, he must have been thrilled. When our astronauts walked on the Moon, they were awed. Their "Moon visit" helped us to know more about our closest heavenly neighbor than we ever knew before.

An Earth year is 365 days and a day is 24 hours long. This is not true for the other planets. Revolution and rotation affect our seasons as well.

How these things happen is explained in Unit F.

Concepts and Words To Be Understood

apparent daily motion	constellation	orbit
astronomical unit	eclipse	revolution
astronomy	latitude lines	rotation
axis	light-year	seasons
compass	longitude lines	tides

Astronomy is the study of outer space and the objects that occupy this space. These objects include planets, natural satellites (moons), stars, asteroids, comets, and meteoroids. Astronomy studies the composition, size, and relative position of these objects to Earth and to each other. Earth is the only known planet to support life. Studying the Earth as part of the universe can lead to a better understanding and appreciation of the Earth.

I. Earth In Space

The Earth is constantly moving in space. There are two basic motions of the Earth in space: **rotation** and **revolution**.

A. Rotation And Revolution

Rotation is the spinning or turning of the Earth on its axis. An **axis** is an imaginary line through the center of Earth, drawn from the North Pole to the South Pole. The Earth spins in a counterclockwise direction around the axis as seen from the North Pole.

Evidence Of Rotation Includes:

- *The apparent daily motion of the Sun across the sky.* The Sun does not move across the sky. It only seems to move across the sky. It happens because the Earth is spinning on its axis.

- *Apparent daily motion of the Moon, stars, and planets.* The Moon, planets, and stars do not move around the Earth. They only seem to do this because of the Earth's spinning on its axis.

- *Free swinging pendulum.* A pendulum that can be set to swing freely appears to change its direction of swing (period). The pendulum does not change its swing. It seems to do so because the Earth is rotating beneath the pendulum.

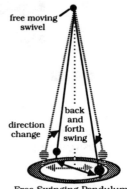

- *Substances such as air and water that move freely over the Earth's surface.* In the Northern Hemisphere, air and water currents are turned to their right because of the Earth's rotation. In the Southern Hemisphere, air and water currents are turned to their left because of the Earth's rotation.

Free Swinging Pendulum

Effects Of Rotation

Rising and Setting of the Sun. The direction of rotation causes the Sun to appear to rise in, or near, the east. It also causes the Sun to appear to set in, or near, the west. Rotation causes the Sun to apparently "rise in the east and set in the west."

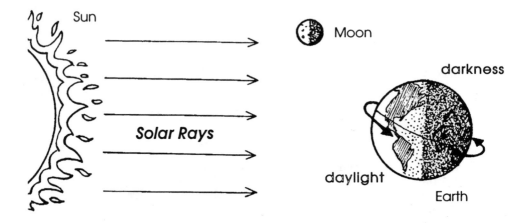

Daylight and Darkness. The rotation of the Earth causes the Earth to turn toward the Sun. This produces daylight. As the Earth turns away from the Sun, darkness is produced. One side of the Earth is always facing the Sun and is light. The other side is always facing away from the Sun and is dark.

Areas within the Arctic and Antarctic Circles are exceptions. During winter in these areas, the Sun does not "rise or set." How does this relate to the expression "Land of the Midnight Sun?"

Length of Day. The rotation of the Earth causes the day to be about twenty four hours long.

Revolution

Revolution is another motion of the Earth in space in relation to the Sun. **Revolution** is the orbiting of an object around another. In this case the Earth orbits around the Sun. An **orbit** is the path an object takes around another object.

Evidence Of Revolution

- *Stars nearer the Earth show a definite change in position.* There are definite changes in the position of stars that are nearer to Earth. This is especially true when the stars nearest the Earth are compared to the position of stars that are farther away from Earth.

- *Some of the stars seem to form a pattern.* These patterns are called **constellations.** Some constellations can only be seen during certain months. As the Earth revolves around the Sun, the part of the Earth having "nighttime" faces a different part of the universe. Sunlight does not block these constellations from our view.

Effect Of Revolution

Length of a year. The Earth takes about 365 days to make one complete revolution around the Sun. This is one year on the Earth.

Questions

1   The apparent rising and setting of the Sun and Moon as seen from the Earth is caused by the
   1   Earth's revolution   3   Sun's revolution
   2   Earth's rotation   4   Sun's rotation

2   Because of Earth's rotation, the Sun appears to rise in the
   1   north   2   south   3   east   4   west

3   The spinning of the Earth on its axis is called
   1   rotation   2   gravity   3   inertia   4   revolution

4   The rotation of the Earth causes all of the following *except*
   1   the apparent daily motion of the Sun across the sky.
   2   all of the seasons on the Earth.
   3   the apparent daily motion of the Moon, planets, and stars.
   4   day and night

5   Air and water are turned to the right in the Northern Hemisphere because of the
   1   Sun's rotation   3   Sun's revolution
   2   Earth's rotation   4   Earth's revolution

6   The Earth's 24 hour day is caused by the
   1   Sun's rotation   3   Sun's revolution
   2   Earth's revolution   4   Earth's rotation

7   The orbiting of the Earth around the Sun is called
   1   rotation   2   gravity   3   inertia   4   revolution

8 The fact that some constellations can be seen only during certain months
proves that the Earth
1 rotates   3 revolves
2 has tides   4 none of these

9 The Earth's year is about 365 days because of the
1 Sun's rotation   3 Earth's rotation
2 Sun's revolution   4 Earth's revolution

10 The apparent change in direction observed in a free swinging pendulum
is caused by the Earth's
1 rotation   3 hours of darkness
2 revolution   4 length of day

B. Seasons On The Earth

As the Earth revolves around the Sun, different parts of the Earth experience different general weather patterns during the year. These cyclic differences are the **seasons** (such as spring, summer, fall and winter).

Causes Of Seasons

The seasons on Earth are caused by these factors:

- *The **tilt of the Earth's axis of rotation**.* Earth's axis is tilted 23 ½
degrees. The Earth's axis always points to nearly the same place in
space. The North Star (Polaris) occupies this spot. The Earth's axis is
tilted toward the Sun during summer in the Northern Hemisphere.
During the winter, the Northern Hemisphere is tilted away from the
Sun.

- *The **revolution of Earth around the Sun**** causes the Sun's direct rays
to fall on different latitudes of the Earth during the Earth's 365 day
revolution.

- *The **rotation of the Earth**** causes the alternation of day and night.

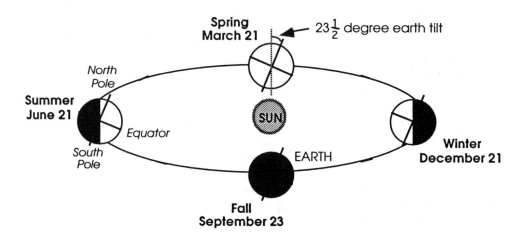

Characteristics Of Earth's Seasons

Summer. During the summer, the Northern Hemisphere is tilted toward the Sun. Because of this, the Sun shines more directly on the Northern Hemisphere and warms it. The days are longer because the Northern Hemisphere is tilted toward the Sun and spends more time in the Sun's light.

Winter. During the winter, the Northern Hemisphere is tilted away from the Sun. The Southern Hemisphere is receiving the direct rays of the Sun.

The Northern Hemisphere receives the indirect rays from the Sun. Because of this, the Northern Hemisphere cools. The days are shorter because the Northern Hemisphere is tilted away from the Sun and spends less time in the Sun's light.

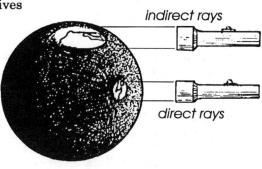

indirect rays

direct rays

Note in the drawing at the right, that the same amount of light (and heat) cover different amounts of the Earth's surface.

Spring and fall. On the first day of spring and the first day of fall, the Earth is not tilted toward or away from the Sun. The Sun shines directly on the equator. This causes equal day and night.

C. Determining Locations On Earth

Different places on Earth can be located in many ways.

A **compass** can be used. The main compass points are North, South, East, and West. The needle of a compass always points toward magnetic North. If you face North, the South is behind you. East is to the right and West is to the left.

Latitude lines are parallel lines that are north and south of the equator. The equator is the parallel that divides the Earth into the Northern and Southern Hemispheres. Latitude lines measure distance in degrees north and south of the equator.

Longitude lines are imaginary lines that are east and west of the Prime Meridian. The Prime Meridian and the 180th Meridian divide the Earth into the Eastern and Western Hemispheres.

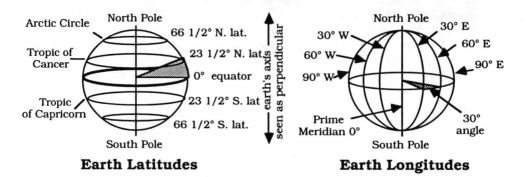

Earth Latitudes   **Earth Longitudes**

The meridian lines measure distance east and west of the Prime Meridian. The 180th meridian is known as the International Date Line.

D. Determining Time Of Day

Hourly time is based on the length of a day on Earth. Noon by Sun time occurs when the shadow cast by a vertical pole is the shortest. This shadow always point in a northerly direction in the continental United States (at noon).

Many years ago, before there were modern clocks, time was determined with a sun dial. When the shortest shadow was cast, the time was 12 noon.

Questions

1   The imaginary line drawn through the center of the Earth from the North Pole to the South Pole is called the Earth's
   1   equator   3   longitude
   2   axis   4   latitude

2   The tilt of the Earth's axis is one of the causes of Earth's
   1   tides   3   seasons
   2   latitude lines   4   longitude lines

3   The Northern Hemisphere is tilted *toward* the Sun when people in California are having
   1   summer   3   winter
   2   fall   4   spring

4   The Prime Meridian and the 180th longitude line divide the Earth into the
   1   continents   3   North and South Hemispheres
   2   seasons   4   East and West Hemispheres

5   What is the amount of tilt from the perpendicular of the Earth's axis in degrees?
   1   23 ½°   2   45°   3   66 ½°   4   90°

Use the illustration at the right to answer questions 6 and 7.
The flashlights represent the rays of the Sun.

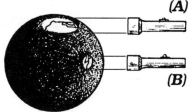

(A)

(B)

6   Countries receiving the indirect rays of the Sun *(A)* would most likely be having which season?
  1   spring
  2   summer
  3   fall
  4   winter

7   The illustration shows the direct rays of the Sun at the Equator (B). When this happens, both the Northern and Southern Hemispheres are having
  1   summer or spring   3   spring, winter, or fall
  2   spring or winter   4   fall or spring

8   The Northern Hemisphere is tilted *away* from the Sun when people in Ohio and New York are experiencing
  1   summer   3   winter
  2   fall   4   spring

9   If you face North, the direction to your left is
  1   North   2   South   3   East   4   West

10 The equator divides the Earth into the
  1   continents   3   North and South Hemispheres
  2   seasons   4   East and West Hemispheres

II. Earth's Moon

The Moon is the nearest natural neighbor to the Earth.

Orbit Of The Moon

The Moon travels in its orbit around Earth. The same side of the Moon is always facing Earth. The Moon's plane of orbit is not usually the same as the plane of the Earth's orbit.

The Moon revolves around the Earth in a counterclockwise direction. The Moon revolves from west to east, just as the Earth revolves around the Sun.

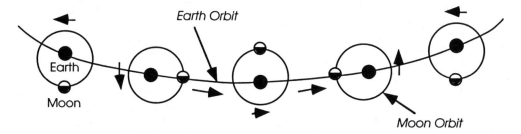

Moon Motion Around The Earth

Causes For The Phases Of The Moon

There are two main causes for the phases of the Moon:

- The Moon produces no light of its own. It can only be seen by reflected light from the Sun.

- One half of the Moon is always lighted by the Sun as it moves around the Earth. The amount and shape of the lighted side seen from Earth determines the phase of the Moon.

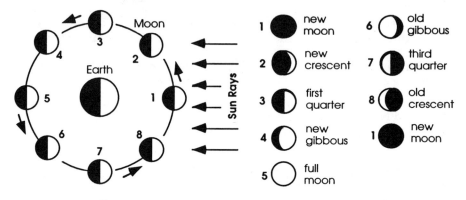

Total cycle from new moon to next new moon
requires 29 1/2 days. Time between phases is 3 1/4 days.

Phases Of The Moon

At the new moon phase, the side facing the Earth is dark and the Moon cannot be seen. The Moon is between the Earth and the Sun. At the full moon phase, all of the lighted side can be seen. This is true because the Moon is behind the Earth. At the crescent phase, only a small sliver can be seen. At the quarter moon stage, one half of the lighted side can be seen. At the gibbous phase, about three-fourths or more can be seen.

Eclipses

The plane of the Moon's orbit is *not* the same as the Earth's orbital plane. Also, the plane of the Moon changes over time. Sometimes the Moon's plane of orbit causes it to be in the Earth's shadow, or vice versa. This is called an **eclipse**.

Lunar Eclipse

Moon

Sun

Earth

Full Shadow

Partial Shadow

Lunar eclipses occur when the Moon passes into the Earth's shadow. A lunar eclipse can occur _only_ at Full Moon phase. When the Moon is completely in the shadow, it is called a **total eclipse. Partial eclipses** happen when only a portion of the Moon gets in the shadow of the Earth.

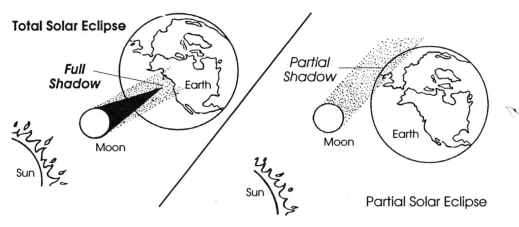

Total Solar Eclipse

Full Shadow

Earth

Moon

Sun

Partial Shadow

Earth

Moon

Sun

Partial Solar Eclipse

A **solar eclipse** occurs when the Moon casts a shadow on the Earth. The Moon is between the Earth and the Sun. This can _only_ happen at the New Moon phase. (**Never look directly at a solar eclipse.** The ultraviolet light rays can damage your eyes.)

Moon And Tides

Tides are the rising and falling of the oceans on Earth. Tides are caused by the gravitational attraction between the Earth, Moon, and Sun. As the Earth rotates, the tides change. High tide occurs when a certain position on the Earth is facing directly toward, or away from, the Moon. The tides move from high tide to low tide (or low tide to high tide) about every 6.25 hours. The Sun does not affect the tides as much as the Moon does.

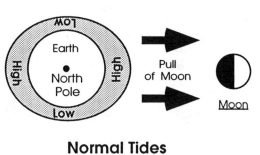

Low

Earth

North Pole

High

High

Low

Pull of Moon

Moon

Normal Tides

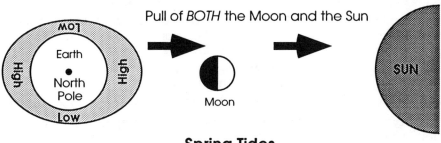

Pull of _BOTH_ the Moon and the Sun

Low

Earth

North Pole

High

High

Low

Moon

SUN

Spring Tides

(When the Moon is new or full, the tide is _unusually_ high)

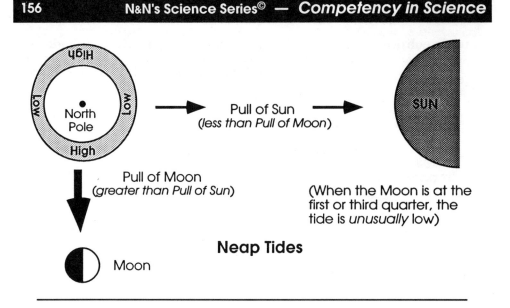

Neap Tides

 Moon

Questions

1   The closest natural neighbor to Earth is
    1   the Sun   3   Mars
    2   the Moon   4   Venus

2   When the Moon is directly between the Earth and the Sun, it is in its
    1   new moon phase   3   full moon phase
    2   quarter moon phase   4   gibbous moon phase

Answer questions 3 through 6 using the following illustration of the Moon's Phases.

1 ●   **2** ◗   **3** ◐   **4** ◖   **5** ○

3   As seen from Earth, the lighted surface of the Moon appears to be
    1   remaining the same   3   decreasing in size
    2   loosing brightness   4   increasing in size

4   The number of days for the Moon to go through these phases is about
    1   5 days   3   14 days
    2   10 days   4   28 days

5   What phase of the Moon is indicated by number 5?
    1   full moon   3   old crescent
    2   new moon   4   third quarter

6   What type of eclipse could occur during the phase represented by number 1?
    1   elliptical   3   orbital
    2   lunar   4   solar

7   The Moon is on the opposite side of the Earth from the Sun. It is in its
    1   new moon phase   3   full moon phase
    2   quarter moon phase   4   gibbous moon phase

8   The Moon revolves about the same rate it rotates; therefore,
    1   the Moon moves around the Earth twice a day.
    2   the same side of the Moon always faces the Earth.
    3   the Moon stays in the same position.
    4   the Moon moves so that both sides can be seen.

9   The phase of the Moon is determined by
    1   how much sunlight shines on the Moon.
    2   how much light the Earth shines on the Moon.
    3   the amount of the lighted side seen from the Earth.
    4   how high the Moon is in the sky.

10 The rising and falling of the oceans every 6.25 hours is called
    1   a tidal wave   3   ebb tide
    2   good surfing   4   the tides

III. Sun And Solar System

A. Sun And Other Stars

The Earth receives most of its energy from the Sun. The **Sun** is many times larger than the Earth. Compared to other stars, the Sun is only an average sized star.

There are many stars smaller and larger than the Sun. The Sun is about 150,000,000 kilometers (93 million miles) from the Earth. This is one **astronomical unit**.

Astronomical Unit

Other Stars. The distance between stars is vast (very great). Because of this distance, a light-year is used to determine the distance between stars. A **light-year** is the distance light travels in one year. Light travels at about 300,000 kilometers per second (186,000 miles per second). Therefore, light travels about nine trillion kilometers (6 trillion miles) in an Earth year.

B. Solar System

The solar system is made up of the Sun, the nine planets, and other bodies that revolve around the Sun.

Location Of The Sun

The Sun is located near the center of the solar system. The planets revolve around the Sun in elliptical (slightly out of round) orbits. Our solar system is a small part of the Milky Way galaxy.

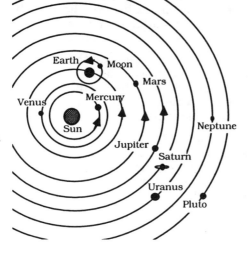

The Solar System

(top view not drawn to scale)

Planets

There are nine planets in the solar system. The planets in order from the Sun are: Mercury, Venus, Earth, Mars, Jupiter, Saturn, Uranus, Neptune, and Pluto. The planets can be seen from Earth by reflected sunlight.

Each planet has its own unique characteristics.

Earth seems to be the only planet that is able to support life.

Other Solar System Objects

Many other objects revolve around the Sun. **Asteroids** are small planet-like bodies that orbit between Mars and Jupiter.

Meteoroids are rock fragments that travel in space. Some of these meteoroids enter the atmosphere and heat up. This produces a light that is called a "shooting star" or a "falling star." If a piece of the meteor does not burn up and reaches the Earth, it is called a **meteorite**.

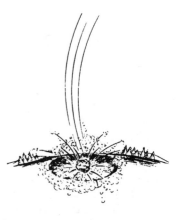

Comets also travel around the Sun in highly elliptical orbits. These comets produce a glowing head and a long tail when they come near the Sun. The tail always points away from the Sun.

Halley's Comet is probably the most famous comet. It returns every 76 years or so. Halley's Comet just passed us a short time ago. If you were not lucky enough to see it, you will have to mark your calendar for the year 2062 It won't be back until then.

Questions

1 The Earth receives most of its energy from
  1 hydroelectric power   3 nuclear plants
  2 the Sun   4 the power plants

2 When compared to other stars, our Sun is
  1 average sized   3 farthest from Earth
  2 the largest   4 the smallest

3 An astronomical unit is the average
  1 distance the Earth is from the Moon.
  2 distance the Earth is from the Sun
  3 time it takes for the Earth to revolve.
  4 time it takes the Earth to rotate.

4 The distance light travels in a year is called a
  1 light-day   3 light-year
  2 light-month   4 light-century

5 The only planet known to support life is
  1 Venus   3 Mars
  2 Earth   4 Mercury

6 The Sun, nine planets, asteroids, meteoroids, and comets make up
  1 the Milky Way
  2 Earth's family
  3 the solar system
  4 everything in the universe

7 We are able to see the other planets in the solar system because they
  1 reflect the Sun's light
  2 provide their own light
  3 reflect the Earth's light
  4 collect cosmic rays

8 The distance between stars in the universe is
  1 one light year
  2 two astronomical units
  3 quite small
  4 very, very great

9 A "shooting star" is really a meteor that has
  1 burned up in space
  2 circled our Moon
  3 entered the Earth's atmosphere
  4 formed a constellation

10 Which solar system member comes closest to the Earth's surface?
  1 comet   3 Moon
  2 meteor   4 Venus

Notes

Area 3
Physical Sciences

- Energy and Motion
  - Chemistry of Matter
    - Energy: Sources and Issues

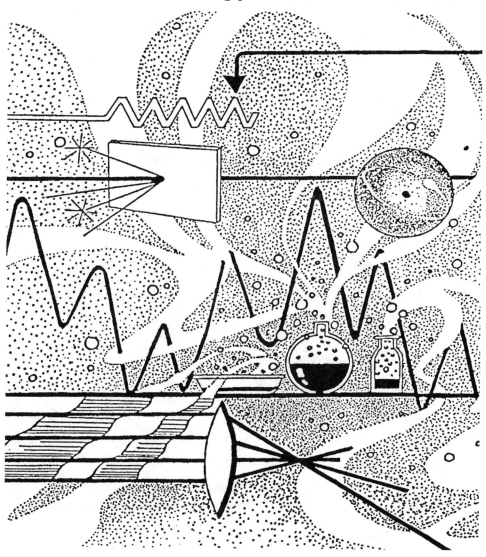

Unit G — Physical Sciences:

Energy and Motion

Energy is needed by all living things. It is used to think, to move, and to play baseball. The study of energy, motion, and the changes energy goes through is the science of Physics. Some energy forms are electricity, heat, light, and sound.

Machines are used to make work easier for us. Two simple machines on which all other machines are based are the lever and the inclined plane. Even the pulley is considered a "rotating lever." The screw is nothing more than a spiral inclined plane.

Unit G includes discussions of what energy is, how it travels, and what it can do to make our lives better.

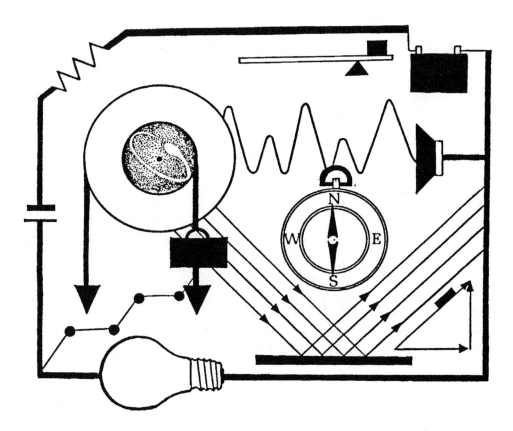

Concepts and Words To Be Understood

created	machine	random
energy	movement	reference object
force	potential energy	transformation
kinetic energy		work

I. Energy

Energy is required to do work or cause change. To understand what energy is, a scientific explanation of work is needed. **Work** is done when something moves. A formula can be used to define work:

Work equals force times distance.
W (joules) = F (newtons) x d (meters)

W = F x d
W = 20N x 10m
W = 200N-m(or joules)

20 N ➔ ➔ ➔ 20 N

10 m

point A   point B

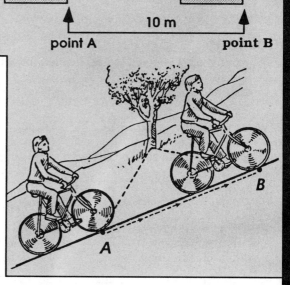

To understand work, the concept of **movement** is needed. Movement can be observed only by using a **reference object** which is assumed to be not moving (stationary).

An object moves because an unbalanced force acts on it. In the illustration (right), the tree is the stationary object. The bicycle moves from point *A* to point *B*.

A **force** is a push or pull exerted on an object. When an object at rest is acted upon by two equal forces in opposite directions, no motion is produced. When unequal forces act on an object, movement results. *Energy can be thought of as a source of force.*

A. Kinds Of Energy

Potential energy is energy that is **stored** to be used later. The potential energy depends on the position or condition of the object having it. Examples of things that have potential energy include water stored behind a dam, hailstones in a cloud, rocks on the edge of a cliff, gasoline in a car's gas tank, and trinitrotoluene (TNT) in a closed container.

Kinetic energy is present in anything that is **moving**. Should the rock on the top of the cliff fall, the potential energy changes to kinetic energy. This happens as the rock crashes to the base of the cliff. Examples of things that have kinetic energy are a speeding motorcycle, a jet plane during takeoff, falling rivers and raindrops, and rolling stones and bowling balls. The **faster** an object moves, the **more** kinetic energy it has.

The water at the brink (top edge) of Niagara Falls has a greater amount of potential energy than kinetic energy. As the water falls over the edge, the potential energy of the water is changed into kinetic energy.

Questions

1   A bag of groceries needs to be carried from the car to the kitchen. What is needed to do this work?
   1 distance   3 matter
   2 energy   4 movement

2   What is needed to detect an object in motion?
   1 some form of matter   3 an object that is not moving
   2 a moving observation deck   4 falling water

3   Moving things have what kind of energy?
   1 chemical   3 nuclear
   2 kinetic   4 potential

4   An object will move when acted upon by
   1 balanced forces   3 equal forces
   2 unbalanced forces   4 reference objects

5   As water moves over the edge of Niagara Falls,
   1 kinetic energy changes to chemical energy
   2 lots of potential energy is produced
   3 potential energy decreases and kinetic energy increases
   4 kinetic energy changes to potential energy

B. Forms Of Energy

There are many forms of potential and kinetic energy. Several examples are chemical, electrical, heat, light, magnetic, nuclear, mechanical, and sound.

•   **Chemical energy** is the energy stored in substances. This energy results from the forces that hold atoms and molecules together. Candle wax, dynamite, and gasoline are examples.

•   **Electrical energy** results from the movement of electrons, usually through a conductor. It is associated with an electric current. Dry cells, storage batteries, and generators are sources of electrical energy.

•   **Heat** is a form of kinetic energy resulting from the random movement of particles. The faster the particles move, the more heat is made. The Sun's rays are changed to heat on the Earth. Stoves and ovens cook food. Furnaces and heaters are used to warm us.

•   **Light** is a part of the energy from the Sun, stars, fires, and man-made objects like light bulbs. Light is the most plentiful energy source of all.

All life on Earth depends on light energy for the process of photosynthesis. Photosynthesis takes place in green plants only.

•   **Magnetic force** is present naturally in iron, nickel, and cobalt. Their particles are thought to be tiny magnets themselves. The Earth acts as a very large magnet and is strongest at the magnetic poles. There are permanent bar and horseshoe magnets.

Electromagnets are found in doorbells, motors, telegraph sets, and junk yards, where magnets move old cars.

•   **Mechanical energy** can be potential energy when not moving, but it usually is thought of as the kinetic energy of moving objects. The energy released by human muscles for walking, running, and playing basketball is a form of mechanical energy. Moving machines and freight trains are additional examples.

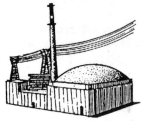

• **Nuclear energy**, also called **atomic energy**, is a very powerful form of potential energy. Very large amounts of kinetic energy can be produced. Stored in the nucleus of the atom, nuclear energy is released when an atom splits apart (**fission**) or joins with another (**fusion**). The atomic and hydrogen bombs and nuclear power plants release atomic energy.

• **Sound energy** is produced when matter vibrates. Vocal cords allow us to speak, while school bells, fog horns, and ambulance sirens convey other messages.

C. Energy Transformation

Energy transformation (conversion) occurs when one form of energy changes to another form. For example:

• The chemical energy of candle wax changes to heat and light when the candle burns.

• Electricity changes to sound when a radio is turned on.

• The chemical energy of gasoline changes to mechanical energy in the engine of a motorcycle.

• The heat from a nuclear reactor changes water to steam. Steam turns the turbines (mechanical energy). Turbines turn the generators (magnetism present) to produce electricity. Now the television set can produce the light and sound so that we can enjoy the programs.

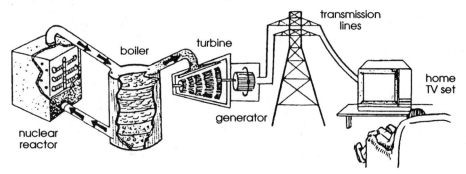

D. Law Of The Conservation Of Energy

The law of conservation of energy states that *energy cannot be created or destroyed by ordinary means, only changed in form.* Much of the energy that is "believed to be lost," is being changed to heat energy. Touch the outside case of a television set before and after use. Note the change in heat. Heat was "lost" while you used the television.

Questions

1   A match head stores energy in what form?
   1   chemical   3   mechanical
   2   magnetic   4   sound

2   In the Sun, hydrogen atoms join to form helium and release lots of energy. This is an example of what form of energy?
   1   electrical   2   magnetic   3   nuclear   4   sound

3   When a radio is turned on, the energy change taking place is
   1   light to heat   3   electricity to nuclear
   2   sound to heat   4   electricity to sound

4   Energy *cannot* be
   1   changed   3   stored
   2   created   4   wasted

5   Electrical energy is changed to mechanical energy by
   1   the Sun   3   a bread toaster
   2   an electric motor   4   a calculator

Concepts and Words To Be Understood

circuit	conductor	electron	insulator
circuit breaker	electricity	fuse	

II. Electricity

Electric current is the result of electrons moving from one place to another. Lightning is a form of electricity produced by friction. This form of electricity is *uncontrolled.* Usable electric current flows through wires and can be started and stopped.

Conductors

Conductors are materials, usually metals, that allow electrons to pass through them easily. Silver is one of the best conductors of an electric charge but is very expensive. Copper is also a good conductor. Copper is cheaper than silver; so, most electric wires are made from copper. Pure water does not conduct electricity, but water with impurities does.

A wet human body conducts electricity. Always be careful, especially when hands are wet, when touching switches and using appliances in the bathroom, garage or basement, and around a swimming pool.

Insulators

Insulator is the name given to a material that does *not* allow electricity to flow through it easily. Glass, plastic, rubber, wool, wax, and special paints are good **insulators** and are called **nonconductors**.

Circuits

Circuits are the *paths followed by electrons* as they travel through conductors. A simple circuit consists of:

1) a source of electricity,
2) a device to use the energy,
3) a switch, and
4) a conducting wire.

Symbols often are used by electricians and physicists to represent parts of circuits. Some common symbols are:

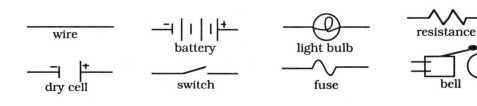

wire   battery   light bulb   resistance

dry cell   switch   fuse   bell

Switches are used to control electricity.

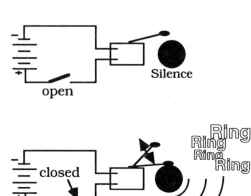

open   Silence

closed   Ring Ring Ring Ring

- A **fuse** or **circuit breaker** is a kind of switch. When it is opened, electricity will not flow through the circuit until is it replaced or reset. These switch-like devices "open" circuits when they are overloaded. Overloaded circuits carry too much electricity. They may overheat and cause fires.

- An **open circuit** has a break or opening in it that does not let the electrons flow. An open switch does the same thing.

- A **closed circuit** has no openings. Therefore, electrons move through the circuit. A switch can be used to start and stop the flow of electricity.

Safety With Electricity

Safety with electricity must be taken seriously. Electricity can be dangerous and can injure or kill a living organism. Some safety rules to follow are:

> - **Disconnect appliances before attempting to repair them.**
> - **Do not throw a switch or plug in an appliance when standing in water or when the body is wet.**
> - **Locate and repair the cause of a "blown" fuse or circuit breaker before turning on electricity. Fires can result from overloaded circuits.**
> - **Be sure that circuits are properly grounded. Grounding of circuits conducts extra electrons to the earth where they can be absorbed. Grounds prevent a large build up of electrons that might cause a fire, serious injury, or death.**

Questions

1   Electrons moving through a wire produce
　　1　current　　　　2　gravity　　　3　light　　　　　4　sound

2   A substance through which electricity will travel is a(an)
　　1　glass rod　　　2　conductor　　3　insulator　　4　plastic tube

3   The best conductor of electricity is
　　1　copper　　　　2　iron　　　　　3　silver　　　　4　tungsten

4   The metal most commonly used to make electric wires is
　　1　copper　　　　2　iron　　　　　3　silver　　　　4　tungsten

5   Substances that do *not* easily carry electric current are called
　　1　conductors　　2　insulators　　3　matter　　　　4　circuits

6   Which of the following is a good conductor of electricity?
　　1　glass　　　　　2　copper　　　　3　plastic　　　　4　porcelain

7   Rubber, glass, and plastic make good
　　1　conductors　　2　insulators　　3　circuits　　　4　light bulbs

8   A complete circuit may consist of a light bulb, switch, wires, and
　　1　a battery　　　2　a magnet　　3　a glass rod　4　an insulator

9   A circuit that is conducting electrons to the earth is
　　1　open　　　　　2　closed　　　　3　grounded　　　4　turned off

10 The flow of electricity in a circuit is controlled by a
　　1　conductor　　2　door bell　　3　light bulb　　4　switch

11 Electric current in a circuit can be controlled with the use of a
　　1　circuit breaker　　　　　　3　switch
　　2　fuse　　　　　　　　　　　4　all are correct

12 Which of the following diagrams best represents an "open circuit?"

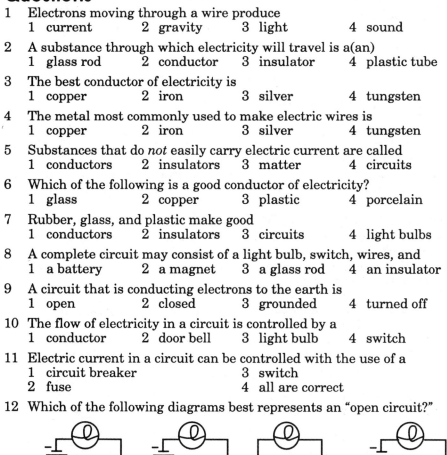

13 The correct symbol for a light bulb is

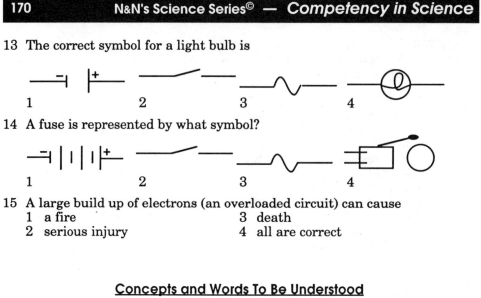

1   2   3   4

14 A fuse is represented by what symbol?

1   2   3   4

15 A large build up of electrons (an overloaded circuit) can cause
1 a fire   3 death
2 serious injury   4 all are correct

Concepts and Words To Be Understood

conduction	convection	kinetic	radiation
contract	expand	phase	theory

III. Heat

Heat is the *total of all the kinetic and potential energy* of the particles in a material. **Heat energy** is the result of the *random* movement of these particles. The faster the particles move, the greater the amount of heat present. We feel heat (temperature) with special cells (receptors) in our skin. **Temperature** is the measure of the average kinetic energy of the moving particles. Rub your hands together. The heat (temperature) you feel is produced by the friction. It is caused by your hands being in close contact.

A. Kinetic Particle Theory Of Matter

The kinetic particle theory of matter can help explain some of the concepts and principles of science. Also, using this theory will help you to better understand heat. Heat is something that we feel but cannot "see." Some parts of the kinetic particle theory are:

1   All matter (solids, liquids, and gases) is made up of tiny particles.

Soap is a Solid
Particles are close together.

Soda is a Liquid
Particles are farther apart.

**Air in a Balloon
is a Gas**
Particles are very far apart.

2 The particles are always moving.
3 There are spaces between the particles (even in solids).
4 Heat energy makes the particles move faster.
5 There is an attraction between the particles that holds them together.

B. Expansion And Contraction

Expansion and contraction happen to substances when the amount of heat energy they have changes. When particles move faster, they have more heat energy. They **expand** and take up more space. The reverse is also true. When heat is lost, particles slow down and need less space. When there is less space between particles, the substance **contracts**.

Expansion joints are needed on bridges because the bridge surface expands and contracts. Spaces are left between concrete sections of highways and sidewalks. This allows for hot weather expansion and cold weather contraction.

Thermometers work because the liquid in the tubes expands and contracts. The amount of liquid movement depends on the amount of heat present.

Celsius Scale
100°   20°   0°

Boiling Pt.   Room   Freezing Pt.
of water   Temp.   of water

212°   68°   32°
Fahrenheit Scale

Water is an unusual substance. Water behaves like most things, most of the time, but at 4°C (39°F) it begins to expand again. Ice takes up more space than the water that makes it up.

C. Phases Of Matter

Phases (states) of matter are determined by the energy of the particles present. When heat energy is added to ice, the **frozen water** turns to **liquid water**. When more heat energy is added to the liquid, **water vapor** or gaseous water, is formed. See Unit H - Chemistry of Matter for further details.

D. Heat Transfer

Heat transfer happens because heat energy flows from areas of higher temperature to areas of lower temperature (high concentration to low concentration). The amount, type, space, or condition of the space between these two areas will determine the type of heat energy transfer. There are three kinds of heat energy transfer:

1) **Conduction** occurs when closely packed particles, especially in solids, bump into each other. A metal spoon gets hot when left in a boiling pot of soup.

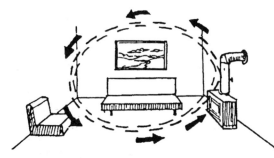

2) **Convection** is the movement of heat energy in liquids and gases. These particles have more freedom of movement.

3) **Radiation** is the transfer of heat through space by infrared waves. Infrared waves are part of the **electromagnetic spectrum.** Radiation can transfer heat energy through empty space (a vacuum). Radiation allows the Earth to be heated by the Sun.

Insulators are substances that slow down the flow of heat energy from one area to another. The use of good insulators is important in the building of houses, schools, and office buildings. Homeowners want to keep the heat **in** or **out**, depending on the season. This can be done by installing proper wall insulation, storm windows and doors, and caulking. These things help prevent unwanted cold air from coming in during winter.

Good insulators are also used in refrigerators, thermos bottles, and ice chests. Insulators are usually *poor conductors* of heat energy. Wood, air, paper, polystyrene foam, and wool resist heat flow or transfer and make good insulators.

Conductors are substances, usually metals, that carry heat energy from one place to another easily. Usually, kettles, pans, and coffee pots are made from copper, iron, or stainless steel. Special glass and ceramic materials are being made that also conduct heat energy well.

In general, *good conductors of electricity are good conductors of heat energy.* Likewise, *poor conductors (insulators) of heat energy are also poor conductors of electricity.*

Good Conductors		Poor Conductors (Insulators)	
Electricity	**Heat**	**Electricity**	**Heat**
silver copper aluminum iron	silver copper aluminum iron	air fiberglass wax plastic foam	air fiberglass wax plastic foam

Questions

1 Heat is considered to be a form of
   1 an animal   2 chemicals   3 energy   4 matter

2 Heating makes particles move
   1 at the same speed   3 faster
   2 in circles   4 slower

3 Rubbing two objects together produces friction. This will make the objects feel
   1 cooler   2 heavier   3 warmer   4 thicker

4 The method of heat transfer where particles bump into each other is called
   1 conduction   2 convection   3 insulation   4 radiation

5 Homes are insulated to keep them
   1 warmer in the winter   3 cooler in the winter
   2 warmer in the summer   4 thicker for wall support

6   Which of the following are good conductors of heat?
1   paper and air   3   copper and silver
2   wood and iron   4   cotton and copper

7   Good conductors of heat are usually
1   good insulators   3   poor conductors of electricity
2   poor wave makers   4   good conductors of electricity

8   Matter expands when heated because its particles
1   get larger   2   break up   3   get smaller   4   move apart

9   When air is heated, it will
1   contract   2   expand   3   sink down   4   not change

10 Heat energy always moves from
1   cool places to warm places   3   high places to low places
2   warm places to cold places   4   low places to lower places

11 A metal screw-on cap of a bottle will not turn when trying to remove it.
It is placed under hot water for a few minutes. The metal cap then turns
easily. This is due to the fact that
1   water is a liquid   3   matter contracts when cooled
2   the metal cap is a solid   4   matter expands when heated

12 The way energy gets to the Earth from the Sun is by
1   conduction   2   convection   3   insulation   4   radiation

13 Humans can feel heat because the skin contains special
1   cells   2   colors   3   layers   4   reflectors

14 The movement of air currents from warm regions to cool regions is an example of what kind of heat transfer?
1   conduction   2   convection   3   radiation   4   evaporation

15 "Foam" cups are used to keep lemonade cold for hours because styrofoam
is a good
1   color   2   conductor   3   insulator   4   strong material

16 When you rub your hands together, they will
1   feel colder   2   feel warmer   3   change color   4   change shape

17 Expansion joints are used in the construction of bridges because
1   they make the bridge look more attractive
2   iron is expensive
3   it adds expense to the initial cost
4   it prevents "buckling" during hot weather

18 Which of the following would represent a solid?
1   a cloud   3   a bar of soap
2   soda in a bottle   4   air in a balloon

19 A thermometer works because
1   the liquid in the tube expands and contracts
2   the air inside can freeze
3   Celsius and Fahrenheit were friends
4   no answer here is correct

20 The only form of heat energy transfer that can travel through empty
space (a vacuum) is
1   condensation   3   conduction
2   radiation   4   convection

21 Which of the following diagrams represents the Celsius scale?

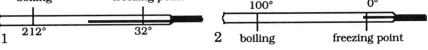

22 Of the following diagrams, which would best represent a solid?

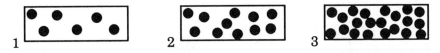

23 Which diagram could represent particles with the highest temperature?

24 Water is an unusual substance because it contracts as most substances when it cools, but at 4°C it

  1 freezes   3 disappears
  2 begins to expand again   4 continues to contract

25 A proposed explanation for "...heat is something that we can feel but cannot see..." is based on experimentation. This information represents a

  1 conclusion   2 summary   3 theory   4 procedure

Concepts and Words To Be Understood

concave lens	frequency	refraction
convex lens	medium	transverse wave
crest	prism	trough
electromagnetic spectrum	reflection	wavelength

IV. Light

Light is a form of energy sensed by the eyes of many organisms. The Sun is the major source of our light. Light from the sun travels to the Earth by special radiant waves. These light waves do not need a medium as sound waves do. Looking much like a water wave, light waves have **crests** and **troughs**. **Wavelength** is measured from a point on one crest (or trough) to the same point on the next crest (or trough).

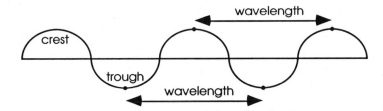

Properties Of Light

The **speed of light** is about 300,000 kilometers per second (about 186,000 miles per second). Light travels in **straight lines** (rays) and can go around a corner only if **reflection** is possible.

The "white light" from the sun can be **separated** into the seven colors of the light spectrum. A triangular piece of solid glass called a **prism** can break apart white light.

There is a definite order to the colors (red, orange, yellow, green, blue, indigo, and violet). The letters **ROY G BIV** can help you remember the order of colors.

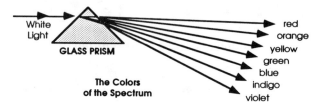

White Light

GLASS PRISM

The Colors of the Spectrum

red
orange
yellow
green
blue
indigo
violet

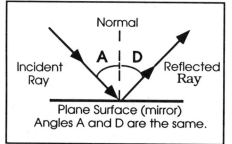

Normal

Incident Ray

A | D

Reflected Ray

Plane Surface (mirror)
Angles A and D are the same.

Reflection

Reflection occurs when a light ray hits a surface and is bounced off. Almost all surfaces reflect some light which permits our eyes to "see" the object. The sky is blue because particles in the atmosphere reflect the blue rays in the Sun's light. Surfaces reflect light at the same angle at which they are hit.

When sunlight hits the leaves of a green plant, the green rays are reflected. Our eyes then see the leaf as "green." The other light rays are absorbed (taken in) by the plant.

Some objects reflect light. Some absorb it. There are substances that allow light to pass through. When this happens, light is **transmitted**. Clear glass and plastic allow almost all light to be transmitted.

Transparent   Translucent   Opaque

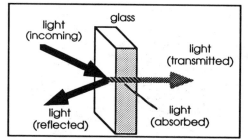

light (incoming)

glass

light (transmitted)

light (reflected)

light (absorbed)

Some materials both transmit and absorb some light. These substances are **translucent**. When all light is absorbed or reflected, the object is said to be **opaque**. Things that are opaque cast shadows.

Smooth, shiny surfaces reflect images. When this happens, the image appears to be the same distance behind the mirror as the object is in front of it.

Refraction
Refraction is the bending of light rays. This is done by a prism when it separates white light. This is caused by the slight change in the speed of light as it passes from one substance to another.

Lenses
Lenses are curved pieces of glass or plastic that are able to **refract** (bend) light rays. Lenses are named for their shape. Note that the convex lens is thicker in the middle than at the edges.

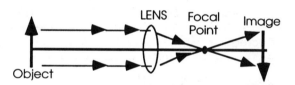

Convex Lens   **Concave Lens**

Convex Lens
A convex lens bends light rays to bring them to a "focal point." An upside down and smaller image forms behind the focal point if the object is far away.

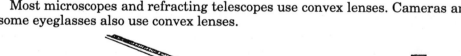

LENS   Focal Point   Image

Object

When the object is close to the lens, the image forms in front of the focal point and will be larger and upright (for example, a magnifying glass). When the object is twice as far as the focal point is to the lens, the image will be the same size as the object. Human eyes have a lens that forms an image on the retina.

Most microscopes and refracting telescopes use convex lenses. Cameras and some eyeglasses also use convex lenses.

Concave Lens

A **concave lens** spreads out light rays. A concave lens is thinner in the middle and thicker at the edges. The major use for concave lenses is in making eyeglasses to correct the vision of nearsighted people.

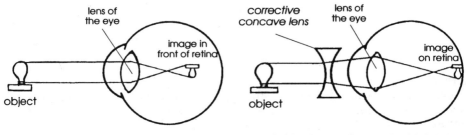

Nearsightedness   **Nearsightedness Corrected With Lens**

Farsightedness is corrected with convex lenses. This allows the image to form on the surface of the retina, rather than behind it.

Electromagnetic Spectrum

The electromagnetic spectrum is a family of waves that includes light. Light is a small portion of the many forms of radiation sent out by the sun. These different kinds of waves are arranged according to their wavelengths and frequencies. The result is the electromagnetic spectrum.

Decreasing ◄─── Wavelength ───► Increasing				
HIGH ◄─── Frequency ───► LOW				
gamma rays	X-rays	ultra violet rays	visible light	infra- red rays	radar microwaves	radio FM TV AM
Diagnosis and Treatment of Diseases and Injuries	Suntan Rays and Fluorescent Lamps	Violet Indigo Blue Green Yellow Orange Red	Baking and Heating Lamps	Cooking, Speed-traps, and Weather Forecasts	Broadcasting, Television, and Ham Radio

Overexposure and/or improper use of any of these waves can cause serious damage to human tissue.

Questions

1   Light is a form of
   1   motion   2   speed   3   energy   4   matter

2   Light can reach us from the sun because it
   1   travels very fast   3   cannot reflect off objects
   2   does not require a medium   4   bounces off objects in space

3   Light travels only in
   1   circles   2   zigzags   3   curved lines   4   straight lines

4   When a light wave hits an object, it may be
   1   absorbed   2   reflected   3   transmitted   4   all of these

5   Wavelength is measured from
   1   top to bottom   3   front to back
   2   crest to crest   4   crest to bottom

6   Reflected light is light that has
   1   been made brighter   3   changed color
   2   bounced off something   4   passed through something

7   The bending of light rays as they pass from one medium to another medium at an angle is called
   1   refraction   2   reflection   3   retreating   4   reflowing

8   Lenses are usually used to
   1   bend light   3   reflect light
   2   block light   4   produce light

9   A lens that is thicker in the middle than on the edges (curved out) is
   1   concave   2   convex   3   triangular   4   prism

10 The lens that brings parallel light rays to a focal point is
   1   concave   2   convex   3   prism   4   mirror

11 A beam of light hits a reflective surface at 45°. The reflected ray will be
   1   25°   2   35°   3   45°   4   55°

12 A triangular piece of glass that can break up white light is the
   1   concave lens   3   prism
   2   convex lens   4   mirror

13 Suntan is caused by
   1   visible light   3   ultraviolet rays
   2   infrared rays   4   reflected rays

14 The electromagnetic spectrum does *not* include
   1   x-rays   3   sound waves
   2   light rays   4   radio waves

15 A substance is said to be transparent if it
   1   stops light from passing through
   2   allows almost all the light to pass through
   3   lets only a small amount of light through
   4   reflects light

16 The proper shape for a concave lens would be

17 Which of the following best represents a prism?

18 Here is a diagram of a wave. What is represented by "c"?
1 amplitude
2 crest
3 trough
4 wavelength

19 When no light can get through an object and a shadow is cast behind it, the object is said to be
1 clear   2 translucent   3 transparent   4 opaque

20 Convex lenses are used in
1 electric motors   3 most microscopes
2 roller coasters   4 computers

21 According to the law of reflection, if angle "a" in this diagram is 60°, what will angle "b" be?
1 30°   3 60°
2 45°   4 90°

22 If an image is seen between a convex lens and the focal point (using a magnifying glass), the image will be
1 upside down and larger   3 upright and larger
2 upside down and smaller   4 upright and smaller

23 A concave lens can be used to correct
1 farsightedness   3 loss of memory
2 nearsightedness   4 all answers are correct

24 Which of the following are used for checking the speed of traffic and in making weather forecasts?
1 gamma rays   3 radar
2 x-rays   4 ultraviolet rays

25 Which electromagnetic waves are greatly used today for cooking?
1 microwaves   3 x-rays
2 radio waves   4 visible light

Concepts and Words To Be Understood

compression	longitudinal wave	noise
expansion	medium	vibrate

V. Sound

Sound is a form of energy produced when matter **vibrates**. When something vibrates, it moves back and forth. The wave that is set up has areas where particles are squeezed close together (compression). Also, there are areas where the particles are spread out (expansion).

The energy that starts the wave and the particles in the matter (medium) move in the same direction. Note: *Particles move in the same direction as energy.*

Sound Travels

Sound waves travel outward in **all directions** from the place where they are produced. When you speak (below left), people all around you hear what you say. This is like a pebble falling into a quiet pool of water (below right). Note that the pattern of waves is very similar.

 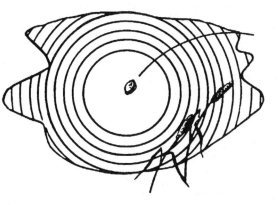

Substance	Speed meters/second	Speed feet/second
air	344	1,100
water	1,460	4,860
wood	3,850	11,500
steel	4,990	16,000

A **medium** (some form of matter) is necessary to carry sound waves. Sound travels faster in substances where the particles are fairly close together.

The distance between you and a **thunderstorm** can be estimated. Air carries sound waves at about 1,100 ft/sec (about 0.2 mile/second) and light travels at 186,000 mi/sec. Therefore, you can assume that you see the lightning at the same time it is produced.

Lightning and thunder are produced at about the same time. If you count the number of seconds between the flash and the time you hear the thunder, the distance between you and the storm can be estimated.

Suppose a flash of lightning is seen and the roar of the thunder is heard about *five* seconds later. You could estimate the storm to be about *one* mile away.

Incidentally, the thunder is caused by cooler air rushing into the vacuum-like space left by the lightning. The lightning heated the strip of air as it passed through.

Music

Music is considered to be sounds that are in harmony and pleasant to hear. *Noise* is sound that is not in harmony and is not wanted. A rock concert might be music to some people and noise to others.

When certain sounds are too loud and last too long, damage to parts of the ear can result. Overexposure to loud sounds has caused deafness in many people.

Questions

1   Sounds are made when objects
    1   stretch   2   sink   3   vibrate   4   become wider

2   The sounds of human speech are made by the vibrating
    1   air   2   hands   3   paper   4   vocal cords

3   What is needed to make an object vibrate?
    1   decibels   2   energy   3   tuning forks   4   a sound

4   The matter that carries a sound wave is the
    1   crest   2   lens   3   medium   4   wavelength

5   Which material will carry sound the fastest?
    1   steel   2   water   3   meter stick   4   air

6   A flash of lightning is seen. Fifteen seconds later the thunder is heard. How far away was the lightning?
    1   1 mile   2   2 miles   3   3 miles   4   4 miles

7   The speed of sound in air is about
    1   1100 feet / second   3   344 meters / second
    2   1/5 miles / second   4   all answers are correct

8   Sounds that are pleasant to hear are called
    1   music   2   noise   3   vibrations   4   eardrums

9   Sound waves travel
    1   through glass only   3   in 90° angles from the source
    2   through a vacuum only   4   in all directions

10 If sounds are too loud and last too long,
    1   musical notes are heard   3   damage to hearing can result
    2   no problem exists   4   the sound is no longer heard

Concepts and Words To Be Understood

efficiency	fulcrum	machine	resistance
effort (force)	input	output	

VI. Mechanical Energy

Mechanical energy can be thought of as the kinetic energy found in moving objects. It can also be referred to as **potential mechanical energy** in things that *can* move. A bicycle does not move until the pedals are turned. A saw does not cut until it is pushed and pulled.

A. Machines

Machines are used to *transfer mechanical energy* from one object to another. Therefore, machines make work easier.

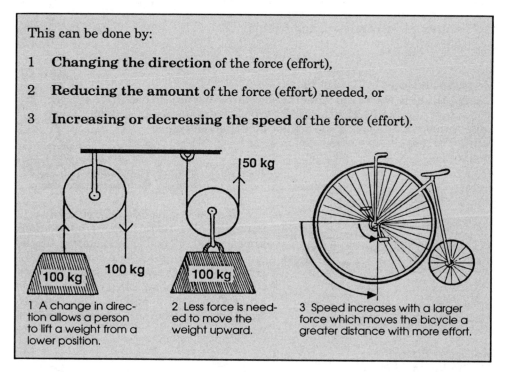

This can be done by:

1 **Changing the direction** of the force (effort),

2 **Reducing the amount** of the force (effort) needed, or

3 **Increasing or decreasing the speed** of the force (effort).

50 kg

100 kg

100 kg

100 kg

1 A change in direction allows a person to lift a weight from a lower position.

2 Less force is needed to move the weight upward.

3 Speed increases with a larger force which moves the bicycle a greater distance with more effort.

All machines that help to accomplish this are based on the principles of the **lever** and **inclined plane**. The **lever** is a rigid bar that rotates around a pivot point called a **fulcrum (▲)**. There are three classes of levers.

1 **Class one** has the fulcrum between the effort (E) and resistance (R). Examples: seesaw, crowbar, and double levers, such as scissors and pliers.

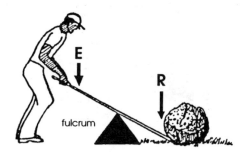

E

R

fulcrum

2 **Class two** has the resistance between the fulcrum and effort. Examples: wheelbarrow, can opener, and bottle cap opener.

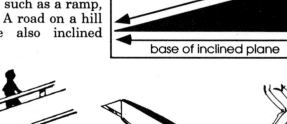

3 **Class three** has the effort between the fulcrum and resistance. Examples: snow shovel, pencil and pen, and fishing pole.

Machines Based On The Lever

• A **pulley** is a grooved wheel that rotates around (not with) the axle. Ropes or chains moving in the grooves of a system of several pulleys make up a block and tackle. This machine can be used to move heavy objects such as car engines.

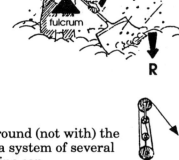

gears

• The **wheel and axle machine** is found in bike pedals, car wheels, door knobs, and pencil sharpeners. These have a wheel and an axle that rotate together. When the wheel rotates, so does the axle and vice versa. Toothed wheels are called **gears** and can be used to transfer force from one wheel to another wheel.

Machines Based On The Inclined Plane

The **inclined plane** is a machine with a sloping surface, such as a ramp, cutting edge, or knife. A road on a hill and a stairway are also inclined planes.

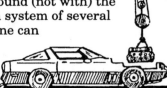

length

height

base of inclined plane

• **Wedge,** a double inclined plane, is two inclined planes back to back. Axes, log splitters, chisels, and most knife blades are wedges.

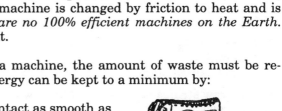

• **Screw** is a spiral inclined plane. Walking up and down a spiral staircase will give you a good idea of a screw. Machine screws, bolts and nuts, and jacks used to raise cars and houses are examples of screws.

The **Law of Machines** states that *under ideal conditions input equals output.* That is: the work put into a machine should equal the work done by the machine. Note that in both cases **work equals force times distance.** But, some of the effort put into the machine is changed by friction to heat and is lost. This explains why *there are no 100% efficient machines on the Earth.* Output is always less than input.

To increase the efficiency of a machine, the amount of waste must be reduced. The amount of waste energy can be kept to a minimum by:

• Making the surfaces in contact as smooth as possible.

• Using oil or grease (lubrication) or waxing surfaces.

• Using wheels and/or ball bearings.

What conditions would make this roller skate an efficient machine?

Questions

1 All simple machines are based on the
   1 lever and pulley
   2 wheel and screw
   3 inclined plane and lever
   4 wedge and pulley

2 Machines can be used to
   1 make work easier
   2 reduce effort needed
   3 overcome a resistance
   4 all answers are correct

3 The point around which a lever rotates is called the
   1 fulcrum
   2 gear
   3 leverage
   4 wheel and axle

4 A wedge is really a double
   1 cross
   2 inclined plane
   3 lever
   4 no answer here is correct

5 The wheel and axle is really a
1 resistance
2 rotating lever
3 revolving wedge
4 none of the above

6 Which class of lever is represented by this diagram?
1 first
2 second
3 third

7 Which class lever has the fulcrum between the resistance and the effort?
1 first   2 second   3 third

8 Which class lever has the resistance between the fulcrum and the effort?
1 first   2 second   3 third

9 An example of a third class lever is the
1 broom
2 snow shovel
3 writing pencil
4 all answers are correct

10 The blade of a steak knife is an example of
1 a pulley
2 an inclined plane
3 a screw
4 a lever

11 The draw strings on Venetian blinds work because of
1 screws
2 pulleys
3 wedges
4 inclined planes

12 Effort is
1 the distance from the fulcrum to the effort of the lever
2 resistance
3 the force used on a lever
4 none of these

13 A good example of the second class lever is the
1 fishing pole
2 seesaw
3 wheelbarrow
4 pulley

14 A force that needs to be overcome before work can be done is often called
1 efficiency
2 effort
3 mechanical advantage
4 resistance

15 A device that is able to transfer energy from one object to another is a
1 glass of water
2 light wave
3 machine
4 vibration

16 In this diagram, what is represented by the symbol ▲ ?
1 effort
2 fulcrum
3 resistance
4 pulley

17 Which of the following would be the wedge?

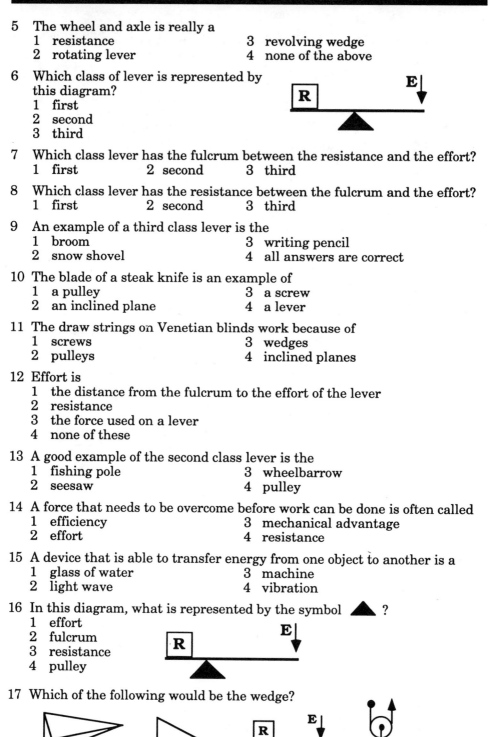

18 The chain on a bicycle is able to transfer energy from the pedal wheel to the rear wheel because of the presence of
1 a handle bar   3 a spoke
2 the pedals   4 gears

19 A spiral staircase is really a
1 rotating lever   3 form of inclined plane
2 wheel and axle   4 double inclined plane

20 The "length" of this inclined plane is measured from points
1 A to B
2 B to C
3 A to C
4 A to B to C

21 A pulley would be represented by which of the following diagrams?

22 Roller skates work better when
1 ball bearings are used in the wheels
2 they are used on smooth floors
3 the wheel and axle connection is kept oiled
4 all answers here are correct

23 The best tool (machine) to use to split a log would be a
1 pulley   3 wedge
2 jackscrew   4 wheel and axle

24 A block and tackle would probably be used to
1 slice a beef roast
2 remove an engine from a car
3 turn a bicycle wheel
4 split wood

25 A bicyclist coasts down a hill. The hill would be an example of a(an)
1 inclined plane   3 wheel and axle
2 gear   4 pulley

Unit H — Physical Sciences:

The Chemistry of Matter

Everything in our natural world is made up of chemicals. The physical and chemical properties of these materials are studied by chemists. How these chemicals will behave and react is of special interest. Where they can be found and what they will do are important pieces of information for mankind.

Pure gases can be collected by displacing water. Solids and liquids can be observed changing back and forth. Laboratory experiments, when performed properly, provide information about the world around us. New discoveries are made every day.

Proper laboratory behavior, the structure of matter, and different types of chemical reactions are explained in Unit H.

Concepts and Words To Be Understood

aerosol   chemicals   toxic   vapors

I. Handling Chemicals Safely

Handling chemicals safely is an important rule to follow. Wherever you are, in the laboratory, at home, or out in the world, careful handling is necessary. Everything with which you come in contact is made of chemicals. Rocks, water, air, plants, animals, and candy bars are composed of chemicals. Many household chemicals, as well as those found in the school laboratory can be dangerous. They must be handled carefully and stored properly.

A. Laboratory Rules

1) **Wear rubber aprons** to protect clothing. Wear goggles or eyeshields to protect the eyes.
2) **Carefully wash** away with a large amount of water any chemicals that are accidentally spilled on skin, clothing, or the desk.
3) **Do not eat or drink** anything in the laboratory.
4) **Use** test tube holders, tongs, spatulas, and other lab equipment properly. Keep them clean.
5) **Observe** odors by fanning gases toward nose. When observing odors, hold the substance at least 12 inches from the nose.
6) **Contact teacher immediately** if unwanted fire occurs.
7) **Follow directions carefully.** **Never** mix unknown chemicals together. They may explode or produce toxic substances.

B. Home Rules

1) **Read labels carefully.**
An **ammonia** bottle label says, "Caution: Harmful if swallowed." A label on the back reads:

Caution - *Do not mix with other household chemicals such as automatic toilet bowl cleaners. Avoid contact with eyes and prolonged contact with skin. Do not swallow. Avoid inhalation of vapors. Use in well ventilated area. Do not use to soak aluminum pans.*

DANGER!
POISON!

The boxes and bottles of common **detergents** state, *"In case of eye contact, flush for 15 minutes with water."* Some even suggest calling a physician.

Similar **warnings** are on containers of weed killers, paints, and other dangerous household chemicals.

It is very important to read the labels on these products. Don't forget to follow the directions given on household products such as polishes, waxes, cleaners, insect sprays, and lighter fluid. Remember, read the label and follow directions on any container that may hold dangerous chemicals.

2) **Do not mix** household chemicals together. Toxic substances or even explosions could result.

3) **Do not heat or puncture** aerosol cans. They may explode! Eyes have been hurt, fingers lost, and other body parts damaged because people tried to heat or puncture these cans.

4) **Keep all chemical containers tightly closed.**

5) **Store household chemicals** in cupboards that can be locked. **Keep them out of the reach of small children and pets.** This includes:

   - all drugs and medicines
   - bleaches and ammonia
   - laundry detergents
   - lye, caustic soda (drain cleaner)
   - lighter fluid and charcoal lighter
   - paint solvents and cleaning fluids

Questions

1   Toxic substances would be those that are
    1 plentiful   2 poisonous   3 pretty   4 purple

2   "Vapors" is another word for
    1 gases   2 liquids   3 solids   4 minerals

3   Substances that can burn should never be used close to flames or sparks
    because they
    1 would get the job done faster
    2 might begin to burn
    3 could turn black
    4 increase chances of bone cancer

4   Mixing unknown chemicals is
    1 a good thing to do   3 always safe
    2 a bad thing to do   4 standard procedure

5   Fanning gases toward your nose is a good way to test for
    1 color   2 noise   3 odor   4 temperature

6   Rubber aprons are worn in the laboratory to
    1 improve lab room appearance
    2 protect clothing
    3 add to lab expenses
    4 make everyone look alike

7   Which is a good laboratory procedure to follow?
    1 Do not eat or drink in a lab.
    2 Wear goggles or eye shields when heating chemicals.
    3 Always wash away spilled chemicals.
    4 All answers are correct.

8   Labels on household chemicals must be read carefully and directions fol-
    lowed because the chemicals
    1 might cost too much
    2 are used up quickly
    3 could be harmful to the user
    4 might remain unused for many years

9   The cupboard in which chemicals are stored should be locked so that
    1 small children or pets cannot get at them
    2 they do not fall out
    3 a speedy check will tell what is there
    4 extra light does not hit them

10 Should some detergent ever get in your eye, you should immediately
    1 smile and forget it
    2 put the box away so no one else gets hurt
    3 throw the box or bottle out
    4 flush the eye with clean water and call a doctor

11 Mixtures of small particles suspended in a liquid or a gas are often sold in
    pressurized cans. These mixtures are called
    1 aerosols   3 scales
    2 compounds   4 vapors

12　When handling and storing household chemicals, it is always wise to
　　1　read the labels carefully
　　2　keep container tightly closed
　　3　store them in locked cupboards
　　4　all answers are correct

13　According to the rules for safety in the laboratory, a very important rule
　　for the student to know is the
　　1　teacher's name
　　2　location of the first aid kit
　　3　time the period is over
　　4　next homework assignment

14　If an unwanted lab fire occurs in the classroom, the *best* thing to do is
　　1　tell nobody
　　2　try to put it out yourself
　　3　inform your teacher immediately
　　4　let it burn and forget about it

15　It would be *unwise* to use cleaning fluids near a (an)
　　1　open window　　　　　　3　driveway
　　2　ventilated cellar　　　　4　flame

Concepts and Words To Be Understood

boiling point　　　　Fahrenheit°　　　　sublimation
Celsius°　　　　　　freezing point　　　theory
condensation　　　　mass　　　　　　　volume
crystal　　　　　　　melting point　　　weight
evaporation　　　　　phases (states)

II. Matter

Matter is considered to be anything that takes up space (volume) and has mass (weight). Under the pull of gravity, mass has weight. Air, the mixture of gases that surrounds the Earth, is matter. This fact can be proven easily.

Weigh an empty balloon on a balance.

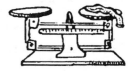

Blow the balloon up and tie the end. Then, weigh it again. When you blew the balloon up, air took up the space inside. This proves that air has volume.

There was a difference when comparing the weight of the inflated balloon to that of the deflated one. This proves that air has mass.

To successfully study matter, the kinetic particle theory of matter needs to be reviewed. The theory states that:

- All matter is made up of tiny particles.

- The particles are always moving in gases, liquids, and solids.

- The particles will move faster when heated.

- There are spaces between the particles.

- Some force holds the particles together.

- The amount of energy possessed by the particles will determine the phase in which the matter will be.

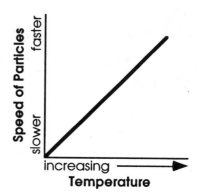

A. Phases Of Matter

There are three common phases of matter: **solid, liquid,** and **gas.** The phase in which matter exists depends on the closeness and speed of its particles.

- A **solid** has particles so close together that they can only vibrate back and forth. They tend to stay in a particular position. The particles resist change from that position. Rocks, bicycles, and desks are solids.

- A **liquid** has particles more loosely packed than solids. There is more space between the particles. The extra space allows them to slide by each other or even spin around.

- A **gas** has much more space between particles. These particles are free to move from one place to another. Air, carbon dioxide, and methane are examples of gases.

All phases of matter (solid, liquid, and gas) must have **weight** and **volume.** All three have definite weights. *Only a solid has a definite volume and shape.*

The phases of matter can change. When they do, energy (usually heat) is taken in or given off. In this way, solids turn to liquids and liquids to solids. Liquids turn to gases and gases to liquids. Study the example of the three phases of water on the next page.

(Note: the particles do not represent density).

The Changing States of Matter

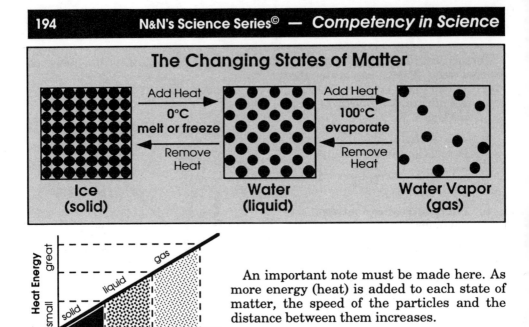

Ice
(solid)

Water
(liquid)

Water Vapor
(gas)

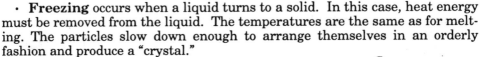

An important note must be made here. As more energy (heat) is added to each state of matter, the speed of the particles and the distance between them increases.

• **Melting** occurs when a solid turns to a liquid. Heat energy is added to the solid substance for this to happen. If the substance is water, the melting takes place at 0° Celsius (°C) or 32° Fahrenheit (°F). Every solid has its own **melting point**.

• **Freezing** occurs when a liquid turns to a solid. In this case, heat energy must be removed from the liquid. The temperatures are the same as for melting. The particles slow down enough to arrange themselves in an orderly fashion and produce a "crystal."

All liquids have their own **freezing point** (temperature) at which they freeze. Salt water freezes at a lower temperature than fresh water. The greater the salt content of the water, the lower the water's freezing point will be.

• **Evaporation** takes place when liquids turn to gases. Heat energy must be added to the liquid to raise it to the boiling point (Every liquid boils at its own specific temperature). More heat energy needs to be added to change the liquid to gas (**heat of fusion**).

The **boiling point** for fresh water is 100° C or 212°F. The bubbles seen in boiling water in a beaker, test tube, or "Pyrex" coffee pot are water vapor (steam). They are not air bubbles, as some people wish to think.

Evaporation may occur at temperatures lower than the boiling point. Because of their constant motion, particles may "escape" from the surface of a liquid. This explains the "disappearance" (evaporation) of a puddle after a rain storm. The drying of the skin after swimming is another example.

• **Condensation** happens when gases turn to liquids. Heat energy is given off. The particles slow down, and a liquid forms. The temperature at which this occurs is the condensation point. Each gas has its own **condensation point**.

Water vapor in the air condenses to form clouds. The droplets of water seen on the outside of a pitcher of cold fruit juice come from water vapor in the air. Water vapor cools enough to condense and collect on the pitcher. They are *not* drops of fruit juice that "hopped out."

Melting point and freezing point are usually the same temperature for any particular substance. This is true also for boiling point and condensation point. The following table shows some examples:

Substance	Melting Point Freezing Point	Boiling Point Condensation Point
Pure Water	0°C	100°C
Glycerine	18°C	290°C
Ethyl Alcohol	-117°C	78°C
Mercury	-39°C	357°C
Tungsten	3370°C	5900°C

Table of the Temperature Changes for Some Common Substances

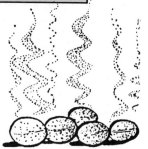

• **Sublimation** occurs when a solid turns directly to a gas, or a gas turns directly to a solid. Sometimes snow will sublimate. "Dry ice" (solid carbon dioxide) never turns to a liquid before it turns to a gas. Moth balls sublimate, making them safe for use next to clothing in storage trunks and closets.

On the next page, there is a **phase change diagram** for water. Note that while the phase is changing, there is no increase in temperature. For example, while ice is melting, 80 calories of heat must be added for each gram of ice until all the ice is melted. Likewise, when the water gets to 100° C, 540 calories of heat must be added for each gram of liquid to change it to water vapor. This is called **heat of vaporization.**

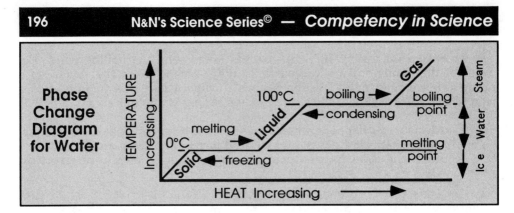

Phase Change Diagram for Water

TEMPERATURE Increasing →

100°C — boiling → boiling point

condensing

melting → Liquid

Gas

0°C — Solid ← freezing

melting point

HEAT Increasing →

Steam / Water / Ice

Questions

1   For anything to be considered matter, it must
    1   occupy space only   3   form crystals
    2   have weight only   4   have weight and take up space

2   A wad of paper is stuffed into a dry glass. The glass is turned upside down and put under the water in a tank. When the glass is lifted straight up and out of the water, the paper inside is still dry. This proved that
    1   air was in the glass   3   air has volume
    2   air occupies space   4   all answers here are correct

3   A bicycle tire gets heavier when you pump air into it because air
    1   is invisible   3   has mass
    2   makes the tire larger   4   is everywhere

4   Matter can appear in three different phases or
    1   containers   2   shapes   3   states   4   volumes

5   In which state of matter do particles have the most energy?
    1   solid   2   liquid   3   gas   4   frozen

6   What must be added to ice to change it to a liquid?
    1   thermometer   2   sound   3   heat   4   light

7   When liquid water turns to water vapor, we say that it
    1   evaporates   2   expands   3   condenses   4   sublimates

8   When we change a liquid to a solid, we say that it
    1   cools   2   freezes   3   melts   4   evaporates

9   When steam turns to water, we say that it has
    1   condensed   2   evaporated   3   frozen   4   sublimated

10   As the temperature of matter decreases, what happens to the speed of the particles?
    1   speeds up   2   slows down   3   stays the same

11   The one single most important factor that seems to decide the state in which matter will be is the
    1   amount of a substance present
    2   container holding the material
    3   location on Earth
    4   temperature of the substance

12 When ice turns to liquid water, we say that it has
    1 melted
    2 gone through a physical change
    3 changed states
    4 all answers are correct

13 Water turns to water vapor at
    1 0° C   2 37° C   3 100° C   4 212° C

14 Sublimation occurs when
    1 a gas changes directly to a solid
    2 a solid changes directly to a gas
    3 both answers 1 and 2
    4 neither answer 1 nor 2 is correct

15 The melting point and freezing point for the same substance are
    1 usually different temperatures
    2 usually the same temperature
    3 always different temperatures
    4 very different

Concepts and Words To Be Understood

| atom | element | nucleus |
| electron | neutron | proton |

III. Structure Of Matter

The structure of matter (material objects) requires the study of **elements**. Elements are the "building blocks" of all things in the universe. The chemicals that make up everything in our natural world are either pure elements or combinations of elements. Some common elements are listed in the following table:

Name	Symbol	Name	Symbol	Name	Symbol
aluminum	Al	hydrogen	H	plutonium	Pu
bromine	Br	iodine	I	potassium	K
calcium	Ca	iron	Fe	radium	Ra
carbon	C	lead	Pb	silicon	Si
chlorine	Cl	magnesium	Mg	silver	Ag
chromium	Cr	mercury	Hg	sodium	Na
cobalt	Co	neon	Ne	sulfur	S
copper	Cu	nickel	Ni	tin	Sn
fluorine	F	nitrogen	N	tungsten	W
gold	Au	oxygen	O	uranium	U
helium	He	phosphorus	P	zinc	Zn

There are now 109 known elements, and a couple of new radioactive ones needing to be named. Less than half of the 109 elements are found commonly under natural conditions. Most elements are solids, two (bromine and mercury) are liquids, and ten are gases. Most elements are found in combination with other elements.

Atoms

An **atom** is the smallest amount of an element that can exist and still be that element. According to the **atomic theory,** atoms are made up of **protons** (p), **neutrons** (n), and **electrons** (e). Protons have a positive charge. Neutrons have a neutral charge. Electrons have a negative charge.

The **atomic nucleus** is the center or core of the atom. It contains the protons and neutrons. The number of protons seems to determine what the element is (see illustration below). A change in the normal number of neutrons produces an **isotope.** Circling the nucleus in various energy levels are the atom's electrons. When there is a change in the normal number of electrons, an **ion** is formed. This is important to know when studying certain kinds of **bonding** (joining of atoms to form compounds).

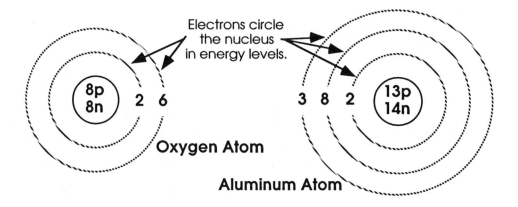

Electrons circle the nucleus in energy levels.

8p 8n   2 6   **Oxygen Atom**

3 8 2   13p 14n

Aluminum Atom

Chemical Bonds

Chemical bonds are responsible for the many **compounds** found on the Earth. Two or more different atoms can join together and form a compound. They do so because of strong, opposite charges between them. Two hydrogen atoms (gases) have positive charges. They are attracted to one oxygen atom, which has a double negative charge. The compound, water (a liquid), is formed.

Another common compound, carbon dioxide, forms when two atoms of oxygen join with one atom of carbon. Carbon dioxide is needed by green plants to make food. It is also the gas that fizzes from soda.

H   H H_2O
   \   /
     O   Water

$O = C = O$ CO_2

Carbon dioxide

In addition to water (H_2O) and carbon dioxide (CO_2), some other common compounds are:

1	Sugar (sucrose)	$C_{12}H_{22}O_{11}$	6.	Sulfuric acid	H_2SO_4
2	Baking soda	$NaHCO_3$	7.	Grain alcohol	C_2H_5OH
3	Quartz sand	SiO_2	8.	Table salt	$NaCl$
4	Cider vinegar	$HC_2H_3O_2$	9.	Ammonia	NH_4
5.	Chalk	$CaCO_3$	10.	Methane	CH_4
	(Limestone has the same formula)		11.	Simple Sugar	$C_6H_{12}O_6$

The numbers after the symbols are called subscripts. They tell how many parts of the element are in the compound. No number indicates one part. Ones (1's) are never written in formulas.

When only one kind of atom bonds together, a pure element exists. Some examples are: the diamond (**carbon**) and the band (**gold**) of an engagement ring.

The filament (**tungsten**) in a light bulb is another example of a pure element.

Chemical Energy

Chemical energy is stored in the union when atoms bond together. Energy is released when bonds are broken and new bonds are formed.

The electrons circling in the outermost energy level about the nuclei of the atoms determine:

- the **amount** of energy stored

- the **type** of compound formed

- the **properties** of the compound

When a log burns, the chemical energy is released as heat and light. This comes from the chemical bonds joining the atoms making up the wood. In this case, the electrons release their hold fairly easily. But, try to burn sugar. It melts when heated.

Questions

1   The smallest amount of an element that can exist is a (an)
    1   atom   2   compound   3   mixture   4   chemical bond

2   The center of the atom is the
    1   energy level   3   electron
    2   nucleus   4   empty space

3   The nucleus of the atom contains
    1   electrons and neutrons   3   neutrons and protons
    2   electrons and protons   4   only neutrons

4   Negatively charged particles circling the nucleus are
    1   electrons   2   neutrons   3   protons   4   ions

5   When all the atoms making up a substance are the same,
    1   a mixture is formed   3   a new combination develops
    2   there is a compound present 4   a pure element exists

6   The number of known elements is
    1   26   2   92   3   103   4   109

7   Most natural elements are found
    1   as pure metals   3   on top of mountains
    2   in combination with others 4   in coal mines

8   Less than half of the known natural elements
    1   are made up of protons, neutrons, and electrons
    2   are solids
    3   are metals
    4   occur under natural conditions

9   Basic "building blocks" of all chemicals in the universe are
    1   elements   2   compounds   3   salts   4   mixtures

10 A chemical combination of two or more different atoms is called a(an)
    1   atom   2   compound   3   element   4   mixture

11 Which of the following is a pure element?
    1   aluminum   2   sugar   3   salt   4   water

12 Which of the following is an example of a compound?
    1   iron   2   sulfur   3   carbon   4   sugar

13 A combination of hydrogen and oxygen forms the compound
    1   acid rain   3   sugar
    2   carbon dioxide   4   water

14 The symbol used for the element chlorine is
    1   Ca   2   C   3   Cu   4   Cl

15 Which compound forms and what properties it has are determined by
    which part of the atom?
    1   protons   2   neutrons   3   electrons   4   nucleus

16 How many protons are indicated for this atom of
    carbon?
    1   12   3   6
    2   2   4   4

17 The correct formula for water is
  1 NaCl   2 H_2O 3 SiO_2 4 H_2SO_4

18 Which elements make up cane sugar (sucrose)?
  1 C, H, O   2 H, S, O   3 Na, H, C, O   4 Ca, C, O

19 The union of atoms when they bond together stores
  1 extra protons   3 chemical energy
  2 more energy levels   4 water

20 Most pure elements are
  1 gases   2 liquids   3 solids   4 mixtures

Concepts and Words To Be Understood

brittleness	ductility	luster	property
conductivity	elasticity	malleability	tenacity

IV. Properties Of Matter

The properties of matter can be used to identify them. A **property** is a characteristic or feature an object has. A property allows the object to be recognized as that object. The **shape** of an automobile easily separates it from a motorcycle or bicycle . In this example, **shape is a property**.

A. Physical Properties

Physical properties deal with the shape, form, or behavior of all substances.

  1 **Phase or state** is solid, liquid, or gas.
  2 **Melting point and freezing point.** This is the temperature at which a substance changes from solid to liquid or liquid to solid.
  3 **Boiling point and condensation point.** This is the temperature at which a substance changes from a liquid to gas or gas to liquid.

  Note: These three properties have been explained in detail in **Section II Matter** (page 194).

  4 **Color** is the way an object absorbs and reflects light.
  5 **Hardness** is the resistance to being scratched.
  6 **Luster** is the shininess of all metals.

bright

dull

7   **Brittleness** is the ease with which something breaks. A cracker will snap apart. A caramel candy bar's particles hold together (stick) more tightly.

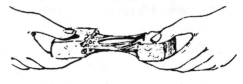

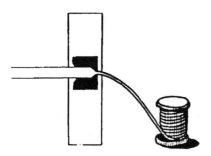

8 **Conductivity** is how well a substance lets heat and electricity pass through it. **See Energy and Motion** (Unit G) for further details (page 167).

9 **Ductility** is a property of metals that allows them to be drawn into wires. Copper wire comes in many sizes which allows for its use in many different ways.

10 **Elasticity** refers to the ability of an object to stretch and return to its original position.   A rubber band or wire coil can do this, but it has an **elastic limit**. When stretched beyond the elastic limit, the object cannot return to its original position.

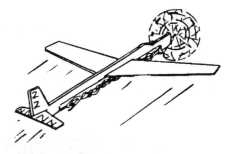

11   **Malleability** is a property of most metals allowing them to be rolled into sheets or pounded into different shapes. Aluminum siding for houses is possible because aluminum is malleable.   Lead sinkers used in fishing can be pounded into various shapes with a hammer.

12 **Odor** is observed by the nose and is a common characteristic of substances. Odor is produced by vapor particles being given off by an object. Steak and turkey, while cooking, produce unique odors. But, so do sulfur and chlorine.

13 **Tenacity** refers to the ability of a substance to resist being pulled apart. The chemical bonds for highly tenacious objects are very strong. The tenacity of a piece of paper is low and permits easy tearing. The tenacity of steel cables is strong enough to support suspension bridges.

B. Chemical Properties

Chemical properties are very different from physical properties. They deal with the make-up of the atom. Chemical properties give the substance the ability to react with other substances or not to react at all. Remember that the **electrons** in the outermost energy level of atoms determine the **properties** of the substance. This is true for elements and compounds.

For example, helium is used in a blimp, such as the "Goodyear" Blimp (used by television networks for "bird's eye views" of sporting events). The gas helium is much lighter than air and does not explode. The lighter than air gas hydrogen is not used in blimps, because it does explode.

To better understand the importance of using helium in a blimp (airship), you should read about the "Hindenberg disaster."

Questions

1 A property of a substance helps to
    1 destroy it   3 identify it
    2 send it upward   4 seal it

2 Solids, liquids, and gases are considered to be
    1 temperature scales   3 lab procedures
    2 phases of matter   4 sources of energy

3 Copper wires are easily made because copper is
    1 ductile   3 malleable
    2 brittle   4 lustrous

4 Aluminum foil is possible because aluminum is
    1 brittle   2 ductile   3 hard   4 malleable

5 Conductivity means that the substance
    1 has a pretty color
    2 lets heat and electricity pass through it
    3 will break easily
    4 can be pounded into new shapes

6   One of the hardest natural substances is a piece of
    1 coal   2 diamond   3 talc   4 sulfur

7   You are given an unknown substance to identify. It has a shiny surface.
    The sample is probably
    1 a metal   2 iodine   3 carbon   4 a nonmetal

8   During a laboratory test, a clear liquid is found to boil at 100°C. You will
    probably name the liquid
    1 alcohol   2 chocolate   3 mercury   4 water

9   Which of the following represents a chemical property?
    1 melting point   3 elasticity
    2 electron energy   4 malleability

10 Helium gas is used in a blimp (air ship) because
    1 it is lighter than air   3 both 1 and 2 are correct
    2 it will not explode   4 neither 1 nor 2 is correct

11 The cables that hold up a suspension bridge are metals that have a high
    1 brittleness   3 malleability
    2 elasticity   4 tenacity

12 A heavy rubber band is stretched around a couple of books. After a while,
    it is removed. It will then
    1 stay stretched   3 break
    2 return to its original position 4 give off a strong odor

13 Odor is a property observed by the
    1 ears   2 mouth   3 nose   4 skin

14 A piece of carbon breaks easily. This is because it is
    1 brittle   2 ductile   3 elastic   4 malleable

15 A substance has a definite weight, shape, and volume. It is classified as a
    1 gas   2 liquid   3 solid   4 plasma

16 A wire coil will return to its original shape if it is not stretched beyond its
    1 freezing point   3 elastic limit
    2 condensation point   4 temperature limit

17 Sheet aluminum is used in some types of work. This is possible because
    the aluminum metal
    1 is brittle   3 has odor
    2 shows elasticity   4 is malleable

18 Chemical properties of a substance are determined by the
    1 protons in the nucleus
    2 electrons in the outermost energy level
    3 size of the neutrons
    4 number of neutrons

19 The resistance of an object to being scratched is best described by its
    1 color   2 hardness   3 luster   4 malleability

20 When observing the color of a mineral, what should be used?
    1 large quantities   3 a fresh surface
    2 sun glasses   4 all answers are correct

<u>Concepts and Words To Be Understood</u>

absorb   electrodes   physical change
chemical change   reaction

V. Changes In Matter

Changes in matter occur in different ways. When a substance changes phase, shape, or size, a physical change happens. When materials form new substances with completely different properties, a chemical change happens.

A. Physical Change

A **physical change** is one in which the **form** or **energy** of a substance changes. The chemical composition of the substance remains the same.

· A **phase change** occurs when a material melts, freezes, evaporates, condenses, or sublimates. This can be observed when a chocolate bar is left in the Sun.

· A **shape change** occurs when the basic form of a material is changed. When a car hits a tree, the form of the car and/or tree will be changed.

· A **change in size** is simply when something gets larger or smaller. For example, you could take a large stone and, with a sledge hammer break the stone into smaller pieces. An artist begins a statue by cutting and chipping away pieces of marble. The "controlled" hammering results in a work of art.

A physical change alone does not result in the formation of any new substances. The stone above is still marble. It has not become a different kind of rock or mineral. Ice can melt to form water, and the water can evaporate to form a gas. The chemical composition is still the same for water in all three states. The energy of the particles has changed, not the chemistry.

B. Chemical Change

A **chemical change** happens when one or more new substances are formed with completely new properties. The tobacco in cigars and cigarettes burns to produce things quite unlike the original tobacco. Some of these are smoke, carbon monoxide, hydrogen cyanide, nicotine particles, and tar (all damaging to the body). Ash is left after burning has ended.

Cake batter contains flour, eggs, butter, and flavoring. When heat is added to it in an oven, a delicious tasting dessert, very different from the original ingredients, is produced.

A chemical change occurs when an egg is fried. The wearing away of marble statues in parks by air pollution is other example of chemical change. The digestion of food by the small intestine and the release of energy from it by the cells are also chemical changes. In all cases, new things with new properties are produced. The properties of the original substance can no longer be observed. The original substance no longer exists.

Chemical changes and energy are closely related.

The **addition** of some form of energy is needed to start some chemical changes.

• A lighted match adds enough **heat** to paper to start it burning. While burning, the paper produces more heat and light. Ashes are left when the burning stops. The paper no longer exists.

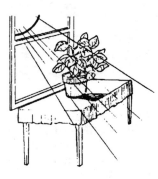

• **Light** from the Sun lets the process of photosynthesis take place. The chlorophyll is able to take in the light energy so that it can be used to combine the water and carbon dioxide to make the simple sugar and oxygen.

• **Electric sparks** from spark plugs are needed in the engines of cars and motorcycles. The spark lets the gasoline vapors explode within the cylinders. The expanding gases push the piston down.

Heat, light, and electricity are needed to start some chemical reactions. There are some reactions that happen without the addition of any energy.

Rust can often be observed on iron fire escapes. When iron comes in contact with oxygen, that is all that is needed to form iron oxide. Iron oxide is the reddish brown material called rust. This is a **slow oxidation** process. Garbage rots for the same reason.

The **release** of heat, light, or electrical energy is involved in some chemical change reactions.

- After being lit, lighter fluid in a lighter burns giving off **heat** and **light**.

- An enzyme (called luciferace) in "lightning bugs" allows the male to **light** up when looking for a mate.

- Electricity is produced by the chemical reaction inside batteries in cars, mopeds, and motorcycles. This electricity can then be used to light the lights, honk the horn, and start the engine.

Energy is **absorbed** during the reaction of some chemical changes. When rock salt is thrown on ice to melt it, the rock salt takes in heat. This lowers the overall temperature of the "salt water." The same principle applies when antifreeze or coolant absorbs heat and lowers the freezing point of the radiator solution. This prevents the cracking of the radiator by the expansion of freezing water.

The **rate or speed** at which chemical changes take place differs depending upon the:

- **Temperature** of the substances. As the temperature rises, so does the speed at which the change occurs. When the temperature "plunges" below zero, a very cold battery is often *too cold* to produce enough electricity to start the car.

A warm bottle or can of soda seems to "explode" when opened. This is due to the escape of carbon dioxide. When kept cold, the carbon dioxide tends to stay dissolved in the liquid.

- **Size of particles** also seems to affect the speed at which a reaction will occur. Small particles usually react more quickly than larger particles.

Coal burning power plants use crushed coal in the furnaces. The powdered coal burns faster; therefore, it produces heat more quickly than lump coal would.

Sliced carrots cook much faster than whole carrots. More surface is exposed to the hot water.

In science laboratories, a mortar and pestle are used to crush lumps of certain chemicals. The small crushed chemical pieces react more quickly than the whole chunky ones.

Questions

1   When a chocolate bar melts, what kind of a change has taken place?
    1 atomic   2 chemical   3 physical   4 nuclear

2   A burning cigarette is going through what kind of change?
    1 atomic   2 chemical   3 physical   4 solid to liquid

3   Which of the following is a physical change?
    1 ice cream melts   3 paper tears
    2 rock is crushed   4 all are physical changes

4   Which is a chemical change?
    1 burning wood   3 soap carving
    2 carved wood   4 ground pepper

5   To start something burning,
    1 more kindling wood is needed
    2 add water to cool substance
    3 cut substance into small pieces
    4 heat must be added to the substance

6   Gasoline explodes in a motorcycle engine because the necessary energy is provided by the
    1 moving piston
    2 electric spark from spark plug
    3 pedal of the rider
    4 steering wheel

7   A chemical change that does *not* require adding energy to get it started is
    1 the baking of a cake   3 the rusting of iron
    2 the burning of coal   4 the frying of an egg

8   A blazing fire would be an example of a chemical change that
    1 takes in energy   3 takes in carbon dioxide
    2 gives off energy   4 gives off oxygen

9   The speed at which a chemical change occurs will increase as the
    1 amount of the substance increases
    2 kinds of substances change
    3 temperature of materials rises
    4 container changes that the materials are in

10 The chemical change going on in a car battery releases what kind of energy?
    1 heat   2 light   3 electricity   4 sound

11 A physical change occurs only when a substance changes in size, shape, and/or
   1 chemical composition   3 phase
   2 amount   4 atomic structure

12 A phase change happens when
   1 you get a haircut   3 ice cream melts
   2 paper is wadded   4 a wood board is sawed in half

13 A shape change occurs when
   1 a horse is formed from modeling clay
   2 a sheet of paper is burned
   3 mirrors "steam up" after a hot bath
   4 a lightning bug lights up

14 After a chemical change takes place, the original substance
   1 is still present   3 no longer exists
   2 increases in size   4 gets smaller

15 When water freezes or evaporates, the compound H_2O
   1 stays the same
   2 forms a new substance with new properties
   3 breaks up to form hydrogen and oxygen
   4 picks up another oxygen atom to form H_2O_2

16 What kind of energy is required for the process of photosynthesis in green plants to occur?
   1 electrical   2 heat   3 light   4 sound

17 Antifreeze is added to car radiators in winter because it
   1 encourages freezing
   2 aids the battery
   3 helps to keep the tires warm
   4 lowers the freezing point of the liquid in the radiator

18 Oxidation occurs when an element unites with oxygen. This happens when
   1 carbon dioxide rushes out of a can of soda
   2 an iron fire escape rusts
   3 plants make food
   4 no answer here is correct

19 A mortar and pestle can be used in a laboratory to
   1 start a bunsen burner
   2 crush lumps of chemicals
   3 light a bulb
   4 bend metals

20 A chemical change can be recognized easily because the
   1 new substances are just like the old ones
   2 new substances have their own new identifying properties
   3 old substances are still present
   4 accompanying "bang" lets you know it happened

Unit I — Physical Sciences:

Energy: Sources and Issues

The availability of energy resources is important for life as we know it today. Fossil fuels, in particular, are used to heat our buildings, run buses, and produce much of our clothing. A great deal of energy is needed every day.

When fossil fuels are gone, they can never be replaced. Their wise use is important. Alternative energy sources must be sought. Nuclear power has great potential but can be dangerous also. The problems of pollution must also be considered.

Unit I presents the sources of energy, their availability, production, transmission, and use.

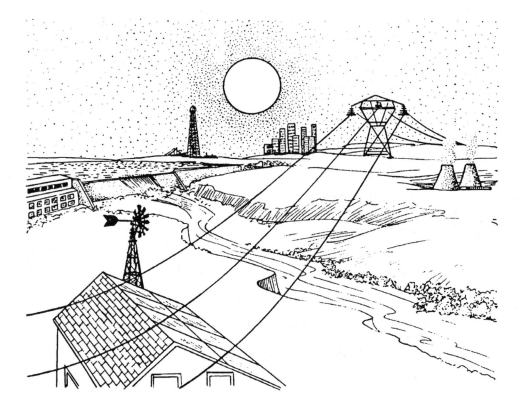

Concepts and Words To Be Understood

anthracite	condensation point	lignite	peat
bituminous	energy	mega-	radioactivity
calorie	fossil fuels	methane	uranium
Calorie	kilo-	nuclear	watt

Energy Units

The study of **energy** and its related sources and issues involves places and problems associated with getting energy and using it. Two units of measurement are required for energy study. They are the calorie and watt.

1) The **calorie** is the metric unit for measuring heat. It is the amount of heat energy needed to raise the temperature of one gram of water one degree Celsius (1° C.). Calories allow for the comparison of amounts of energy obtained from the use of foods and fuels.

2) The **watt** is the standard unit used to measure **electrical power**. Watts indicate the rate at which work is done. The power in a system can be measured by multiplying the voltage by the current (amperes) or

Watts (W) = Volts (V) X Amperes (I)

Related to the watt, is the **watt-hour**. Watt-hours are the units that the power companies use to charge for electricity. A 40 watt bulb lit for one hour would use 40 watt-hours of electricity.

The prefixes **kilo-** and **mega-** are also needed:

Kilo- means 1000 and added to calorie gives the kilocalorie (1000 calories). The energy from foods is measured with the Calorie (spelled with a capital C). It is a kilocalorie. A kilowatt-hour (1000 watt-hours) is used to measure the rate of electricity used in homes and factories.

Mega- added to a base word indicates one million units. Megacalories and megawatts are used to indicate large quantities.

I. Changing Energy Needs

The daily per person energy requirement has increased greatly over the years. Early humans depended on the Sun and then on fire for their energy sources. As farming methods developed, more energy was needed.

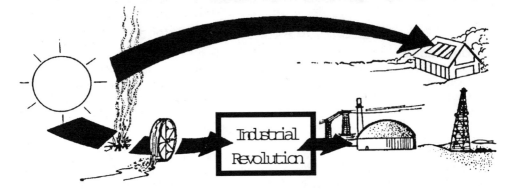

The 19th Century Industrial Revolution caused the need for still more energy. Modern day needs for electricity and fossil fuels have pushed energy demands to extremely high levels (note the comparison on the graph at the bottom of the page).

The use of electrical energy appears to double about every ten years. There appears to be an obvious conclusion here. As the world's use of energy increases, the need for sources of fuel to provide the energy also increases.

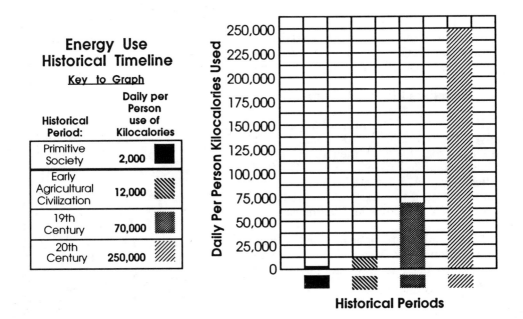

Energy Use Historical Timeline

Key to Graph

Historical Period:	Daily per Person use of Kilocalories	
Primitive Society	2,000	■
Early Agricultural Civilization	12,000	▨
19th Century	70,000	▩
20th Century	250,000	▱

Historical Periods

The great demand for energy in today's world increases as the world's population increases. This increases the demand for new technological products. One-fourth of our annual **energy consumption** goes for **transportation**. Here, transportation means: *the moving of people and products from one place to another.*

Large amounts of energy are needed also for **heating** homes and factories. Much energy is used in **agriculture** for raising, harvesting, processing, packaging, and selling foods. America's **industries** use huge quantities of energy, especially electricity.

The major source of energy today is **fossil fuels,** primarily oil. Fossil fuels were formed over millions of years from the remains of dead plants and animals. These prehistoric plants and animals were able to capture the Sun's energy for us to use today.

Questions

1   The metric unit used to measure the amount of heat needed to raise the temperature of one gram of water one degree Celsius is the
   1 atom   2 calorie   3 liter   4 watt

2   The daily per person use of energy in the 20th century as compared to energy use in the 19th century has
   1 stayed the same   3 greatly increased
   2 decreased steadily   4 increased slightly

3   Today, the consumption of electrical energy appears to be
   1 leveling off   3 staying the same
   2 decreasing   4 doubling every 10 years

4   The daily per person use of kilocalories in the 19th century was
   1 2,000   2 12,000   3 70,000   4 250,000

5   The type of graph used to show the energy time-line (opposite page) is a
   1 bar graph   3 pictogram
   2 line graph   4 circle graph

A. Fossil Fuels

- **Oil**, found as crude oil, is a mixture of chemical compounds containing carbon and hydrogen. Oil requires much refining before it can be useful. Refined crude oil provides us with many useful products:

- **Gasoline** is the principal product of oil used to power motorcycles, cars, buses, airplanes, and trucks.

- **Heating oil** is another major product used to heat office buildings, factories, and homes.

- **Kerosene** is an oil by-product used for jet fuels, cooking, and heating.

• **Natural gas** (primarily **methane**), is found usually near oil deposits. Methane is a chemical compound composed on one carbon atom bonded to four hydrogen atoms. This is a clean-burning fuel used for industrial heating as well as home cooking and heating.

$$\text{H} \overset{\bullet}{\underset{\bullet}{\text{C}}} \text{H}$$

with H above and H below the central C.

Pipelines are used to transport natural gas from where it is found to where it is used. For transport over oceans and other large distances, another method is used. The natural gas is cooled to its condensation point (about 160°C) which reduces the volume from 615 cubic feet (as a gas) to 1 cubic foot (as a liquid). This saves space making it much easier to transport by freighter or tank truck. Use the kinetic particle theory to explain why this happens.

• **Coal** was formed from the remains of giant mosses, ferns, and trees. They were covered by water and mud and did not decay. **Peat**, a low-grade fuel, was the first thing to form from this. Many years of pressure on the peat turned it to **lignite**, a brownish-black coal. Over time, by additional heat and pressure, **bituminous** coal was formed. It is a soft, black coal that burns with more heat than lignite. Unfortunately, this soft coal has a high sulfur content. The hardest coal with the lowest amount of impurities and the highest amount of heat rating is **anthracite**.

Dead plants
covered by
swamp water.

Over the years,
great pressure
is applied.

After a very
long time,
coal deposits form.

Fortunately, the Earth holds a large reserve of coal. Perhaps there is enough for more than 2,000 years. Even so, it must be used wisely. The primary use of coal today is as a fuel to heat water to produce electricity. Another major use is for industrial heating.

· **Products from fossil fuels** number in the hundreds and many of them are **not** used for fuel. The following drawing indicates some modern-day items:

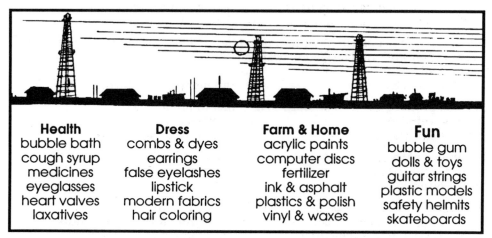

Health	Dress	Farm & Home	Fun
bubble bath	combs & dyes	acrylic paints	bubble gum
cough syrup	earrings	computer discs	dolls & toys
medicines	false eyelashes	fertilizer	guitar strings
eyeglasses	lipstick	ink & asphalt	plastic models
heart valves	modern fabrics	plastics & polish	safety helmits
laxatives	hair coloring	vinyl & waxes	skateboards

Fossil fuel reserves will not last forever. Estimated fossil fuel reserves appear in the following table:

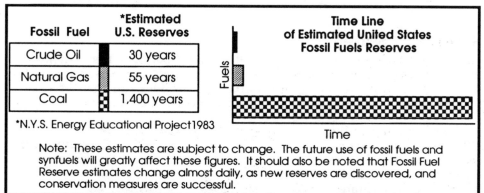

Fossil Fuel	*Estimated U.S. Reserves	Time Line of Estimated United States Fossil Fuels Reserves
Crude Oil	30 years	
Natural Gas	55 years	
Coal	1,400 years	

*N.Y.S. Energy Educational Project 1983

Note: These estimates are subject to change. The future use of fossil fuels and synfuels will greatly affect these figures. It should also be noted that Fossil Fuel Reserve estimates change almost daily, as new reserves are discovered, and conservation measures are successful.

Today, most of the energy demand in the United States is met by fossil fuels. Serious problems may lie ahead unless changes are made and conservation measures taken.

Questions

1   The principal product that we get from oil is
   1   alcohol   2   gasoline   3   heating oil   4   kerosene

2   Natural gas is primarily
   1   alcohol   2   heating oil   3   kerosene   4   methane

3 Which of the following groups contains only fossil fuels?
   1 oil, natural gas, coal   3 wood, natural gas, methanol
   2 coal, wood, oil   4 natural gas, coal, wood

4 Which two elements make up the gas methane?
   1 helium and carbon   3 hydrogen and carbon
   2 carbon and oxygen   4 hydrogen and chlorine

5 Oil was formed over millions of years from the
   1 formation of igneous rocks   3 action of Moon and Sun
   2 plant and animal remains   4 bodies of dinosaurs

6 The remains of ancient giant mosses, ferns, and trees that were covered by water and mud formed deposits of
   1 coal   3 oil
   2 electricity   4 all answers are correct

7 The primary use of coal today is as a fuel to produce
   1 electricity   3 methane
   2 home heating   4 pressure to pump water

8 Which of the following burns with the highest heat content?
   1 anthracite coal   3 lignite
   2 bituminous coal   4 peat

9 Which of the following is produced from fossil fuels?
   1 cough syrup and laxatives   3 fertilizers and acrylic paints
   2 lipstick and bubble bath   4 all answers are correct

10 At the present rate of use, which fossil fuel will last longest?
   1 coal   2 gasoline   3 oil   4 natural gas

B. Moving Water

Moving water is an energy source that is almost pollution free. When water falls, its kinetic energy increases. This kinetic energy can be used to turn turbines. The mechanical energy of the turning turbines can then be used to turn generators (containing magnets) which produce electric current.

At the beginning of the 20th century, hydroelectric power was the main source of electricity in the United States. This was electricity produced by falling water. Only 15% of the total energy produced in the United States today is made by hydroelectric plants. Such plants are found on the Colorado, Tennessee, and Niagara Rivers.

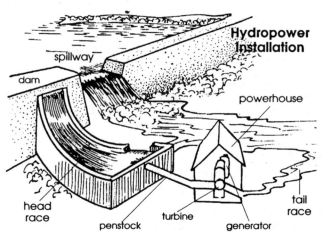

C. Nuclear Energy

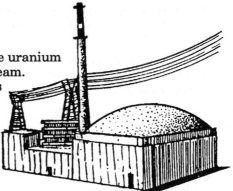

The **nuclear energy** contained in the uranium atom can be used to change water to steam. The steam is then used to turn turbines which turn generators to produce electric power. In the process of fission, a neutron is freed from the nucleus of the uranium atom. This neutron bombards another nucleus releasing two neutrons. These two neutrons hit other atoms and release two more neutrons each and so on. This is referred to as a **chain reaction**. Nuclear energy is sometimes called **atomic energy**.

Only a small percentage of electricity used in our country is produced by nuclear power. However, nuclear power plants can be found in many states in the United States.

D. Electrical Energy

Electrical energy, as used today, must be produced from other energy sources. Some sources are falling water, fossil fuels, or uranium. This is why electrical energy is often referred to as a **secondary energy source.** The nature of electricity, the flow of electrons, permits fairly easy transmission from place of production to place of use. Conductor wires made of copper or aluminum are used for transmission lines.

Our present-day society greatly depends on very large quantities of electricity. Try to live without it for a day. You would have

- no lights, TV, radio, or video games.
- no appliances to cool food and soda.
- no clothes washers or dryers.
- no electric fans, stoves, heaters, elevators, or escalators.
- no subways.

Questions

1 Moving (falling) water is an especially good energy source because it is
   1 found everywhere on the Earth
   2 plentiful
   3 small in volume
   4 almost pollution free

2   Presently, what percentage of the total energy need in America is provided by plants that use falling water to generate electricity?
    1 15%   2 30%   3 50%   4 75%

3   When nuclear energy is used to heat water to turn turbines and generators, the energy is released from what kind of atom?
    1 hydrogen   2 oxygen   3 sulfur   4 uranium

4   Nuclear fission occurs when
    1 electrons are released   3 protons are taken in
    2 neutrons are released   4 neutrons are taken in

5   Which of the following is *not* a natural source of energy?
    1 coal   3 natural gas
    2 electricity   4 nuclear energy

Concepts and Words To Be Understood

environment   particulate   pollution   thermal

II. Environmental Problems

Environmental problems associated with energy production are numerous. They need to be studied carefully. **Pollution**, the adding of unwanted things to the environment, is of major concern.

A. Air Pollution

Air pollution results when fossil fuels are burned, and the wastes are not disposed of properly.

When fuels burn, many things are produced besides heat and light. Some of the pollutants produced are smoke, sulfur dioxide, carbon monoxide, and carbon dioxide, to mention just a few.

• **Acid rain** is a direct result of burning fossil fuels, especially those containing sulfur. There is a lot of sulfur in soft coal. The sulfur joins with oxygen as the fuel burns to form sulfur dioxide.

The sulfur dioxide then bonds with a water molecule to produce sulfurous acid. This acid easily captures another oxygen atom from the air to make sulfuric acid. The acid then dissolves in raindrops. This acid rain water "burns" the plants and the fish in lakes. All over the world, many forests, lakes, and forms of animal life are being destroyed gradually by acid rain.

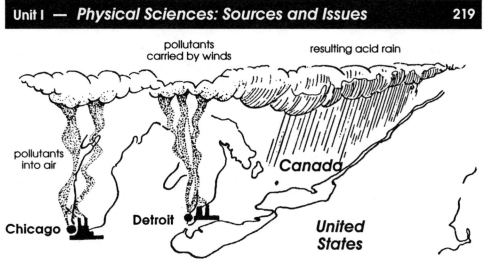

International Effects of Air Pollution

· The **greenhouse effect** is caused by light energy (short wavelength) entering an area. After entering, it is changed to heat energy (longer wavelength) and is trapped by some barrier.

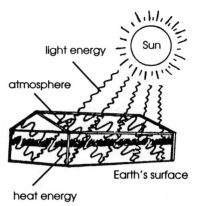

A serious problem could exist if very large amounts of carbon dioxide (too much to be used by green plants) are given off by cars, homes, and factories. This build up of carbon dioxide produces a heat screen in the atmosphere. A result is an overall increase in the temperature of the Earth. This could lead to the melting of the polar ice caps.

B. Land Pollution

Land pollution results when the surface of the Earth is damaged.

· **Strip mining** is used when coal and other ore deposits are close to the Earth's surface. Topsoil and other unwanted materials are cleared away. Then, the coal is removed. If the area is not reclaimed after the coal is removed, a lasting scar results.

· **Garbage dumps** in many states, including New York and New Jersey are now being controlled. In areas where they are still found, offensive odors and sights mar the environment. Rat populations increase in these places.

• **Pesticides and herbicides** used in large-scale farming can pollute the land. These chemicals are often dangerous to all living things.

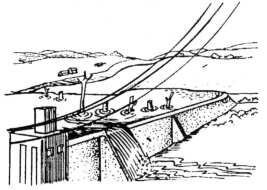

• **Pipelines**, especially those above ground, have changed the ecology of certain areas.

• **Dam construction** to make artificial lakes, so that hydroelectric power plants can be built, has a rather permanent effect on the environment. The habitats of many plants and animals are changed, forcing them to move, adapt, or die.

C. Water Pollution

Water pollution results when factories, cities, and ships dump their wastes into rivers, lakes, and oceans.

• **Industrial and city wastes**. Some of these wastes are **toxic** (poisonous) to living organisms. When dumped into nearby bodies of water, these wastes have caused serious problems. People, plants, and animals in the area are affected. They may have difficulty surviving.

• **Oil spills** from freighters and wells have had disastrous ecological effects. Offshore drilling for natural gas and oil has created much controversy. Disasters associated with the transportation of crude oil and natural gas have caused much water pollution.

Accidents at sea where tankers have hit reefs or other ships result in huge quantities of crude oil being released. Being lighter than the water, this oil floats on the surface. Sometimes, the oil washes toward the shore destroying wildlife and beaches.

D. Thermal Pollution

Thermal pollution happens when abnormally large amounts of heat are added to the atmosphere or nearby bodies of water. Nuclear and coal burning power plants can be guilty of adding hot water to the environment. This changes the balance of nature in the area. For example, game fish prefer cooler areas and avoid regions where water temperature is too high for them.

E. Nuclear Pollution

Nuclear pollution can be disastrous, especially when large amounts of radiation leak from the power plant.

The 1979 Three Mile Island accident in Pennsylvania and the 1986 Chernobyl accident in Russia are examples of nuclear disasters.

Fortunately, the Three Mile Island "meltdown" was controlled quickly with minimum radiation released.

The "meltdown" at Chernobyl took longer to control. It released into the environment much more radiation than the Three Mile Island accident. The long-term effects of radiation are not yet known. Already birth defects and deaths have been linked with the nuclear accident at Chernobyl.

The safe storage, transport, and disposal of **nuclear waste** is a major problem. Bone and lung cancers are being linked to overexposure to this type of waste.

Questions

1 Adding unwanted things to the environment is called
   1 condensation   3 pollution
   2 generation   4 reflection

2 A major cause of air pollution is
   1 burning fossil fuels   3 dumping wastes into rivers
   2 mining of coal   4 landfills

3 Sulfur dioxide given off when fossil fuels burn is a major cause of
   1 acid rain
   2 the greenhouse effect
   3 garbage dumps
   4 temperature increase on the Earth

4 Scars left by mining and garbage dumping result in what kind of pollution?
   1 air   3 water
   2 land   4 noise

5 An oil tanker hits a reef putting a hole in the side. Crude oil spills out. What type of pollution is most likely to occur?
   1 air   3 thermal
   2 nuclear   4 water

6 Water pollution can result from
   1 city wastes dumped into lakes
   2 dumping chemicals into rivers
   3 oil spills from freighters
   4 all answers are correct

7 Thermal pollution can be caused by the
   1 strip-mining of coal
   2 heated water from power plants
   3 building of a dam or pipeline
   4 no answer here is correct

8 Radiation from a nuclear disaster might cause
   1 cleaner teeth for people   3 healthier digestive systems
   2 deaths and birth defects   4 brighter futures for children

9 Lung and bone cancers could result from exposure to
   1 carbon monoxide   3 nuclear waste products
   2 city garbage dumps   4 thermal pollution

10 The environmental problems linked to energy production are
   1 of no special concern
   2 not as serious now as they were
   3 thought to be more serious than they really are
   4 numerous and need careful study

11 Excessive amounts of carbon dioxide in the air could result in the
   1 building up of mountains   3 melting of the polar ice caps
   2 shrinking of the oceans   4 continental movements

12 Industrial waste dumped into rivers usually results in
   1 a change in the river's ecology
   2 increased numbers of fish
   3 the clearing up of the water
   4 the widening of the river banks

13 Oil spills are dangerous because the oil
   1 dissolves and disappears   3 washes up on beaches
   2 sinks to the ocean's bottom   4 can pass into the air

14 The proper disposal of which type of waste is the most serious problem?
   1 waste paper   3 nuclear waste
   2 heated water   4 aluminum cans

15 A closed car is parked in the direct sunlight in the summer. It gets very hot inside. This is the result of
   1 air pollution   3 nuclear pollution
   2 the greenhouse effect   4 acid rain

Concepts and Words To Be Understood

biomass   nonrenewable resources
breeder reactor   renewable resources
conservation   synfuel
geothermal

III. Conservation

Conservation is the wise use of our energy sources. It is one possible answer to the energy problem. Much can be accomplished by reducing wastes and improving efficiency. Some conservation practices include:

- car pooling
- reducing home temperatures
- using lights only when needed
- producing more efficient cars
- using buses and trains whenever possible
- cooking with a microwave oven

Alternatives to the ways things are done, as well as the best use of our natural resources, must be studied.

A. Nonrenewable Resources

Nonrenewable resources are those that are *not* replaced during the time span of human history. Once fossil fuels and uranium are used up, they are gone forever. They *cannot* be replaced!

- Wise use of present supplies is essential.
- Development of synthetic fuels for future use is needed.
- Breeder reactors, when used and managed properly, could extend the use of uranium-238 as a fuel for thousands of years.

B. Renewable Resources

Renewable resources replace themselves. This recycling occurs in a relatively short period of time by natural processes.

1. Sunshine is the primary source of energy for the Earth. Sunlight is available in unlimited quantities.

Passive solar energy systems collect heat from the Sun without the use of mechanical devices. Structures are built with large south-facing windows and longer than usual roof overhangs. This permits lots of sunlight to enter in the winter. In the summer, when the Sun is higher in the sky, the overhang blocks many rays.

During the day (left), the sunlight enters and is absorbed by interior materials of the house. During the night (right), the stored heat is released and keeps the house warm.

Active solar energy systems use collectors and storage tanks. These solar systems capture the Sun's energy in a collector filled with a fluid. The fluid might be water or air. After being heated, the fluid is pumped through pipes to a storage tank. Further pumping allows the heat energy in the fluid to make water hot, as well as heating and cooling living and working spaces.

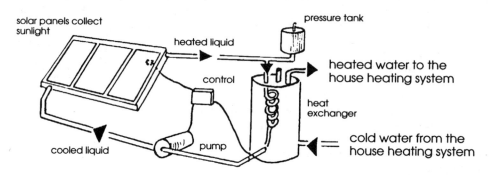

Solar cells are made of silicon, cadmium sulfate, and other materials that have atoms whose electrons can be knocked loose by sunlight. When this happens, the electrons can be made to flow as electric current. Telephones in remote areas are presently being powered by solar cells. Future cars may be powered by electricity that has been produced in this way. Perhaps you have used a solar calculator to do your school work.

2. **Biomass** refers to the remains, wastes, or by-products of plants and animals. Biomass can be used to produce **heat** from burning.

Wood has been a source of energy for many years. If a new tree is planted for each one cut down, there will be a continuous supply.

Much of the **garbage** that we make is burnable. A typical city's garbage is about 50% paper products and wood. In some places, city garbage is being burned to heat buildings. This process gets rid of many burnable wastes.

Synfuels are "man-made" fuels such as methane. They can be made from:

• garbage, sewage, industrial waste, and farm and forest residues.

• wood, corn, sunflowers, or any other plentiful crop. The crop is mashed and fermented with microscopic organisms. Then, it is purified by distillation.

• coal, oil shale, and tar sands. This process is a very expensive one. It probably will not be used until necessary.

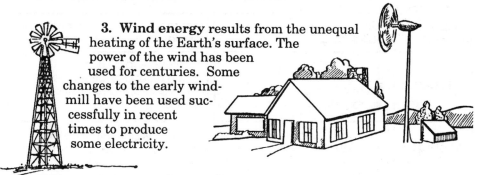

3. Wind energy results from the unequal heating of the Earth's surface. The power of the wind has been used for centuries. Some changes to the early windmill have been used successfully in recent times to produce some electricity.

4. **Geothermal energy** is heat that comes naturally from the Earth. It is usually superheated steam. In some places, it is being used for heating and electrical energy production. Not widespread, this can only be found where hot rocks and water are close enough to the Earth's surface to be useful. Old Faithful geyser in Yellowstone National Park is an example of uncontrolled thermal energy.

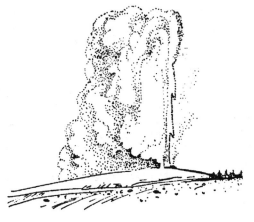

5. Fresh water is one resource that is often taken for granted. Clean water is needed by every living thing to survive.

Care must be taken to preserve adequate supplies. Contaminated lakes and streams must be cleaned up. Conservation is needed to meet our present needs and provide for the future.

There are **both advantages and disadvantages** associated with the use of every nonrenewable and renewable resource. The following chart compares these advantages and disadvantages of the major energy sources:

Resource	Some Advantages	Some Disadvantages
Crude Oil	Major source of gasoline. Hundreds of non-fuel products are made from it.	Nonrenewable. At current level of use, will soon run out. USA is dependent on foreign sources.
Natural Gas	Clean burning and sulfur free.	Nonrenewable. At current level of use, will run out next century.
Coal	Plentiful, although nonrenewable. Over a century of coal supply left.	Nonrenewable. Burns with much sulfur dioxide waste. Land damaged after strip mining.
Sunlight	Unlimited supply and nonpolluting.	Amount varies with time of day and location. Expensive to produce the solar cells.
Biomass	Can be used for garbage and wastes. Reduces size of landfills. Lowers sulfur emission to atmosphere.	Initial high expense to set up the processing plant.
Wind	Free energy, when blowing. Little negative environmental effect.	Wind may not be always blowing. High cost of storing the energy made.
Uranium	Large quantities available.	May have radioactive contamination from a mishap. Hard to get rid of wastes in a safe way. Threat of terrorism.

Questions

1 The wise use of our energy sources is known as
  1 condensation   3 evaporation
  2 conservation   4 restriction

2 Which of the following would be a good way to conserve fuel?
  1 car pool
  2 raise inside home temperature
  3 keep house lights on all night
  4 no answer here is correct

3 A resource that cannot be replaced during the time span of human history is said to be
  1 abundant   3 renewable
  2 nonrenewable   4 plentiful

4 An example of a nonrenewable resource would be
  1 coal   2 solar   3 wind   4 wood

5 If a resource can be replaced in a relatively short period of time, it is said to be
  1 coal   3 renewable
  2 nonrenewable   4 petroleum

6 The primary source of energy on the Earth is
  1 coal   3 the Sun
  2 oil   4 uranium

7 Solar collectors are able to change
  1 electricity to sound   3 sunlight to sound
  2 heat to light   4 sunlight to heat

8 Solar cells made of silicon and other materials are able to change
  1 sunlight to electricity   3 electricity to heat
  2 heat to electricity   4 electricity to light

9 Solar cells provide the electric power for
  1 most American cars   3 some calculators and cars
  2 mining equipment   4 many windmills

10 The remains, wastes, or by-products of plants and animals are referred to as
  1 biomass   3 synthetic fuels
  2 conservation   4 a nonrenewable resource

11 Which of the following is a renewable resource?
  1 biomass   3 wood
  2 wind   4 all are renewable

12 Synfuels, especially methane, can be made from
  1 garbage   3 oil shale
  2 corn   4 all answers are correct

13 The unequal heating of the Earth's surface results in what kind of energy?
  1 biomass   3 nuclear
  2 geothermal   4 wind

14 The geyser Old Faithful in Yellowstone National Park, results from
   1 geothermal energy   3 synfuels
   2 solar energy   4 wind

15 Enough fresh water for future use can be provided if
   1 new solar cells are developed
   2 factories stop discharging wastes into rivers and lakes
   3 synfuel production is increased
   4 enough hot rocks are left in the Earth

Area 4

Science, Technology, and Society

Unit J — All Sciences:

Science, Technology, and Society

Modern devices, such as the robot and artificial heart, are the results of much scientific research. Science provides the basic information while technology tries to develop uses for this information. Because of this, life styles today are very different than they were 10, 100, or 1000 years ago.

Society must make decisions about mass transportation, genetic engineering, and energy production. The future of mankind depends on decisions made today. Trade-offs and changes might have to be made. Because everyone is affected in some way by modern devices, everyone needs to be concerned.

Some technological systems and their affects on society are presented in Unit J.

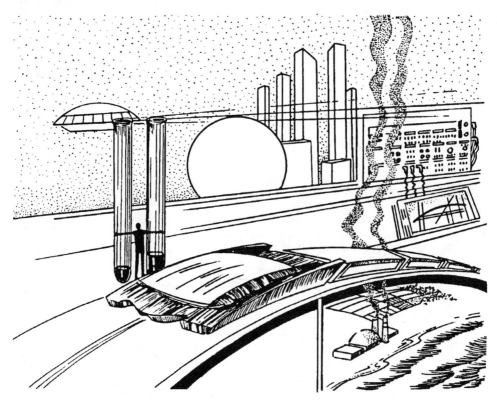

Unit J — Science, Technology, & Society

Concepts and Words To Be Understood

complex	model	science
component	open loop system	society
closed loop system	prototype	system
flow chart	resource	technology

Introduction

Science and Technology are human activities that have existed for a long time. In fact, they have been around since the time man began to find uses for his discoveries. Early man learned that fire could cook meat and make it taste better.

Science can be defined as *a process of solving problems*. Therefore, facts help us to gain an understanding of and predict the outcome of events in our natural world.

Technology is the *process of using resources, discoveries, inventions, and scientific knowledge to develop new products and/or processes*. These new things then are used to meet the needs and wants of our modern day society.

Science and technology are closely related. Basic (pure) science is the "grass-roots" research that provides new scientific knowledge and modifications of previous knowledge. Technology (applied science) uses this knowledge to develop and improve ways that society (people) can better use the discoveries. This, in turn, leads to new devices and/or processes which are used to discover new scientific data and principles. Science provides information while technology finds uses for the information (engineers might be called scientific technologists).

Technology recognizes the need for seven basic resources:

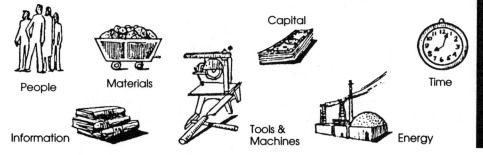

People   Materials   Capital   Time

Information   Tools & Machines   Energy

Categories Of Technology:

1) **Information technology** satisfies the need to communicate ideas and process information. For example, satellites and television bring the news events of the world "right into our living rooms." Computers record and keep the information needed by stores, banks, hospitals, schools, and almost every business. Home computers help with daily work, games, and entertainment.

2) **Biologically related technology** satisfies biological needs. For example, to slow down the growth of harmful bacteria, food processing plants pasteurize the foods before packaging. Modern medicines have reduced infections following surgery. Organ transplants have allowed people to live longer and have a better quality of life. New medical instruments, like the "Cat Scan" (special X-ray machine), help doctors to determine the cause of a problem. This added information enables the doctors to treat their patients quickly and effectively.

3) **Physical technology** satisfies physical needs for shelter, transportation, production of clothing, and other essentials. For example, new homes and apartments are now more comfortable due to better building materials, insulation, and appliances. New cars, buses, and planes are safer and stronger because of technological design and new construction materials. Many new fabrics make our clothes more comfortable, fire resistant, warmer or cooler, and better looking.

Questions

1   Using scientific information to meet the needs and wants of society is
    referred to as
    1   populations   3   science
    2   resources   4   technology

2   *Basic science* supplies us with new
    1   products   3   closed loop systems
    2   scientific knowledge   4   natural resources

3   What is determined by the seven technology resources?
    1   The natural resources of the country.
    2   The number of people in the society.
    3   The composition of the atmosphere.
    4   The technological development of the country.

4   Of the seven technology resources, which of the following represents
    "capital?"

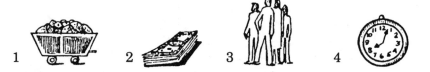

1   2   3   4

5   Which of the three categories of technology satisfies the needs for shelter,
    transportation, and production of clothing?
    1   biological   2   physical   3   informational

I. Technological Systems

Problem Solving In Technology

- **Identify need.** Is there an accurate way to get waste paper into a basket?
- **Develop a plan or idea.** Think of ways to solve the problem. Would folding the paper help?
- **Research the plan or idea.** What additional information is needed? What type of paper is best? What other information is needed?
- **Develop a design.** Design an airplane to help solve the problem.
- **Build a prototype.** Make an airplane from the design.

- **Test the prototype.** How many times did the airplane go into the basket?
- **Evaluate the prototype.** How did the airplane perform? Are changes needed for the airplane to perform better?
- **Accept the prototype and produce it.** If the prototype is accepted, it is then ready for production. If not, begin again.

Open Loop Systems

In open loop systems, a device may be started but it *cannot* automatically stop or change. You have to turn on and turn off the system. For example, turn on the TV. It plays until it is turned off.

Closed Loop Systems

Closed loop systems use feedback produced by sensors to adjust control signals. This automatically changes the process component. The five parts of a closed loop technology system are illustrated below:

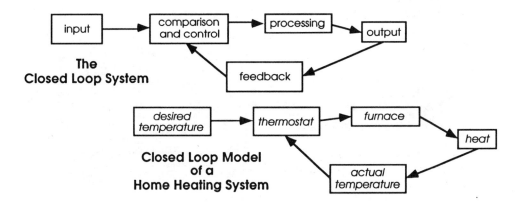

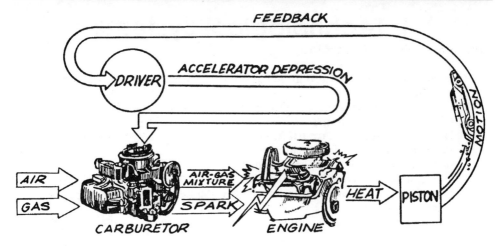

Complex Processes Or Devices

A complex technological process or device consists of a number of simpler technological processes or devices working together as a system. Many processes work together for an automobile to run.

Other complex technological devices and products include personal computers, "TV dinners," CD players, "boom boxes," and telephone and satellite networks.

Can you name some of the processes involved?

Technological Products

Technological products affect everyone in some way. Alarm clocks wake you up in the morning. After a shower, you may use a blow dryer to dry your hair. Breakfast can be eaten with the help of a fork, knife, and spoon. A bus could pick you up and take you to school. After school, you may relax while watching TV or listening to your stereo or "boom box."

Environmental Effects

The environment is affected in some way by technological processes or devices.

Paved highways make travel easier and safer. Remember that automobiles and motorcycles burn fossil fuels. Burning fossil fuels adds carbon dioxide to the air. Added amounts of carbon dioxide allow light energy to enter the atmosphere but trap heat energy. This tends to increase the overall temperature of the Earth and decrease air quality (see Greenhouse Effect - Unit I, page 219).

Bulldozers level the land for many reasons and often destroy the habitats of many plants and animals. Light bulbs brighten dark places but use energy to do so.

Questions

1 The first thing that must be done before a problem can be solved is to
  1 identify a need   3 test a prototype
  2 build a prototype   4 research a plan or idea

2 An open loop technological system
  1 is unable to adjust automatically to desired outcomes
  2 automatically adjusts to process changes
  3 can change without outside help
  4 all answers are correct

3 The way in which a home thermostat works is an example of
  1 an open loop system
  2 a closed loop system
  3 both and open and closed loop system
  4 neither an open nor a closed loop system

4 A number of simple technological processes or devices working together form what type of technological system?
  1 closed loop   3 open loop
  2 complex   4 simple machine

5 Which of the following represents a complex technological device?

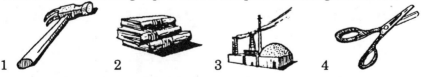

  1   2   3   4

6 How would new windmills affect the environment?
  1 Amount of sunlight would be decreased
  2 Too much water would be pumped
  3 The skyline would change
  4 Winds would be stopped

7 Which process produces a negative effect on the environment?
  1 building paved highways   3 clearing land with bulldozers
  2 driving more automobiles   4 all of these

8   Which of the following is a true statement?
1   Most people do not interact with technological products.
2   Almost all technological products are dangerous for people to use.
3   Wants and need of people seldom affect production of products.
4   Everyone interacts with the products of technology in some way.

9   Which flow chart does *not* represent a closed loop system?

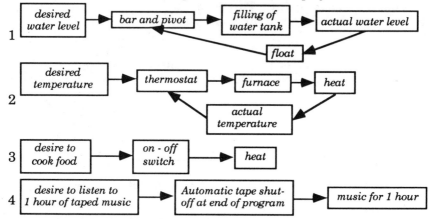

10 Of the usual five components of a closed loop system, which are essential
    for automatic adjustment?
1   Comparison and control and input
2   Feedback and comparison and control
3   Input and feedback
4   Output and input

Concepts and Words To Be Understood

global   lifestyle   robot

II. Interaction Of Science, Technology, And Society

Science, technology, and society are closely related. When any one component changes, there will be an effect on the other two.

For example: When the population (number of people in a society) increases, there is a greater demand for food, shelter, and clothing. One reason for
this population increase is modern medical technology. Organ transplants
also have helped increased the average life span of humans.

The invention of the steam engine and cotton gin greatly affected industry
and society. More work could be done faster and with fewer workers. Products became cheaper to make and buy. But, jobs were lost, and many farm
workers left the farms and looked for factory jobs in the cities.

The chart below shows some effects that **Science, Technology,** and **Society** have on each other:

Science and technology can not solve all of society's problems. Pollution is still a global problem. Many people around the world are dying of starvation. Numerous areas on Earth have too many people in them. They are overpopulated. Science and technology can help, but people (society) themselves must solve these problems.

Science	Technology	Society
laws of motion	space travel	new products, greater knowledge of universe
electricity	electrical appliances	more leisure time
electromagnetic waves	radio and TV	home entertainment, better informed people
chemistry	man-made materials	new products
radioactivity	nuclear medicine	better health
nuclear fission	nuclear power plants	reduced dependence on fossil fuels
structure of matter	microelectronics	increased capability to solve problems

Changes brought about by society might include the following:

more money for medical research	medical research	new medicines and diagnostic techniques
prohibiting genetic engineering laboratories	restricted research	slow down of new technological developments

Improvement And Refinement

Improvements and refinements in technology have produced many new products. These products have greatly affected the lifestyles of people.

Space program developments have provided a variety of products that can be used by ordinary people.

- Freezer-to-oven ceramic dishes
- Football masks equipped with radios
- Cordless drills and other instruments
- Rechargeable cardiac pacemakers
- Hang gliders
- Food processing methods

The **selective breeding** of plants and animals has improved our lives:
- Cattle that have more muscle than fat
- Corn with larger kernels and sweeter taste
- Humans can give birth to children as a result of *in vitro fertilization*

Technological Improvements

- Use of satellites and radar increases the accuracy of weather forecasting.
- Improved telecommunications permits direct-dialing around the world.
- New airplanes, cars, and trains travel faster today than ever before.
- Pictures of documents are sent via telephone through the Fax machine.

Medical advances have reduced the rate of, or eliminated, some causes of death. Other causes of death have increased in rate, some because of technology. Note the following chart:

Ten Leading Causes of Death in the United States in 1900		*Ten Leading Causes of Death in the United States in 1980*	
Cause	**Deaths per 100,000 Population**	**Cause**	**Deaths per 100,000 Population**
Pneumonia & Influenza	215	Heart Disease	340
Tuberculosis	185	Cancer	185
Diarrhea	140	Accidents	95
Heart Disease	130	Stroke	85
Stroke	110	Pneumonia & Influenza	40
Kidney Disease	85	Diabetes	35
Accidents	75	Liver Disease	30
Cancer	65	Artery Disease	25
Senility	55	Suicide	20
Diphtheria	40	Homicide	15

Shorter working hours and longer lives have allowed people more leisure time. This, in turn, encourages development of new industries.

Questions

1 Science, technology, and society are related in such a way that
   1 each one does not affect the other
   2 all will stay constant
   3 when one changes, it affects the other two
   4 if one changes, the others remain the same

2 Technological advances have had what effect on human life spans?
   1 shortened them   3 kept them the same for years
   2 lengthened them   4 had no effect on them

3 The leading cause of death in the United States in 1900 was
   1 accidents   3 pneumonia and influenza
   2 diphtheria   4 stroke

4 The leading cause of death in the United States in 1980 was
   1 cancer   3 liver disease
   2 heart disease   4 suicide

5 The three most common causes of death in 1900 were caused by
   1 disease germs   3 poor diet
   2 drug abuse   4 stress

Business And Industry

Science and technology affect business and industry. Some old jobs have been lost. Other jobs remain but must be changed. However, many new jobs have been made. The changes in old jobs and the creation of new jobs require new training and more education.

- Robots have replaced workers on assembly lines. Where this happens, robot maintenance jobs are created. The cost of making the products is reduced.

- The chain saw made the logger's job easier but reduced the number of loggers needed.

- The fields of electronics and computers have created many new jobs for the educated modern person.

Attitudes

Attitudes of individuals or society toward a technological product affect its use.

- Nuclear energy development has been controversial. This is an abundant natural resource that could last for many years to come.

- Many people are concerned about possible disasters, radiation leaks, and disposal of nuclear wastes.

- Wearing of seat belts in cars has saved lives. Seat belts also prevent serious injury. Many states have a law requiring seat belt use. However, some people question the "seat belt law." Have seat belts helped you?

New medicines have saved the lives of many people. Often, animals are used in the research that proves whether or not the new medicine will do its job safely. But, some people object to the use of animals in research. This is another problem brought about by a conflict between technology, science, and society.

Milk can be processed using very high temperatures and quick cooling. The milk is placed in specially lined packages. In this way, it can be kept on store shelves without refrigeration for six weeks. Once opened, it must be refrigerated. Would you buy and drink this milk?

Global Effects

Global effects of technology result when a process or product crosses international boundaries. **Acid rain** produced by chemical wastes from industries in Chicago and Detroit is affecting parts of Canada.

Satellite television transmission allows Americans to watch the Olympic Games as they are happening in France, Spain, or Norway at the same time as they are taking place.

Radiation fallout from the nuclear plant disaster at Chernobyl, Russia, affected people in Sweden, Poland, Germany, Italy, and other European countries.

Many foods, clothes, and resources used in the United States today, come from foreign lands. Also, the United States exports many products to other countries. Therefore, what affects the rest of the world also affects Americans. And, what affects Americans affects the rest of the world.

Questions

1   Weather forecasting today is more accurate than years ago because of the use of
   1   cameras   3   telephones
   2   satellites   4   telescopes

2   The number of technological products available today is
   1   greater than in 1950   3   remaining the same
   2   lower than in 1960   4   changing only slightly

3   The use of seat belts in automobiles
   1   is a waste of time and money
   2   adds unnecessary cost to cars
   3   should be used only to hold down packages
   4   has been proven to be a good idea

4   A global effect is caused when what type of boundaries are crossed?
   1   city   2   state   3   national   4   international

5   The future of technology and technological products requires that
   1   all countries cooperate with each other
   2   everybody mind their own business
   3   cooperation exists only when necessary
   4   new atomic and hydrogen bombs be developed

III. Decision Making

Technology And Choice

People need to make choices daily regarding products of technology.

- What foods should I buy and eat?
- How should I spend my "free" time?
- Should I drive the car downtown or take the bus?
- Which job or career should I take?
- Will I listen to the radio or watch television?

Advantage And Disadvantage

There are advantages and disadvantages related to the use of every technological product. Chemotherapy uses special chemicals to treat some diseases. Many lives have been saved by its use. Unfortunately, some people lose their hair because of it. In time, the hair usually grows back. This is a disadvantage of chemotherapy.

Disadvantages tend to be tolerated when the advantages outweigh them. Disadvantages often lead to burdens when they affect more people and large areas of the Earth. In general, burdens are more lasting than disadvantages.

Devices And Process Evaluation

Continuous evaluation of technological devices and processes is needed. Possible bad effects on present and future generations and the environment must be considered. For Example:

- In the year 2000, what will be the effects of herbicides and insecticides that are used today?

- Are those living in 2020 going to experience skin cancer because the ozone layer in our atmosphere is being destroyed now?

- Can the Earth's atmosphere take all the extra pollution given off by so many automobiles without great harm?

Decisions

Decisions concerning the use of a technological processes or devices must be made. They need to be based on their short-term and long-term consequences. Often short-term benefits are chosen without regard to long-term problems.

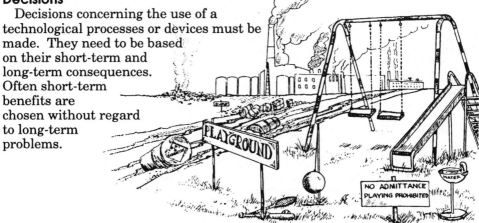

Technological Process or Device	Benefit	Burden
mass transportation	less pollution, less energy used	large cost, personal inconvenience
robotics	modernized and efficient industry	loss of jobs
drugs	treat diseases	dependence through abuse
computers	increased ability to process data	loss of jobs, health problems possible
space travel	increased knowledge and new products	high financial cost
life-sustaining devices	keep people alive	how to decide when to use or remove them
organ transplants	increased life span	cost, decision as to who receives them
radioactive isotopes	medical treatment and diagnosis	increased risk of cancer
automobile	increased mobility	increased pollution, more deaths
chemical fertilizers	increased agricultural yields	fish killed in lakes

Technological Process or Device	Short-term Benefit	Long-term Burden
nuclear energy	electricity	radioactive waste
insecticides	higher agricultural yields	extinction of helpful species while target pests acquire immunity, contamination of water
artificial sweeteners	convenience for diabetics and dieters	possible increased risk of cancer
strip mining	increased fuel supply	unusable land, water pollution
nitrites	prevention of botulism	increased risk of cancer
man-made packing materials	fresher food	nonbiodegradable waste in landfills
logging	increased supply of wood products	deforestation of forests and tropical jungles
burning coal	low cost for heat and electricity	contamination of air without purifiers

Questions

Use the two charts on Benefits and Burdens to answer the following questions.

1   Which technological product could prevent botulism but might increase the risk of cancer?

   1   radioactive isotopes   3   nitrites
   2   coal   4   robotics

2   Valium is a drug taken to relieve pain from kidney problems. A year after the kidney is cured, the person craves and continues using the drug. The burden in this case is

   1   dependence through abuse   3   increased air pollution
   2   good disease treatment   4   loss of employment

3   Our space program has provided much information about the Earth and the solar system. A burden of this program would be

   1   number of people involved   3   high cost of the program
   2   new product development   4   astronaut training

4   A burden resulting from nuclear energy development is the

   1   energy derived from it   3   number of atoms present
   2   radioactive waste   4   production of electricity

5   The future of mankind depends on the

   1   continuous evaluation of technological devices
   2   occasional testing in laboratories
   3   discussion with foreign rulers
   4   rioting by society

Modification And Termination

A technological device or process may be modified or terminated when advantages are overshadowed by disadvantages.

Short-lived or Terminated

- The insecticide DDT causes serious pollution to the environment.
- Sailing ships have been replaced with faster, safer steamships.
- Thalidomide is an anti-nausea drug. It settles the stomach and prevents throwing up. This drug was found to give serious birth defects to unborn babies when taken by their pregnant mothers.

Modified or Reduced

- A change in planting patterns to prevent erosion.
- Use of unleaded gasoline to reduce air pollution.
- Solar heating plants to reduce use of fossil fuels.
- Making many glass, plastic, and aluminum containers "returnable" has helped clean up the environment. Also, it has helped reduce the amount of landfill wastes and conserved our mineral resources.

"Trade-offs"

Decision-making about complex technological issues usually involves trade-offs (compromises) among several alternatives. Often these trade-offs are made between benefits and burdens for society and/or the environment (see chart on the next page).

Issues	Trade - offs
Transplant a human organ.	Who should receive the transplant? Who should pay for the operation?
Build a dam in a river to produce electricity.	What should be done about the plants and animals that will be destroyed?
Burn coal and not oil for electrical power needs.	How and who should clean the air? Coal produces more "dirty" pollution than oil or nuclear power plants.
Use computer robots to make cars.	What work will the laid-off assembly line workers do? Who will retrain the workers?

Questions

1   Strip mining coal increases the fuel supply and leaves a hole in the Earth's surface. Re-claiming the land and planting trees in the area would be an example of a
   1   long-term burden   3   trade-off
   2   short-term benefit   4   no answer here is correct

2   When the advantages of a technological device or process are overshadowed by the disadvantages, the device or process needs to be
   1   produced more quickly   3   sent to the Moon
   2   stored for a year   4   modified or eliminated

3   Decision making about technological issues usually involves
   1   chemists in a laboratory   3   trade-offs
   2   millions of people   4   state governors

4   The resolution of any technological issue may not be acceptable to everyone or every group within a society. This is because
   1   everyone is willing to compromise
   2   trade-offs are fun
   3   most people enjoy the burdens
   4   people all over the world hold different values

5   Organ transplants are common today to save human lives. The short supply of organs and high cost of operations are problems faced by society. Such issues require
   1   modifications   3   termination
   2   short-term benefits   4   trade-offs

IV. Applying The Principles of Science and Technology

The United States space program is an excellent example of science, technology, and society working together. This joint effort has been able to put satellites in orbit. Astronauts have traveled safely to the Moon and back. These accomplishments required much technological research and development. Society had to approve of the program and then "pay the very large bill."

Unmanned Space Programs

Unmanned spacecraft have been sent to study the Sun, Moon, and all known planets except Pluto. Someday, even Pluto will be observed by a space probe. Reaching the outer parts of the solar system is a complex undertaking.

Astronaut (Manned) Space Programs

Early astronaut programs tested human ability to withstand space launch, weightlessness, and Earth reentry. Some of the highlights of later space programs included walks in space, landing of humans on the Moon, and their safe return to Earth. Other accomplishments are a long-term space laboratory and reusable spacecraft (space shuttle). Astronauts are chosen carefully and must undergo a rigorous training program to perform their missions.

Benefits And Value Of The Space Programs

Information About Earth. Weather satellites provide weather data from every part of the Earth's surface. Communications satellites receive and send out television, telephone, and other signals. Earth survey satellites provide information on Earth's resources, agriculture, air pollution, and many other surface features used in mapping.

Information from Beyond the Earth. Some orbiting satellites and space probes are efficient observatories that gather data about the universe. This has led to new discoveries that have helped us better understand our own planet.

Spin-offs. The development of computers was speeded by the needs of the space program. Some products developed for space programs have found uses in medicine, household items, and industry. Technological products and processes developed for the space programs are being adapted continuously for our everyday use.

Concerns And Burdens Of The Space Programs

The ability to place nuclear weapons into space orbits may increase the danger of nuclear war. This ability carries a great responsibility to avoid such a conflict. The high financial costs of these space programs may result in the need to "trim down" or cut other necessary social programs.

There are always the real possibilities of malfunctions and human errors. The *Challenger disaster* in 1986 is a tragic example. System modifications were required before any more launches were scheduled. The need for caution is always present. Yet, society must realize that risks are often necessary if progress is to be made.

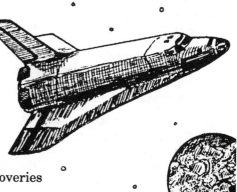

Future Space Programs

• Earth orbit satellites and space probes to other solar system bodies can continue to provide important new discoveries and information.

• An orbiting space station may be our next major space effort. The space station could be used to study space medicine.

• Space factories could use the weightless and airless conditions of space to manufacture products that cannot be made on Earth.

• Many other space programs are possible. In the future, there may be a Moon base and space colonies. But, for now, humans need Earth as their home base and must do everything possible to protect and preserve it.

Questions

1   Reaching the outer parts of the solar system is a complex undertaking. To do this, the United States space program uses
  1   manned spacecraft *only*
  2   unmanned spacecraft *only*
  3   *both* manned and unmanned spacecraft
  4   *neither* manned nor unmanned spacecraft

2   Non-stick cooking surfaces, such as Teflon, have been developed as a result of space technology. This is an example of a space technology
  1   spin-off   2   burden   3   mistake   4   disadvantage

3   Which statement best answers concerns about the Challenger space shuttle disaster?
  1   The United States should stop its manned space program.
  2   The burdens of the space program far outweigh the benefits.
  3   Society must realize that risks are often necessary if progress is to be made.
  4   Information from beyond Earth is not important enough to risk possible disasters.

4   For the United States space program to be successful, science, technology, and society have to work together. Which of the following is a main contribution of society to the space program.
  1   Development of valuable and profitable "spin-off" products.
  2   Approval and payment of the space program.
  3   Direct control over the methods of spacecraft launching and recovery.
  4   Decisions over which kind of spacecraft should be used for each different kind of space mission.

5   The direction of future space research and missions is a decision that should be made by
  1   scientists *only*
  2   the demands of higher technology *only*
  3   the concerns of society *only*
  4   science, technology, and society *together*

Science Competency Practice Tests

1   A proper environment must supply an organism with certain things. Which of these groups includes the things an organism must get from a proper environment?
1   air, proper altitude, energy source, and nonrenewable resources
2   food, oxygen, rock caves, and proper temperature
3   proper temperature, food, water, and oxygen
4   water, light, abiotic things, and minerals

2   Which of the following organisms would be able to carry on photosynthesis?

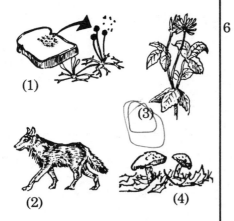

3   In the following food chain, which organism is the producer?
grass - rabbit - fox - bacteria
1   grass
2   rabbit
3   fox
4   bacteria

4   Your family decides to build a new house in the country away from the city. Before buying a new lot for the house, an essential survival feature to find out is the
1   number of sidewalks
2   snow depth in winter
3   number of neighbors
4   source of the water

5   The top part of a rotting log is lifted. Some sow bugs scurry away. Others roll up in a ball. These actions show that the sow bugs are
1   digesting food
2   excreting wastes
3   reproducing
4   responding to a stimulus

6   Some insects go through a four stage life cycle. Which is the correct order for these stages?
(1)

(2)

(3)

(4)

20　A doctor tells a patient that he has a poison ivy rash on his arm. The rash was probably picked up by
1　breathing in polluted air
2　direct contact with a plant
3　being bit by a rabid dog
4　swimming in contaminated water

A　　　　B

21　A student looked under his microscope and viewed picture A. He then adjusted the microscope to get picture B. What adjustment did the student make? The student
1　let in more light
2　switched to a higher magnification (objective)
3　switched to a lower magnification (objective)
4　focused the microscope

22　The main idea of these illustrations is that
1　volcanoes are dangerous
2　running water makes many gullies
3　volcanoes make water run
4　forces are at work changing the Earth's surface

23　Rock fragments result when bedrock breaks down. Very fine rock fragments are the basis for
1　glaciers
2　igneous rocks
3　soil
4　volcanoes

24　A diamond is the hardest natural mineral. This property makes diamonds ideal for
1　creating earrings and necklaces
2　making rock-cutting drill bits
3　making settings for engagement rings
4　shaping bicycle tires

25　Study the above illustration. Suppose this represented the floor of the Atlantic Ocean. Which statement best describes the science concept pictured here?
1　All rivers empty into the ocean.
2　Land features can be found underwater.
3　Plateaus and plains are only found on dry land.
4　Waves erode the land.

26　Rain, snow, hail, and sleet are forms of
1　solar radiation
2　atmospheric pressure
3　precipitation
4　weather fronts

27 A student is to find the density
of a mineral. The sample has an
odd shape. A graduated cylinder
is filled to the 25 ml mark. The
sample is lowered in. The new
water level is at 35 ml. The
volume of the sample is
1   10 cm³
2   25 cm³
3   35 cm³
4   60 cm³

28 Earthquakes occur when large
blocks of rocks move along
breaks or cracks in the Earth's
crust called
1   zones
2   faults
3   joints
4   fractures

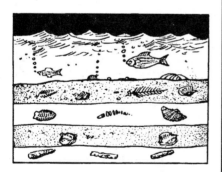

29 The illustration above shows the
formation of fossils. Fossils tell
us much about the Earth's past.
They are found mainly in
1   iron mines
2   igneous rock
3   sedimentary rock
4   desert environments

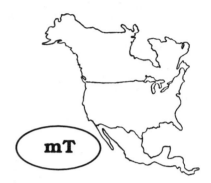

30 The characteristics of the air
mass in the illustration above
would be
1   cold and dry
2   warm and wet
3   wet and cold
4   dry and warm

31 A "beach party and picnic" are
planned. A low pressure area is
expected to be over the picnic
area when you get there. It
would be wise to take a
1   big blanket to spread out on
the sand
2   bottle of suntan lotion
3   raincoat and umbrella
4   pair of sun glasses

32 Weather satellites, radar, and
computers have helped
meteorologists in weather
forecasting. These devices show
that
1   the high cost is not worth the
effort
2   science and technology help
advance one another
3   input and output are
necessary
4   accidental discoveries are
made every day

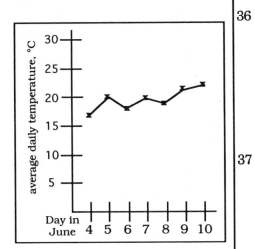

33 This graph shows the average daily temperature for Someplace, USA. What was the average temperature for June 6th?
1   15° C
2   17° C
3   20° C
4   25° C

34 The energy source that causes weather changes is the
1   kind of clouds
2   precipitation that forms
3   Sun's radiation
4   water cycle

35 Warm air is less dense than cold air. Based on this statement, which of the following observations is true?
1   Warm air sinks, and cold air rises.
2   Warm air rises, and cold air sinks.
3   Both warm air and cold air rise.
4   Both warm air and cold air sink.

36 Body heat is lost through the head. Therefore, you should keep your head covered during a
1   tornado
2   heat wave
3   thunderstorm
4   winter snow storm

37 The Sun appears to rise in the East, cross the sky, and set in the West. This "apparent" motion is caused by the
1   attraction of the Moon
2   Earth's gravitation
3   revolution of the Earth
4   rotation of the Earth

38 If the Earth stopped rotating, what would be most affected?
1   day and night hours
2   length of an Earth-year
3   Earth's location in the solar system
4   shape of the Earth's orbit

39 What is associated most closely with the time it takes to revolve once around the Sun?
1   daylight hours
2   TV viewing time
3   your age
4   your birth date

40 When would an astronaut on the Moon be able to see a "shooting star?"
1   at night
2   during landing
3   early morning
4   never

41 The part of the Moon that is always lighted is
1 one fourth
2 one third
3 one half
4 three fourths

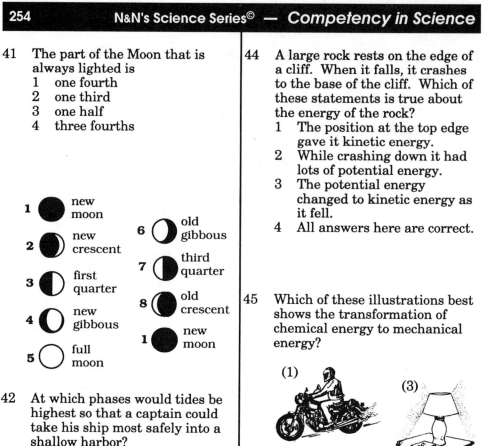

42 At which phases would tides be highest so that a captain could take his ship most safely into a shallow harbor?
1 1 and 3
2 1 and 5
3 4 and 6
4 2 and 8

43 Before Galileo first used a telescope to study the heavens, eyes alone were used. Refracting, reflecting, and radio telescopes have allowed astronomers to "see" into deep space. This shows that technological devices have helped scientists to
1 discover new knowledge
2 lower the number of required reports
3 reduce costs
4 regulate new schedules

44 A large rock rests on the edge of a cliff. When it falls, it crashes to the base of the cliff. Which of these statements is true about the energy of the rock?
1 The position at the top edge gave it kinetic energy.
2 While crashing down it had lots of potential energy.
3 The potential energy changed to kinetic energy as it fell.
4 All answers here are correct.

45 Which of these illustrations best shows the transformation of chemical energy to mechanical energy?

(1)

(3)

(2)

(4)

46 A thermometer works because the liquid in it
1 easily boils and freezes when necessary
2 expands when heated and contracts when cooled
3 is plentiful and cheap
4 is affected by changes in pressure but not changes in heat energy

47 A skateboard works especially
    well when it has
    1   a lip on the end
    2   a smooth top
    3   ball bearings in the wheels
    4   skids instead of wheels

48 When an object vibrates, it most
    likely will produce
    1   electricity
    2   nuclear energy
    3   magnetism
    4   sound

49 A photo-developing room has no
    door. Instead, specially placed
    panels are used. These panels
    stop light from entering the
    darkroom to keep the film being
    processed from spoiling. What
    principle of light explains this?
    1   Light rays are dangerous for
        photographers.
    2   Light rays travel in straight
        lines.
    3   Most building supplies are
        translucent.
    4   Radiant energy does not
        need a medium through
        which to travel.

50 Which of these devices would be
    most helpful in preventing a
    house fire?

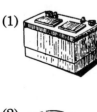
(1)

(2)

(3)

(4)

51 Conductors are substances that
    1   allow electricity to pass
        through easily
    2   permit only small amounts of
        electrons to pass through
    3   resist the passage of heat
    4   stop the movement of
        electrons and heat

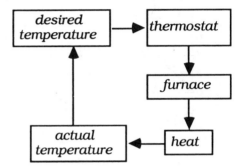

52 Above is a model of a closed loop
    system. Which part is the
    "feedback" component?
    1   actual temperature
    2   furnace
    3   heat
    4   thermostat

53 The students in a chemistry lab
    began choking and coughing.
    Their eyes began to "burn."
    Everyone left the room to get
    fresh air. This situation was
    probably the result of a student
    1   doing what the teacher said
        to do
    2   following directions exactly
    3   mixing together unknown
        chemicals
    4   performing an experiment
        according to the chemistry
        book

Questions 54 and 55 are based on the graph below. The results of a laboratory investigation appear in the graph below.

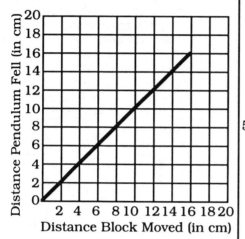

Distance Block Moved (in cm)

54   What are the two variables?
1   speed of block and direction of pendulum
2   distance of pendulum swing and distance the block moved
3   time taken by block compared to swing time
4   weight of block and pendulum mass

55   What do you think is the cause for the wood block moving as seen in the graphed results?
1   The wood block was on a rough surface.
2   The string holding the pendulum mass had all the force.
3   Kinetic energy increased as the mass fell from farther away.
4   The pendulum period decreased from the start of the investigation.

56   Everything in our natural world is made up of
1   matter
2   gases
3   liquids
4   solids

57   A student is studying the properties of matter. What do you predict will happen when the balloon is inflated and placed back on the balance? The balance pan on which the inflated balloon is placed will
1   bob up and down
2   go up
3   go down
4   stay unchanged

58   An example of a chemical change would be
1   baking a birthday cake
2   denting a car fender
3   melting a chocolate bar
4   turning a bicycle wheel

59   Which of the following could be used to measure the mass (weight) of an iron object?

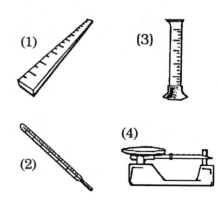

60 You decided to take a hot shower. The bathroom mirror "steamed up." This happened because
 1 ice formed on the glass
 2 water splashed on the mirror from the sink
 3 energy was absorbed by the mirror
 4 water vapor in the air condensed on the mirror

61 Potatoes are to be prepared for dinner. They must be ready to eat in 15 minutes. (Usually, potatoes take a long time to cook.) To cook the potatoes faster, they must be
 1 cut into smaller pieces
 2 placed on a large burner
 3 put in a large pot
 4 submerged in more water

62 These diagrams all represent the same volume and mass of iron. Which illustration represents the iron that will rust the fastest?

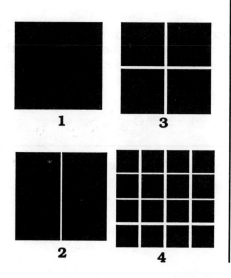

Questions 63 and 64 are based on the following paragraph:

A community fought against a nuclear power plant being built nearby. People were concerned about a possible nuclear accident. Another concern dealt with handling and storage of nuclear waste. Finally a coal burning power plant was built. Now the people are concerned about air pollution control.

63 This situation shows that
 1 a complex process is made up of simpler ones
 2 every technological process affects the environment in some way
 3 technological products can have a global impact
 4 there may be problems with closed loop systems

64 Emission control stops much waste before it enters the atmosphere. This would be considered as
 1 a harmful procedure for people involved
 2 harmful for wildlife
 3 too expensive
 4 good conservation

65 A shortage of crude oil would affect society greatly because
 1 more heating oil would be available
 2 pipelines would not be able to carry the load
 3 so many different kinds of products are made from it
 4 the price of a gallon of gasoline would go down

66   Fossil fuels were formed from
1   the remains of past plants and animals
2   atomic explosions
3   the changing of igneous rock into sedimentary rock
4   the exploration of outer space

67   Garbage dumps and heating expenses could be reduced if cities would
1   buy a larger coal supply
2   fill in the waste dumps
3   use biomass as a fuel
4   use more oil to burn the wastes

Questions 68 through 70 are based on the following paragraph:

Engineers were drilling an oil well. While doing this work, they took temperature readings of the Earth's crust at different depths. The results were: at the surface - 15° C; at 2 km down - 88° C; at 4 km down - 151° C; at 6 km down - 205° C; at 8 km down - 257° C.

68   To make the results easier to read and better organized, the engineers should have
1   guessed the temperatures for other depths
2   made many more temperature readings
3   taken temperature readings at different depths
4   recorded the information on a data table

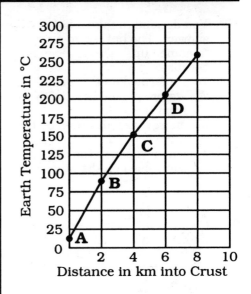

Use the graph above to answer questions 69 and 70.

69   Which letter represents the temperature at 4 km down in the Earth's crust?
1   A
2   B
3   C
4   D

70   What is the difference in temperature between the Earth's surface and 6 km into the crust?
1   73° C
2   136° C
3   190° C
4   242° C

End of Practice Test #1

1   A student wishes to become a good football player. To be sure his body grows properly and damaged cells can be repaired, he must
1   eat a balanced diet
2   follow coach's "play" directions
3   get course grades of 90+
4   maintain a good attitude

2   What condition would cause organisms to respond in these ways?
1   extreme temperature changes
2   too much bright light
3   the intrusion of humans
4   a drastic decrease in species numbers

3   Outside winter temperatures in northern states might drop below zero. Humans in very cold areas would survive by
1   buying new clothes
2   twist-dyeing jeans
3   washing clothes more often
4   wearing heavier clothes

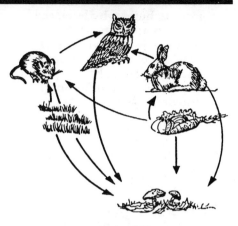

4   The illustration above is of a food web. The mouse and the rabbit would be considered to be
1   carnivores
2   consumers
3   decomposers
4   producers

5   Mushrooms are decomposers in the natural environment. They would
1   add to world hunger
2   add toxins to the atmosphere
3   destroy available nutrients
4   return nutrients to the soil

6   Living things have been found to inhabit the bottom of the ocean. NO green plants are found there. These organisms are probably
1   producers
2   decomposers
3   nutrients
4   photosynthetic plants

Answer questions 7 through 9 based on the following diagram and paragraph:

Humans decide to dam up a river to build a hydroelectric power plant. An artificial lake behind the dam will destroy the habitats of many plants and animals. The lake will provide a new habitat for different plants and animals.

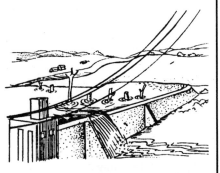

7   Organisms living in the area before the dam was built will not be able to live as they did before the dam was built. Either they will die or they will have to
1   adapt to life in water
2   eat as much food as possible
3   produce many young
4   remain dormant for a long time

8   This situation indicates that
1   building the dam had advantages and disadvantages
2   new projects benefit everybody
3   production of electricity was not the main issue
4   the burden was on society

9   Decision making about such a complex technological issue usually involves
1   a closed loop system
2   science and technology but not society
3   terminating a product
4   trade-offs

10   What two things MUST animals get from green plants?
1   carbon dioxide and food
2   food and oxygen
3   oxygen and carbon dioxide
4   water and salt

11   A student needs to learn the importance of taking in carbon dioxide by plant leaf stomates. A good technique to use would be
1   dyeing the leaf red
2   pinning black paper to the top of the leaf
3   rubbing oil on the underside of the leaf
4   placing the leaf in pure oxygen

12   The endocrine and nervous systems function together to
1   coordinate and control body activities
2   digest and distribute digested food
3   exchange and excrete wastes
4   repair and reproduce new cells

Use the diagram of the human digestive system to answer questions 13 and 14.

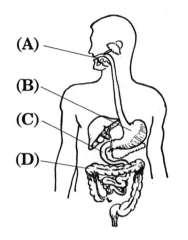

(A)
(B)
(C)
(D)

13 Which letter represents the place where the physical digestion of food begins?
    1   A
    2   B
    3   C
    4   D

14 A disease requires surgery to remove some of the organ labeled "D." This means the person would have difficulty
    1   getting digested food into the blood system
    2   mixing foods to increase digestion
    3   storing solid wastes
    4   swallowing food

15 Following a serious car accident, a person is in danger of bleeding to death. To save the person's life, a doctor orders a
    1   blood transfusion
    2   couple of aspirins
    3   vaccination
    4   wholesome meal

16 Emphysema can be caused by cigarette tar clogging the air sacs. Which activity would make this situation worse?
    1   drinking pineapple juice
    2   eating a chocolate bar
    3   rinsing with mouthwash
    4   breathing polluted air

17 The body organs that eliminate liquid wastes and control water and mineral balance are the
    1   arteries
    2   kidneys
    3   lungs
    4   teeth

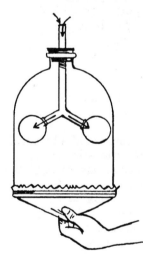

18 A model of the lungs is made as shown above. An experimenter pulls down on the rubber sheet. What do you PREDICT will happen to the balloons when the rubber sheet is PUSHED UP? The balloons will
    1   get bigger
    2   collapse
    3   break
    4   stay the same as they are

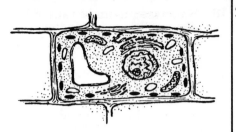

19 While doing microscope work, a student observed the cell shown above. Most likely, she was looking at a
1 bacterium
2 monkey bone cell
3 human brain cell
4 onion plant leaf cell

20 The only form of reproduction that leads to possible variation in the next generation is
1 asexual
2 budding
3 mitosis
4 sexual

21 A baker mixed a batch of bread dough that did not "rise" as expected. He probably forgot to add
1 bacteria
2 mold
3 protozoa
4 yeast

22 Bedrock is broken down to form rock fragments and soil. Organic materials are added to the soil by the
1 decaying of plant and animal life
2 fracturing of boulders
3 freezing of water to ice
4 receding of glaciers

23 A student is doing microscope work. He needs to know how many mold spores are in his field of vision. The number in 1/4 of what he sees is 15. They seem evenly distributed in the rest of the field of vision. What would be a good technique to get the total number?
1 multiply 15 by 2
2 multiply 15 by 4
3 count the rest individually
4 guess the number based on the count of 15

24 The above illustration shows a rock being tested. The bubbles that form indicate that the kind of rock being tested is most likely
1 granite
2 shale
3 igneous
4 limestone

25 Table salt is dissolved in a cup of boiling water. The solution is allowed to cool. What do you predict will happen?
1 The salt and water will evaporate.
2 Crystals will form when the water evaporates.
3 Nothing will happen.
4 The salt will disappear.

26 A variety of products are made from mineral resources. Modifications and modern technology have produced many new products not available twenty years ago. This has caused
1   attitudes of people to remain the same
2   decreased benefits for society
3   decreased choices for people
4   lifestyles to change

27 Drinking water can become "undrinkable" because
1   bedrock is folded to form mountains
2   fossils may be found nearby
3   ground water contains carbon dioxide
4   toxic chemicals are dumped on the ground

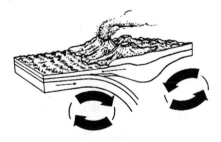

28 Study the diagram above. The large crustal plates seem to "float" on the mantle. The Plate Tectonics Theory states that this might be due to
1   abnormal lateral pressure
2   convective currents
3   drifting continents
4   earthquakes and volcanoes

29 Fossils help to explain
1   the development of life
2   climates of the past
3   prehistoric environments
4   all of these answers

30 High pressure air masses tend to bring
1   stormy weather
2   no change in weather
3   fair weather
4   unpredictable weather

Use the paragraph to answer questions 31 and 32.

A local weather station recorded the following temperatures on April 15th:

> 1 PM - 50° F
> 3 PM - 38° F

Other information reported that the barometer indicated air pressure was falling. A change in wind direction was indicated by the wind vane. The wind speed indicator shows an increase in wind speed.

31 What was the difference in temperature from 1 PM to 3PM?
1   12° rise
2   12° fall
3   38° rise
4   38° fall

32 Which of the following activities would be best suited if scheduled for 4 PM that day?
1   baseball
2   field hockey
3   table tennis
4   soccer

Use the following illustration of an experiment and the paragraph to answer questions 33 and 34.

An experiment is performed with a healthy tomato plant and a dead twig. Both are watered. A clear plastic bag is placed over each and tied at the stem. Both are placed on a window sill. An observation is made the next day. Water droplets appeared on the inside of the bag over the live plant. The bag over the twig was dry.

33 The dead twig was included in the experiment to provide
1 busy work
2 a comparison
3 an extra variable
4 more expense

34 This experiment shows what science concept?
1 Dead twigs do not give off moisture.
2 Moisture gets into the air by transpiration.
3 Plastic bags are handy for doing experiments
4 Precipitation occurs around tomato plants.

Use the following diagram to answer questions 35 and 36.

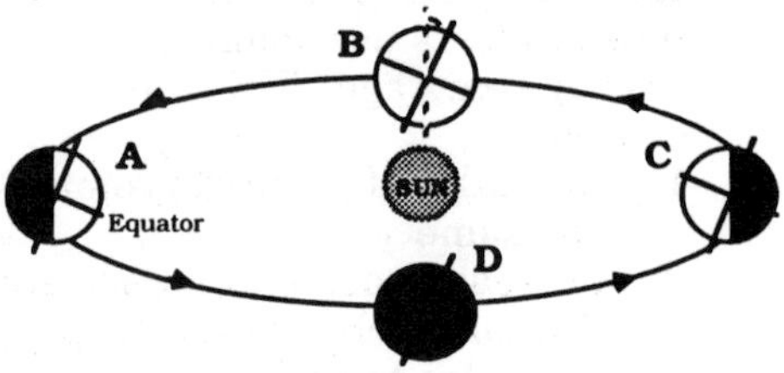

35 The tilting of the Earth's axis is the main reason why the Earth has
1 a calendar
2 day and night
3 seasons
4 years

36 At which position would the Northern Hemisphere be having winter?
1 A
2 B
3 C
4 D

37 The prediction is made that a "High" will remain over your area for at least three weeks. You just finished planting seeds and young plants in your vegetable garden. A wise action for you to take would be to
1 cover the seeded rows with thick plastic
2 dig up the seeds and replant them later
3 put fertilizer around the plants
4 water the garden thoroughly

38 Weather observers are able to
    use modern technological devices
    to make better predictions.
    Radar, computers, and weather
    satellites provide data that help
    by giving
    1   air mass top shapes
    2   atmosphere conditions for a
        broader area
    3   clear local area pictures only
    4   absolute humidity of stratus
        clouds

39 A sundial casts a short shadow
    at noon in Washington, D.C.
    This shadow and one cast by a
    vertical stick in the Rose Garden
    at the White House will point
    toward the
    1   North
    2   South
    3   East
    4   West

40 The amount of the lighted side of
    the Moon's surface as observed
    from Earth determines the
    1   phases of the Moon
    2   seasons
    3   length of day
    4   how long the night will last

41 Light travels at 186,000 miles
    per second. You are to find out
    the distance light travels in one
    year. To do this, you would have
    to multiply 186,000 times the
    number of
    1   minutes in an hour
    2   days in a month
    3   weeks in a year
    4   seconds in a year

42 The only planet of our solar
    system that appears to be able to
    support life is
    1   Venus
    2   Earth
    3   Mars
    4   Jupiter

43 "Spy" satellites have permitted
    nations to "keep an eye" on each
    other. This indicates that a
    technological product (satellite)
    can
    1   be very expensive
    2   study the center of the Earth
    3   destroy the ozone layer
    4   have a global impact

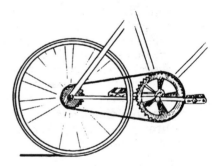

44 Machines make work easier by
    changing the direction of a force,
    reducing the effort needed, or
    changing speed. Look at the
    diagram above. What happens
    when a force is applied to the
    pedal wheel?
    1   Only the direction of force is
        changed.
    2   There is an increase in the
        effort needed.
    3   The distance of the effort is
        increased.
    4   There is a change in the
        speed of the effort force.

45 A weight-lifter uses much energy to lift weights over her/his head. When is "work" being done by the weight-lifter?
1 sizing up the weights before "pumping" them
2 raising the weights from the floor to overhead
3 holding the weights overhead
4 letting the weights drop to the floor

46 Study this diagram of a lightning storm. A hiker saw a flash of lightning. She heard a clap of thunder 15 seconds later. About how far from the storm was the hiker?
1 1 mile
2 2 miles
3 3 miles
4 Cannot tell from the information given.

47 A rock fragment that enters the Earth's atmosphere and heats up produces a
1 meteor
2 asteroid
3 star
4 comet

48 The law of machines states that work put into a machine is equal to the work gotten out of a machine. The first steam engines were less than 10% efficient. This means that 90% of the input was lost. What would cause this?
1 There was a poor operator.
2 The belts were too tight.
3 The steam boiler was on all night before use.
4 Much of the input effort was changed by friction to wasted heat.

49 Why is the heater in this illustration able to make the room warmer?
1 Cold air forces warm air to sink.
2 Warm air forces cooler air to rise.
3 Heat flows from a warm areas to cool a one.
4 Heat flows from a cool area to a warm one.

50 The diagram below represents a simple circuit. Which number represents the "source of electricity?"

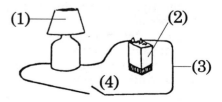

51 It is dangerous to touch electric switches when standing in water or when the body is wet. Why?
1   A lot of work is involved in replacing the switch.
2   Arms and hands are good insulators.
3   Plugs rust easily with the extra water.
4   The body acts like a conductor through which the electricity flows.

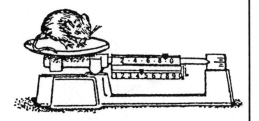

52 What is the mass of the mouse?
1   4.5 g
2   8.45 g
3   90.0 g
4   94.5 g

53 Television and video screens emit ultraviolet rays when operating. Overexposure to these rays can cause cataracts in the eyes when the person gets older. People must be aware that technological products may have
1   complex systems that make up simpler ones
2   consequences that spread around the world
3   short-term benefits and long-term burdens
4   problems that should not be worried about

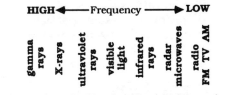

HIGH ◄———— Frequency ————► LOW

gamma rays X-rays ultraviolet rays visible light infrared rays radar microwaves radio FM TV AM

Decreasing ◄—Wavelength—► Increasing

54 According to the diagram, what happens to the frequency as the wavelength decreases?
1   gets louder
2   goes down
3   goes up
4   stays the same

55 The student in the above diagram above is doing an experiment. Chemicals are being heated in a test tube over a burner. What is the student doing wrong?
1   flame should be bigger
2   not close enough to the flame
3   shorter tongs would be better
4   not wearing goggles

56 How close together particles are and how fast they move will determine the
1   amount of wasted energy
2   chemical properties of the matter
3   size of the compound
4   phase of the matter

57 The small circles in these diagrams represent "particles." Which diagram would represent a SOLID?

(1) 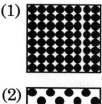 (3)

(2) 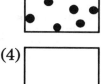 (4)

58 You are going on an overnight camping trip. Rain is expected before you reach the forest. Meals will be prepared over a log fire. To be sure to be able to start the fire, you should keep
1 food in airtight plastic bags
2 matches in a watertight container
3 old newspapers available
4 wood logs piled up early

59 Suppose the data from one of your experiments indicated the "prediction" was wrong. As a science student, what would you do?
1 Make an excuse for the failure.
2 Redo the experiment to see if there was an error in procedure.
3 Stop there and write up the experiment.
4 Tell the teacher you are not interested any more.

60 A thermometer is placed in a beaker of heated water. A student reads and records the temperature every minute for five (5) minutes. In this case, the student was making a(n)
1 decision
2 inference
3 observation
4 prediction

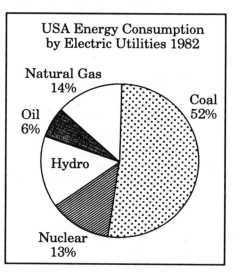

USA Energy Consumption by Electric Utilities 1982

Natural Gas 14%
Oil 6%
Coal 52%
Hydro
Nuclear 13%

61 According to the graph above, which type of energy was used most to produce electricity in the USA?
1 coal
2 nuclear
3 oil
4 water

62 The water in a farm pond starts to freeze. To do this the water must
1 give up energy
2 keep a steady energy level
3 produce energy
4 take in energy

63 Researchers have found that metals are malleable. (They can be rolled into sheets.) Different forms can come from these metal sheets. Which American industry depends on this metal property for its products?
1   making electric transmission wires
2   manufacturing nylon stockings
3   producing automobiles
4   weaving wool sweaters

64 Reserves of coal are much greater than natural gas and oil. Coal mining can be dangerous and expensive. Wastes from burning coal are linked with "acid rain." Burning coal is potentially less dangerous than nuclear mishaps. This situation emphasizes the concept that every technological process/product has
1   benefits and burdens associated with it
2   no problem with complex processes
3   disadvantages that do not make a difference
4   bad effects that should be forgotten

65 The primary source of energy for the Earth is
1   crude oil
2   coal
3   the Sun
4   uranium

66 Greenhouses are able to change solar radiation to usable heat energy. The same thing happens in a closed car in summer. This is why, when the windows are closed, it is not good to leave
1   babies and pets in the car
2   the doors unlocked
3   the radio volume turned high
4   leather seats covered

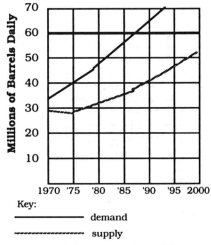

Key:
—————————— demand
~~~~~~~~~~~~ supply

(Note: graph is representative only)

67 The graph above shows that millions of barrels of oil are used every year. The best interpretation of the graph is that
1   energy supply is greater than demand
2   demand for energy is greater than supply
3   supply and demand are equal
4   demand and supply will meet in the future

Base your answers to questions 68 and 69 on the table and graph of data collected during the following experiment:

Two shoe boxes with thermometers inside are exposed to a 200 watt lamp. One box is covered with clear plastic. The other box is not covered.

Minutes	Covered Box Temperature in ° C	Open Box Temperature in ° C
0	20	20
1	21	21
2	22	22
3	24	23
4	26	24
5	29	25
6	32	26
7	36	27
8	40	28
9	45	29
10	50	30

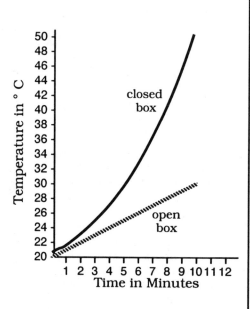

68 Which line on the graph indicates the temperature change inside the covered box?
1   x axis
2   y axis
3   broken line
4   solid line

69 Which statement best describes the science concept shown in the experiment?
1   Active solar energy systems use collectors and tanks.
2   Solar energy can be converted to electricity.
3   Sunlight can be changed to heat energy.
4   Sunshine is the primary source of energy on Earth.

70 Windmills have very little (if any) pollution connected with their use. Except for the cost of installation, wind is free. A disadvantage related to the use of "wind energy" is that it
1   depends on the rise and fall of the tides
2   is easy to store large quantities of power
3   is nonrenewable
4   may not always be available, since the wind may not blow

Abrasive: (112) able to wear away or rub off.

Absorb: (176) to take into.

Acid rain: (133, 218, 240) weak acid produced by dissolving gaseous pollutants with precipitation.

Adapt: (42) change of an organism that makes it more fit to live in its environment.

Adrenaline: (75) hormone secreted by the adrenal glands.

Advantage/Disadvantage: (226, 241) similar to benefits and burdens; relationships about technological advances.

AIDS: (92) Acquired Immune Deficiency Syndrome.

Air Mass: (126) a very large section of air that has the same characteristics of moisture and temperature as the surface over which it formed; *continental*: air mass that forms over land; *maritime*: air mass that forms over water; *polar*: air mass that forms over higher latitudes; *tropical*: air mass that forms over lower latitudes.

Algae: (29) single cell green plant cells, containing chloroplasts and cell walls.

Alternative: (10) another possibility; a choice of two or more things or procedures.

Alveoli: (72) air cells of the lungs found at the end of bronchioles.

Analysis: (23) careful study of data.

Antibody: (96) disease fighting protein produced by the body which reacts with a foreign substance in the body to destroy it.

Anticline: (118) upward fold of rock layers.

Aorta: (68) the largest artery in the human body.

Apparent daily motion: (147) movement of the Sun, Moon, and stars "around" the Earth; the observed movement is caused by the Earth's rotation; they appear to move around the Earth, but do not.

Apply: (23, 244) to put to use.

Artery: (68) blood vessel which carries blood from the heart to the organs.

Asexual reproduction: (31, 32) form of reproduction requiring only one parent.

Astronomical unit (AU): (157) the average distance the Earth is from the Sun (150,000,000 kilometers or 93,000,000 miles).

Astronomy: (7, 147) study of planets, stars, and other objects in space and their characteristics (composition, size, position in space).

Atmosphere: (125, 133, 135) layers of gases that surround the Earth.

Attitude: (7, 239) how a person thinks and looks at things.

Axis: (147) imaginary straight line running through the Earth from the North Pole to the South Pole.

Bacteria: (29, 49, 90) single cell organisms with a simple cell structure and no nucleus.

Beetle, life cycle: (36) stages of development from egg, through larva, pupa, and adult.

Behavior: (62) inborn, acquired, conditioning, and habits all controlled by the brain.

Benefit/Burden: (241, 245) the good and the bad about technological advances.

Biological weathering: (109) the breakdown of rock through the action of living things.

Biomass: (225) remains, wastes, or by-products of living organisms.

Blood: (69, 96) liquid tissue of body containing plasma, blood cells, nutrients, and wastes.

Blood cells: (56, 69) red blood cells (carry oxygen) and white blood cells (fight disease).

Brain: (60) main control center of human nervous system; cerebrum, cerebellum, medulla.

Breakage: (101) cleavage or fracture of a mineral or rock.

Breathing: (71) inhalation and exhalation to obtain oxygen and excrete carbon dioxide.

Bronchial tube: (72) a division of the trachea leading to the lung.

Budding: (32) a form of asexual reproduction in which a single cell organism divides into two unequal parts.

Calorie: (211) (with a capital "C") a kilocalorie; unit used to measure the energy in foods.

calorie: (211) (with a small "c") amount of heat energy needed to raise one gram of water one degree Celsius.

Canning: (94) preserving food by processing it in cans or jars.

Capillary: (69) microscopic blood vessel; connects arteries and veins; surrounds body cells; location of nutrient and waste exchange.

Carbohydrate: (38) specific nutrient group composed of sugars and starch.

Cardiac muscle: (59) special muscle under involuntary control found only in the heart.

Carnivores: (46) meat eating consumers; often predators.

Cartilage: (57) a dense but flexible fibrous connective tissue.

Cell: (55, 81) the unit of structure of living things, performs all physiological activities.

Cell membrane: (82) also called *plasma membrane*; a membrane separating the contents of a cell from its immediate surroundings.

Cell Theory: (81) cells are the basic unit of structure and function, and cells come from cells.

Cell wall: (83) rigid structure composed of cellulose that surrounds plant cells.

Cellulose: (83) a carbohydrate, made by plants, that is used to make cell walls.

Convection: (137, 172) movement of heat in liquids and gases from high to low heat areas.

Convection currents: (116) movements of liquid or gases that are produced by temperature differences.

Conversion: (166) (transformation) changing to a different form or property; result of changes made through technological processes.

Convex: (177) lens that is thicker in the middle than on the edges.

Cranium: (57) the skull.

Crest: (175) high point on a wave.

Crust: (104) the thin, solid outer layer of the Earth.

Crystal: (102) a solid that has a definite shape due to an orderly arrangement of atoms or molecules.

Cytoplasm: (82) area of the cell between the plasma membrane and the nucleus which contains water and organelles.

D ata: (10, 21) facts and figures; often the results of experiments.

(Singular - datum)

Data table: (21) system of columns and rows on which data are recorded and/or organized.

Daughter cells: (23, 85) offspring by mitosis or budding, exactly like parent.

Decomposer: (45, 49) organism that breaks down organic matter into inorganic molecules.

Deficiency: (93) the lacking of something, like vitamins or minerals.

Density: (102) number of particles in a specific space.

Deposition: (112, 118) sediments that settle out of water or air.

Desert: (43, 130) a very dry, often sandy region receiving less than 10 inches of rainfall per year.

Destructional forces: (99, 108) forces that wear down the Earth's surface.

Dew: (137) water vapor that condenses directly onto an object.

Diabetes: (75, 93) disease caused by high blood sugar levels and insufficient insulin.

Diaphragm: (72) curved sheet of muscle between the chest and abdomen, responsible for breathing.

Diffusion: (67) movement of substances from high to low concentrations.

Digestion: (31, 63) a process by which food is broken down for use by the body.

Digestive system: (63) organs used in the intake, breakdown, and absorption of nutrients.

Disinfect: (93) to destroy disease germs with a substance such as alcohol or iodine.

Disease: (92) an unhealthy condition, sickness, or malfunction.

Dormant: (43) inactive, resting, as in seeds before starting to grow; volcanoes before erupting.

Ductility: (202) property of metals that allows them to be drawn into wire.

Dysentery: (92) group of disorders in which there is diarrhea produced by irritation of the bowels.

Earthquake: (114, 116) violent shaking of the Earth's crust due to movement along a fault.

Eclipse: (154) a partial or total blocking out of one heavenly body by another.

Ecosystem: (48) the relationship between plants and animals and the environment in which they live.

Efficiency: (185) comparison of the amount of work actually done by a machine compared to the amount of work put into the machine.

Effort: (183) work put into a machine.

Elasticity: (202) ability of an object to stretch and return to its original position.

Element: (100, 197) a substance consisting of only one kind of atom.

Electron: (198, 203) negatively charged particle circling the nucleus of an atom.

Electricity: (165, 167, 224) flow of electrons through a conductor.

Electromagnetic spectrum: (172, 178, 217) the wide range of wavelengths from lower frequencies such as radio waves, short wave, AM, FM, TV, and radar to infrared rays, visible light and ultraviolet, and, finally, the shorter wavelengths of x-rays and gamma rays.

Endangered: (51) in danger of becoming extinct.

Endocrine system: (60, 74) hormone chemical control system used to regulate life activities.

Energy: (38, 49, 133, 163, 212) *physical*: the ability to do work or cause change.

Environment: (30, 41, 42, 235) the surroundings including both physical and biological conditions.

Enzyme: (63) a protein produced by cells that causes or speeds up chemical reactions in a plant's or animal's life functions.

Era: (122) a long period of geologic time, such as the Pre-Paleozoic era, the Paleozoic era, the Mesozoic era, and the Cenozoic era.

Erosion: (52, 111) removal and transport of the surface of the Earth by water, wind, or ice.

Esophagus: (64) muscular tube that connects the pharynx with the stomach.

Evaporation: (100, 135, 194) process by which liquid becomes a gas.

Excretion: (31, 65) the process by which organisms remove wastes.

Excretory system: (65) liver, kidneys, skin, and lungs; used to remove cell wastes.

Exhalation: (72) process by which air is removed from the lungs.

Expand: (108, 171) to increase in size or volume; to take up more space.

External fertilization: (35) joining of sperm and egg cell outside the body of the female.

Extinct: (50) something that does not exist now, but once did.

Extrapolation: (22) going beyond known points on a graph to make a prediction about future happenings.

Extrusive rock: (104) surface formed when hot molten material cools and hardens.

Fat: (38) oily substance found in animals or plants.

Fault: (116) a crack or fracture in the crust of the Earth due to movement in the Earth's crust.

Faulting: (117) the movement that occurs in rock layers when the crust is pulled apart or pushed together.

Feces: (31, 64) undigested waste material eliminated through the anus.

Feedback: (233) information obtained by monitoring the output of a system.

Ferment: (91) when yeasts change sugars into alcohol and carbon dioxide.

Fertilization: (35, 86) joining of an egg and sperm.

Flowering plant life cycle: (36) sexual reproduction of plant from egg to seed and fruit.

Fog: (136) a cloud on or close to the ground.

Food chain: (45) sequence of organisms, beginning with the producers, through which food energy is passed in an ecosystem.

Food web: (46, 50) series of interconnecting food chains that end with decomposers.

Force: (163) a push or pull.

Fossil: (120) evidence of a once-living organisms found preserved in rock.

Fossil fuels: (213, 218) oil, natural gas, and coal formed from bodies of ancient plants and animals.

Fracture: (101) when a mineral breaks along an uneven surface; breaking of an object.

Fragments: (100, 105) broken down bedrock due to agents of weathering.

Frequency: (178) the number of complete vibrations per second.

Friction: (112, 185) the force that resists movement of two objects in contact.

Frog life cycle: (35) development of frog from egg mass through tadpole to adult.

Front: (128) a boundary between two air masses; *cold:* when a cold air mass moves into a warm air mass; *occluded:* when a cold front overtakes a warm front; *stationary:* between air masses that are not moving; *warm:* when a warm air mass moves into a cold air mass.

Frost: (137) water vapor that sublimates (gas to solid) directly onto an object.

Fulcrum: (183) point around which a lever rotates.

Fungi: (29, 38) classification kingdom of plantlike organisms that lack chlorophyll.

Fuse: (168) device with a thin metal strip that breaks when a circuit carries too much electricity.

Gene: (77, 82) section of DNA transmitted by each parent to offspring which determines hereditary characteristics.

Generation: (86) a group of organisms born and living together at the same time.

Genotype: (87) the genetic makeup of an organism.

Geologic history: (122) a scale of time that divides the history of the Earth into large time periods called eras.

Geology: (7, 120) study of the Earth, its origin, history, and changes.

Glacier: (112) a moving mass of ice that forms over a long period of time.

Gland: (74) mass of tissue which secretes enzymes or hormones.

Gram: (17) metric standard for mass measure.

Graph: (21) a picture of data; compares two or more variables.

Gravity: (112) attraction of one object for another; force that pulls everything toward the center of the Earth.

Greenhouse effect: (219) trapping and changing light energy to heat energy usually in a "glassed in" space.

Ground water: (111) the part of rainfall that sinks into the ground becoming an underground water supply.

Growth: (30) increase in the size or number of cells.

Habit: (62) a learned behavior that occurs "automatically."

Habitat: (42) particular area in an ecosystem where a specific plant or animal lives.

Hardness: (101, 201) the ability of a mineral to resist being scratched.

Heart: (67) main pumping organ of the human circulatory system; 4 valves and 4 chambers.

Heat energy: (165, 170, 194, 206, 211) energy resulting from the random movement of particles of matter.

Herbivore: (46) a plant eating consumer, such as a cow, grasshopper, and most insects.

Hibernate: (43) to spend winter (cold periods) in a sleep-like state (dormant).

High pressure area: (127) a high pressure air mass with clockwise rotation of winds (in the Northern Hemisphere).

Hormone: (74) chemical messenger released by the endocrine glands.

Humidity: (130, 136) amount of water vapor in the air; *absolute humidity:* amount of water vapor in the air at a given temperature; *relative humidity:* ratio of the amount of water vapor in the air at a certain temperature compared to the maximum amount the air can hold at that temperature.

Hurricane: (140) see weather storms, very violent large storm; see warnings and safety.

Hyperactivity: (74) excessively active.

Hypoactivity: (74) lack of activity.

Hypothesis: (9) a possible answer to a problem; a prediction.

Igneous rock: (104) rock formed from liquid magma; intrusive and extrusive; see volcanism.

Immunity: (96) resistance to disease.

Impulse: (60) electrochemical message started by a stimulus that causes a response.

Inclined plane: (183, 184) a simple machine with a sloping surface.

Industrial waste: (220) unwanted materials discharged from factories and industries.

Infection: (92) spread of a disease.

Inference: (17) explanation of an observation; not a direct observation.

Ingestion: (31) process of taking in food to be digested.

Inhalation: (72) activity by which air is forced into the lungs.

Inorganic: (91, 100) materials that are not living and have never lived.

Input: (185, 233) work put into a machine; data, materials, resources, or instructions entered into a system.

Insulator: (168, 172) substance that does not allow electricity or heat energy to pass through easily; a nonconductor.

Insulin: (75, 93) material secreted by glands on the pancreas to regulate the body level of sugar.

Internal fertilization: (36) fertilization of an egg by sperm within the body of the female organism.

Interpolation: (22) estimating between two known points on a graph.

Interpretation: (10, 23) explanation of a hypothesis, observations, and/or data.

Intrusive rock: (104) formed when magma cools and hardens under the surface.

Invertebrate: (29) animals without backbones.

Involuntary muscle: (59) smooth or cardiac muscle controlled by the autonomic nervous system.

Joint: (57) part of the skeleton where two or more bones meet; allows for movement.

Joule: (123) basic metric unit of work (energy); same as a newton-meter.

Kinetic energy: (164) refers to movement or energy of motion.

Kinetic particle theory: (170, 193) concerns the organization of matter.

Kingdom: (29) largest category in the classification system.

Knot: (130) unit of speed used for ship and wind speeds; represents one nautical mile (6,080 feet an hour).

Laboratory safety and tools: (15, 189) procedures and tools necessary for safety in the lab.

Latitude lines: (151) Parallel lines circling the globe north and south of the equator that are used to measure latitude. The 0° parallel is the equator.

Lava: (100, 104, 119) magma that breaks through the Earth's surface.

Law of Superposition: (121) way of determining the relative age of sedimentary rock layers; the oldest layer is on the bottom and the youngest layer is on the top.

Lens: (177) materials that cause light waves to bend.

Lever: (183) a simple machine consisting of a rigid bar turning on a fulcrum.

Life activities: (30) includes all processes necessary to keep an organism alive.

Lifestyle: (237) includes an individual's religious, family, social, and work roles.

Ligament: (57) tough, fibrous connecting tissue which connects and holds the bones together at the joints.

Light-year: (157) the distance light travels in a year.

Liter: (17) metric standard for measuring volume (capacity).

Locomotion: (31) the act of moving from one place to another.

Longitude lines: (151) meridians that run from pole to pole and are used to measure longitude. 0° meridian is the Prime Meridian; 180° meridian is the International Date Line.

Low pressure areas: (127) usually associated with precipitation and storms; see weather.

Lung: (72) major organ of the respiratory system; gas exchange at air sacs (alveoli).

Luster: (102, 201) how a mineral reflects light from its surface.

Lymph: (69) watery fluid present in and around body tissues.

Machine: (183) a device that helps make work easier.

Magma: (100, 104, 118) hot, molten , liquid rock below the Earth's surface.

Malleability: (202) property of most metals to be changed in shape.

Mammary glands: (77) found in mammals only, produce milk necessary for infants.

Mass: (16, 17, 192) amount of material in an object.

Matter: (192, 201, 205) anything that has mass and takes up space.

Measurement: (17) instruments and scales used to determine shapes, sizes, and weights.

Mechanical advantage: (183) benefit realized by using a machine; the measured amount that a machine multiplies force.

Mechanical energy: (165, 183) form of energy that can be potential or kinetic.

Medium: (181) substance through which sound travels.

Meiosis: (85) a type of cell division; occurs only in the testes and ovaries for the production of sperm and eggs for sexual reproduction.

Melting point: (194, 201) temperature at which a solid changes into a liquid.

Meniscus: (16) curve on liquid surface in a graduated cylinder.

Menstruation: (75) breakdown of endometrial membrane; monthly discharge from the uterus of the female.

Metamorphic rock: (105) rock that has gone through changes in temperature and pressure.

Meteorologist: (131) scientist who studies and predicts (forecasts) the weather.

Meter: (17, 18) metric standard for line measure.

Metric System: (17) measurement system based on ten (10).

Microbe: (90, 92) a small living organism seen only through a microscope.

Microörganism: (81, 87, 90, 93) microscopic organism; microbe.

Microscopic: (87) can only be seen through a microscope.

Mid-ocean ridge: (115) a large system of volcanic mountains on the floor of the ocean.

Migrate: (44) to move from one place to another.

Mineral: (39, 100, 106) a naturally occurring, inorganic, solid element or compound that has a fixed atomic pattern giving it a definite shape.

Mineral Chart: (40) list of the common minerals, sources, and values.
Mitochondria: (83) the parts of the cell which carry on respiration.
Mitosis: (85) a type of cell division involving one parent only; identical daughter cells produced; involved in growth; asexual reproduction.
Mixture: (192) two or more things together, both keep their own characteristics.
Model: (233) a representation of an object or concept such as a model rocket, diagram, graph, or definition.
Moh's Scale of Mineral Hardness: (101) scale of how a mineral resists scratching.
Monera: (29) the Kingdom composed of organisms such as bacteria and blue-green algae.
Moon: (153) Earth's natural satellite.
Mountains: (106, 112, 114, 117) uplifting of the Earth's crust.
Movement: (163) change of position of an object in relation to a reference point.
Mucus: (71, 95) a gummy substance secreted by the mucous membranes.
Muscular system: (59) includes, skeletal, involuntary (smooth) and cardiac.
Music: (182) sounds that are pleasant to hear; harmonious sounds.
Mutation: (86) sudden change in the chromosomes, passed on to offspring.

N

Nervous system: (60) body system that coordinates and controls body activities (along with the endocrine system).
Neuron: (61) a nerve cell; *sensory, associative (interneuron), and motor.*
Neutron: (198) a part of an atom's nucleus having mass and no charge.
Newton: (163) basic metric unit of force (weight).
Noise: (182) sounds that are discordant, unpleasant to hear.
Nonpathogenic: (90) microörganisms that do not cause disease.
Nonrenewable resource: (53, 223) materials that cannot be replaced once they are used up.
Nuclear membrane: (82) the membrane surrounding the nucleus of a cell.
Nucleus: (82; 198) the central part of a living cell containing the chromosomes; *atomic nucleus*: center portion of the atom (protons and neutrons) around which electrons orbit.
Nutrient: (38) any compound used by the cell for its metabolic (life) activities.

O

Observation: (15) recording of a happening using all human senses;
qualitative : gives the general worth or description of something;
quantitative: gives the exact value; a measurement.
Ocean wave: (113) the regular rise and fall of water produced by friction of the wind on the surface of the water.
Offspring: (31, 34, 86) children; young of an organism(s) resulting from some form of reproduction.
Omnivores: (46) consumer organisms that eat both plant and animal nutrients.

Open loop system: (233) system that may be started or stopped but cannot automatically stop or change.

Optical illusion: (10) something "seen" which does not exist.

Orbit: (149, 153) the path an object travels as it moves around another object, like the Earth moving around the Sun.

Ore: (103) mineral resource that can be mined, usually for profit.

Organ: (53) group of tissues working together to perform some function.

Organelle Chart: (84) comparison of the plant and animal cell structures.

Organelles: (84, 89) structures in the cytoplasm of a cell that carry on cellular activities.

Organic: (91, 100, 109) materials that are living or were living at one time.

Organism: (29, 42, 45, 56, 81) single living thing.

Osmosis: (67) the special diffusion of water through a membrane of the cell.

Output: (185) actual work done by a machine or system.

Ovary: (34, 76) female sex gland.

Oviduct: (76) tube from the ovary to the uterus.

Oxidation: (49, 109) uniting of an element with oxygen.

P

ancreas: (64, 75) organ which secretes both digestive enzymes and hormones.

Pasteurization: (94) reducing the number of microörganisms in milk by heating.

Pathogenic: (92) disease causing microörganisms.

Pelvis: (57) hipbone region of the body.

Penis: (76) male external genital organ.

Peristalsis: (64) a contractual or squeezing muscle movement of hollow organs in the body.

Perspiration: (66) liquid released by the sweat glands to cool the body.

Pharynx: (64) the throat; connection of the nasal cavity (nose), oral cavity (mouth), and the esophagus (food tube).

Phase: (171, 201) the state of a material, solid, liquid, or gas.

Phase of Moon: (154, 195) portion of the Moon seen from the Earth.

Phenotype: (87) the physical characteristics of an organism based on its genotype or genetic make up.

Photosynthesis: (37, 83) Process by which carbon dioxide, water and minerals are converted into simple carbohydrates.

Physical change: (205) a change in the phase, shape, or size of matter.

Physical weathering: (108) the breakdown of rock without a change in the chemical composition.

Pistil: (34) female part of flower; contains ovary and egg(s).

Plains: (106, 117) broad, flat surfaces of undisturbed, horizontal rock layers at a low elevation.

Planning: (8) area of science skills dealing with recognizing a problem, predicting, selecting procedures.

Plasma: (69) fluid part of the blood.

Plasma membrane: (82) see cell membrane; major membrane of the cell.

Plateaus: (106, 118) horizontal rock layers that have a high elevation.

Plate Tectonic Theory: (116) the theory that states the crust of the Earth is made up of pieces called plates that "float" on the mantle.

Platelets: (56, 69) cell fragments that play an important part in the clotting of the blood.

Pollutants: (133) substances found in the atmosphere as a result of human activity and natural events.

Pollution: (52, 64, 133, 218) adding unwanted, harmful substances to the environment.

Population: (48) all organisms of the same kind living in a certain place.

Porous: (82, 112) having holes or openings; allows materials to move through easily.

Potential energy: (164) stored energy; energy at rest as a result of its state or position.

Precipitation: (131, 137) moisture (liquid or solid) that falls from clouds in the form of rain, snow, sleet, or hail.

Predator: (46, 50) an animal (consumer) that kills and eats another animal.

Predict: (9, 22) forming an educated guess as to what might happen; to form a hypothesis.

Prey: (46, 50) In a food chain, the organism which provides the food for a predator (consumer).

Prism: (176) solid triangular piece of glass or quartz which separates white light into colors.

Problem solving: (8) process of identifying, selecting, trying out, and evaluating alternative answers that will fulfill a desired goal.

Process: (233) action component of a system.

Producers: (45) organisms with the ability to produce their own food (green plants).

Product: (215, 234) anything or object produced by an action or operation.

Property: (101, 201, 203) a trait or characteristic used to describe matter.

Proton: (198) part of an atom's nucleus having mass and a positive charge.

Protein: (38) the nutrient needed for the growth and repair of cells and tissues.

Protista: (29) Kingdom composed of simple organisms with an organized nucleus.

Protoplasm: (81) the material basic to all living matter; a semi-fluid substance.

Prototype: (233) a pre-production model.

Protozoa: (29, 92) simple single cell organisms having characteristics similar to both plants and animals; such as amoeba, paramecium, and euglena.

R

Radiation: (172) movement of heat through space by infrared waves.

Reaction: (60) a change in behavior in response to a stimulus.

Receptor: (61) special structure sensitive to certain stimuli.

Reference object: (163) apparently stationary object used to compare movement of another object.

Reflection: (176) when light or sound bounces off a surface; angle of incoming ray and reflected ray are the same.

Reflex: (31, 67) the rapid inborn nervous reaction of the spinal cord.

Refraction: (177) bending of light rays passing through substances of different densities.

Regeneration: (32, 33) replacement of lost body tissue in animals.

Relationship: (23, 49, 52) a connection to another person, idea, or concept.

Relative age: (121) determining if the age of a rock layer is older or younger than another rock layer.

Renewable resource: (52, 224) any energy source that can be made from living material that can be "re-grown."

Reproduction: (31, 32, 34, 50, 238) process by which organisms produce copies of themselves.

Reproductive system: (34, 76) male and female; organs and glands; necessary for offspring.

Resistance: (183) force needing to be overcome before work can be done.

Respiration: (31, 41, 49, 70) life process: makes energy from food; may involve breathing.

Respiratory system: (70) body organs used in the exchange of respiratory gases.

Resource: (231) component necessary for technology.

Response: (31, 60, 62) reaction to a stimulus.

Revolution: (149, 150, 153) the orbiting of an object around another such as the Earth's revolution around the Sun.

Robot: (239) multi-functional device to perform physical tasks in response to command input.

Rotation: (147, 150, 155) spinning or turning of an object, like the Earth, on an axis.

Saliva: (63) fluid secreted by the salivary glands of the mouth; chemical digestion of carbohydrates.

Saturated: (136) holding as much of something as can be held under certain conditions.

Science: (7, 231, 236) process of solving problems to gain a better understanding of and predict the outcome of events in our natural world.

Scientific method: (8) a way of solving problems using a controlled experiment.

Seasons: (150) summer, fall, winter, and spring; result of Earth's tilt.

Secretion: (31, 74) substance released by cells or organs; such as mucus and oils.

Sedimentary rock: (105) rock laid down through the process of erosion; may contain fossils.

Sediments: (105, 112) fragments deposited by water, wind, and glaciers.

Sensitivity: (31, 60) ability to react to a change (stimuli).

Sexual reproduction: (31, 34, 76) joining together of sperm and egg, producing an offspring.

Shore current: (113) currents that flow parallel to the shore or coast.

Skeletal system: (56) 206 bones of the body and joints; locomotion, protection, and support.

Skin: (66, 95) outer covering of the body; defends against disease; removes heat, etc.

Society: (52, 231, 236) a group of people having common traditions, institutions, and interests.

Soil: (52, 110) organic material mixed with rock fragments.

Solar radiation: (130) heat and light from the Sun.

Solar System: (157) planets, asteroids, and comets revolving around Sun.

Species: (31) group of organisms having similar characteristics, with the ability to interbreed.

Sperm: (34, 76) male fertilizing cell.

Sperm ducts: (76) tubes used for passage of sperm.

Spinal cord: (60) extension of the brain; involved in reflexes.

Spore: (33) small, tough reproductive cell produced by molds and other organisms.

Staining technique: (89) process used to make cells more visible to a light microscope.

Stamen: (34) male part of the flower.

Standard: (17) a fixed unit to which other units can be compared.

Streak: (102) color of fine powder produced when rubbing a mineral against unglazed porcelain (streak plate).

Sterilization: (93) to make free from germs.

Stimulus: (31, 60) a change in the environment that causes an impulse (such as touch, heat, light, and odor).

Sublimation: (137, 195) a gas turns directly to a solid; also, a solid turns directly into a gas.

Succession: (48) the changes in an environment from primary to climax organisms.

Synclines: (118) down-folds in rock layers.

Synfuel: (225) synthetic (man-made) fuels made from sources such as biomass.

System: (55) a regularly interacting or interdependent group of items forming a unified whole; a group of organs working together.

Systems of the Body Chart: (78) listing of all system, organs, and functions.

T

Technology: (231, 236) process of using scientific knowledge to develop new products or processes to meet the needs and wants of society.

Temperature scales: (17, 171) comparison of the Celsius and Fahrenheit scales.

Tenacity: (203) ability of a substance to resist being pulled apart.

Tendon: (57) tough connective tissue by which muscle is attached to bone.

Testes: (74, 76) male reproductive glands.

Theory: (81, 115, 170, 190) an idea or explanation, supported by evidence that has not been proven true; a proposed explanation for a happening based on experimentation and facts.

Tidal Hypothesis: (121) idea that states that the Earth and other planets may have formed when a star passed too close to the Sun and pulled material away that formed the planets.

Tides: (155) rising and falling of the oceans due to the gravitational pull of the Moon and Sun.

Tissue: (55) group of cells working together to perform a particular function.

Tornado: (139) Low pressure center with the strongest winds; violent storm.

Trachea: (72) windpipe; tube through which air is transported to the lungs during breathing.

Trade-off: (243) process or end result of reaching a workable compromise.

Transpiration: (135) process by which the leaves of plants release water vapor into the air.

Trough: (175) low point on a wave.

Uterus: (76) womb; female organ in which fetus develops.

Urine: (65) fluid produced in kidneys; made from the combination of water, salts, and urea.

Vacuole: (83) ball like organelle containing nutrients of substances essential to the cell.

Vagina: (76) muscular tube which connects the uterus to the outside of the female body through which the fetus is born.

Values: (7, 243) beliefs and attitudes held by society or an individual.

Variable: (9) a condition in an experiment that changes.

Variation: (31, 86) trait found in one organism of the species that is not found in other organisms of the species.

Vegetative propagation: (32) a form of asexual reproduction in plants.

Venereal disease: (93) a contagious disease that is typically acquired through sexual contact, such as gonorrhea, herpes, and syphilis.

Vein: (68) blood vessels that carry blood back to the heart.

Verify: (11) to prove correct.

Vertebrate: (29) animals with a backbone.

Vibrate: (175, 180) to move back and forth rapidly.

Villi: (64) small, finger-like projections found in the small intestine.

Virus: (29, 93) extremely small particle, composed of DNA or RNA surrounded by protein and capable of reproducing only inside of another organism.

Vitamin: (39) chemicals found in foods that are necessary for proper bodily function.

Vitamin Chart: (39) chart of the most common vitamin names, sources, and functions.

Vocabulary- word parts: (24) common parts of words used in science to make other words.

Volcanism: (115) the movement of molten rock at or near the Earth's surface.

Volume: (16, 18) capacity; amount of space taken up by something.

Voluntary muscle: (59) also called striated and skeletal; muscles of the skeletal system.

Water (hydrologic) cycle: (41, 135) the constant transfer of water in the liquid, gaseous, or solid state between the atmosphere and the Earth.

Watt: (211) basic unit used to measure electric power.

Watt-hour: (211) unit used by power companies in charging for electricity.

Water table: (112) level below which rocks are saturated with water.

Wavelength: (175, 178) distance between a point on one wave to an identical point on the next wave.

Waves: (113) produced by wind blowing over the surface of water.

Weather: (125) a condition of the atmosphere in relation to temperature, moisture content, wind, and pressure.

Weather features: (126) weather features observed over a wide area at the same time.

Weather forecasting: (131) process of predicting weather based on symbols, techniques; work of meteorologists.

Weathering: (108) a natural process that wears down or breaks rock into smaller pieces by chemical, biological, or mechanical (physical) processes.

Weather warning: (141) indication that hazardous conditions are either imminent or occurring.

Weather watch: (141) indication that hazardous weather conditions described may occur.

Weight: (16) pull of gravity on the mass of an object.

Wind chill: (142) combination effect of temperature and wind.

Wind: (112, 130, 225) movement of air due to the unequal heating of the Earth's surface by the Sun.

Work: (163, 183) a force moving through distance.

Notes:

Notes: